Challenging Catholics

Challenging Catholics

A Catholic-Evangelical Dialogue

Dwight Longenecker
and John Martin

paternoster
press

British Library Cataloguing in Publication Data

A catalogue record for this book is available from
the British Library

ISBN 1-84227-096-6

Cover design by Campsie
Printed in Great Britain by
Cox and Wyman, Reading

Contents

Preface

Challenging Catholics is based on a twelve part radio conversation conducted by John Martin and Dwight Longenecker for London's Premier Radio. The original idea was to produce a punchy dialogue between two informed Christian laymen – an Evangelical and a Catholic.

Dwight Longenecker and John Martin both came to England twenty years ago, from opposite ends of the globe. Dwight was brought up in an Evangelical home in the USA. He studied Speech and English at a fundamentalist university, before coming to England to prepare for the Anglican ministry at Wycliffe Hall, Oxford. He served for ten years in that ministry, as a curate, a chaplain at Cambridge and a country parson. In 1995 he and his family were received into full communion with the Catholic Church. Dwight now works for the St Barnabas Society – a charity which gives assistance to clergy who wish to become Catholics. He also works as a freelance writer and broadcaster. His first book, *The Path to Rome*, was published in 1999; his second book, a commentary on the Rule of St Benedict for Christian fathers, came out in February 2000. Dwight lives with his wife Alison and their four children in Chippenham, Wiltshire.

John Martin was born in rural Australia of a Presbyterian father and Brethren mother. He was first educated through the Correspondence school of New South Wales, then attended Saint Andrew's Cathedral school in Sydney. He completed his BA and studied for a Diploma of Education at Macquarie University in Sydney, where he was President of the Students' Union and the Evangelical Union. He has held posts as

Travelling staff-worker for the Australian Fellowship of
Evangelical Students, Training Officer for the Association of
Youth Organisations, and Information Officer for the Anglican
Diocese of Sydney. In 1979, he came to England to be Director
of Communications, Anglican Communion Office, London
(1979-85). He went on to do consultancy work (1986-88),
before becoming editor of the Church of England Newspaper.
He works now as a research and PR advisor to the Church
Mission Society, is on the advisory boards of several Christian
magazines and is a regular broadcaster. John has written six
books, including *Gospel People: Evangelicals and the Future of
Anglicanism* (SPCK 1997). He lives at Bow in the East End of
London. He is church warden of St Mary's Anglican church,
where he occasionally preaches, and Chair of the Council for
an Anglican Group Ministry involving the seven parishes of
Bow. He also plays cricket in the North East London league.

Foreword

In 1965, after Archbishop Michael Ramsey visited Pope Paul VI, the Anglican Roman Catholic International Commission was established. As the Bishop of Arundel and Brighton I was co-chairman of that commission. Over the years the ARCIC members have worked hard to establish the common ground on which the Anglican Church and the Roman Catholic Church can work together towards full communion. The way has not been easy, but none of the work has been wasted, and by God's grace our two churches are closer together now than they have been for centuries.

At the same time ecumenical discussions have been initiated and continued with all the major non-Catholic Christian groups. Catholics have found it difficult to establish formal discussions with Evangelicals because, by its nature, Evangelicalism is de-centralised and diffuse. Nevertheless, good progress has been made. On a formal level, the Pontifical Council for Promoting Christian Unity has held three sessions of discussions with the World Evangelical Fellowship's Theological Commission. The final communiqué from their meeting in 1999 stated, 'As we listened jointly to the Scriptures, prayed together, and spoke the truth to one another in love, we recognized and rejoiced in the fellowship we have in Christ based on our common faith in Him. The riches of this gift are such that all who share in it cannot regard each other as strangers much less treat each other as enemies.'

Another historic milestone has been the *Joint Declaration on the Doctrine of Justification* which was signed in Augsburg on 31 October 1999. This agreement between the Catholic Church

and the Lutheran World Federation shows that there is basic
agreement between us on the fundamental questions of salvation and justification. This agreement between Lutherans and
Catholics has important and far-reaching ramifications for our
continued theological discussions with all Evangelical groups.

There is more that unites our two traditions than divides. In
many social and moral issues Catholics and Evangelicals
speak with the same voice. On doctrinal matters and questions
of worship, as we talk and listen to one another more carefully in the spirit of Christian charity, we are beginning to
understand each other's beliefs.

Cardinal Avery Dulles calls for Catholics to take now a
more creative initiative. He calls for an ecumenism of 'mutual
enrichment'. The time is ripe, he writes, 'to welcome the more
traditional and conservative churches into the dialogue. For
the Catholic Church it may not prove easy to reach a consensus with either the Orthodox or the conservative Evangelicals,
but these churches and communities may have more to offer
than some others because they have dared to be different.
Catholics have the right and duty to challenge the adequacy of
some of their positions, but they should be invited to challenge
Catholics in their turn.[1]

Challenging Catholics does just that. This book complements
the work which has gone on in official talks and through the
work of theologians. The authors bring a fresh angle to the
debate. While both of them have studied the issues and know
their theology, neither writer is a professional theologian.
Dwight Longenecker was brought up in an American
Evangelical home and came to Catholicism through the
Anglican ministry. John Martin was brought up in an
Evangelical home in Australia and has settled within
Evangelical Anglicanism. As professional writers they know
how to maintain a readable style. As laymen they discuss the
issues that separate and unite Evangelicals and Catholics with
candour and humour. Their tone is charitable, optimistic and
forward looking.

The dawning of the third millennium of the Christian faith
is a time for hope and joy. *Challenging Catholics* shares in that

hope for the future by helping Evangelicals and Catholics to better understand one another. I believe this book will contribute a small part in my larger hope that in this new millennium the Holy Spirit will lead us into that fullness of unity in the Church for which Christ himself so fervently prayed.

Cardinal Cormac Murphy O'Connor

---

1 Avery Dulles, *The Craft of Theology: From Symbol to System* (New York, Crossroads, 1992), 780

Foreword

Two lively Christian minds engage in honest, sometimes passionate, debate: that is the shape and substance of this book, and often the sparks fly! The discussion between the Anglican Evangelical, John Martin, and the Roman Catholic, Dwight Longenecker, focuses on the claims of the Roman Catholic Church. The dialogue partners are both very able, well informed and good communicators. They have interesting background histories with surprising links. John Martin, the Australian writer, was raised in a mixture of Brethren and Presbyterian cultures, before finding Anglicanism a context for his evangelical faith. Dwight Longenecker, the American, came from a background in the Mennonite tradition and a fundamentalist university, before taking the path to Anglicanism and then to Rome. Such a curiously shared background enriches the discussion and debate.

They probe the main points of disagreement between Anglicans and Romans at a depth perhaps masked by the often jolly and courteous language. The discussion manages to achieve a very difficult task – to get to the very serious issues in everyday language. These two are in colourful shirts chatting over a coffee, not in grey academic dress! The twelve chapters come to the reader in well organised fashion, beginning with the question of the Bible and sources of authority, before getting into the way we are in touch with God through Jesus. The saints, Mary, the Reformation are debated before a final chapter tries to point us to the future of the church.

To have a shot at painting a 'big picture' of the debate, I would say that the 'fence around the law' might work as an image. They debate Rabbinical idea as a way of trying to defend the Roman Catholic additions to the faith, not directly found in Scripture. The Rabbis famously added layers of rules to the Torah, a fence around the law, as a double check against anyone even getting near to breaking the holy law book itself. Basically, Dwight argues that Roman Catholic 'additions' are logical outworkings of Scripture itself, natural developments as Cardinal Newman said – in fact Dwight's position reflects Newman pretty exactly for readers of 19th century literature. What to the Roman Catholic is a natural development surrounding Scripture, to the Reformation had become a dense thicket preventing people from getting at the simple gospel of Jesus. This thicket needed to be pruned away to allow access.

If we take this model of the disagreement, a fair number of the topics fit into place. Scripture itself, says Dwight, is inspired – but is not in itself understandable, it needs the church's specially ordained teaching ministry of bishops and popes to interpret it. Is that claim a natural development, or a distortion muffling the message and preventing a natural reading? Or on the question of Mary: is prayer to Mary, the deceased mother of Jesus, a natural outworking of the spirituality of the New Testament – or is it a distorting development getting in the way of direct access to God the Father through the Son and Spirit? Other topics could be given the same treatment. Dwight says at the end that he denies little of what John affirms, but he wants to add his Roman Catholic elements on, elements he claims are given by his infallible teaching priesthood – itself of course an additional layer, according to John! John wants very much to ensure that the prophets and apostles, whose voice we hear in Scripture, can speak to the church clearly so as to reform it – including its ordained bishops, priests and popes.

How does the common background shared between Dwight and John affect the discussion, if at all? John thinks that the Bible stands for itself as basically clear in its message, but with areas of disagreement in secondary matters being acceptable. Dwight dislikes this sort of pluralism and insists that there must be one true interpretation and one visible organization teaching it, based in Rome. He thinks the multiplicity of Protestant churches counts against them, although he does consider the Eastern Orthodox as a possible contender for the title. John's view of catholicity is relaxed about many different expressions of the faith. In fact many 'liberal' Roman Catholics would be happy with this also, and we need to remind ourselves that Dwight, a convert, represents the more conservative strand of his church, and that 'cradle Catholics' are freer than converts to hold dissenting views.

Readers might ask themselves how 'experience' plays a part in the formation of the theologies of Dwight and John. Curiously enough Dwight uses his feelings more than we might have imagined in reaching his conclusions. His acceptance of Mary as a focus of veneration came with a feeling of happiness, a key factor in cementing this Roman Catholic teaching in his mind. John speaks of the Holy Spirit as a helper in interpretation, and a guide in life. Similarly, how important is 'history' to our debating partners? The history of the papacy, for example, is admitted even by Dwight to be rather mixed. But that does not count as a reason for him to deny its specially inspired and infallible nature. John, naturally, is rather more sceptical about making any human historical institution 'indefectible' or 'infallible'. John reaches a lot of agreement with Dwight that the history of the Reformation, in England at least, involved a lot of unfair attack on the Roman Catholics. Here the reader is reminded that this is a very English discussion and that the experience of many other European peoples was rather the reverse.

John, at the end, takes a careful look at the way the cultural winds are blowing and does not think that high claims to infallibility will be credible for long. He believes that the Spirit blows and reforms the Church, and will again, to produce new ways forward. Dwight sticks to his position, hoping for reunion under the papal structure to unite the many under a single church rule.

You will share this fizzing debate with real enjoyment and gain. Congratulations to Dwight and John for getting this unusual discussion into print so that we can all join in!

The Rev Dr Tim Bradshaw
Anglican minister, tutor at Regents Park College Oxford and
member of the English Anglican-Roman Catholic Commission

Introduction

John: As we've got to know each other, it's emerged that you and I began our journeys several thousands miles apart culturally and geographically, but not all that distant spiritually. Our destinations are different, although I suspect we've discovered new things on the way that we share in common.

Let me begin at the beginning. My Australian father and mother met at what turned out to have been a very conservative evangelical missionary and Bible training college. He was a Presbyterian elder at the time. What took him there was an evangelical conversion. My mother's family was Brethren, with Cornish Methodist roots. A key influence was the Keswick movement – an evangelical movement based on a Bible teaching conference in northern England. I'm told my mother went to college having responded to a Keswick-style call to missionary service, a regular set piece at the Katoomba Convention, west of Sydney. Some years later my father, on holidays in the mountains west of Sydney, came upon the Convention tent, was befriended, had a conversion experience, accepted baptism by immersion (having earlier been baptised as a baby) and – man of action that he was – immediately travelled to Sydney to enrol at Bible college. Dad didn't share her missionary call and when they married, my mother, a city girl, bravely agreed to adopt the life of a farmer's wife in an isolated rural community. They faithfully ran the local Sunday school. He became a regular lay preacher and on his day could be very good. Let me give you a broadbrush version of the faith I was brought up in. It lived uneasily with its twin Brethren and Presbyterian roots. My parents ran a Sunday school in the local Presbyterian church but they hung loose to just about everything else that went on there. My father often stated that the Presbyterian Church had turned away from its historic faith and he thus paid only token financial contributions and declined to take any official position. My parents rejected its practice of infant baptism, thought services too formal and said the preaching lacked both Bible exposition and a clear gospel message. They attended, somewhat grudgingly because it had one important attribute – it was unrivalled in the district as 'the best boat to fish from'.

Then when Sunday school and the morning service were over we would all pile into the car and speed (as fast as an incredibly bumpy road would allow) to the nearest big town to a 'lively' evangelical church. There my sister, brother and I went through yet another course of Sunday school, spectated at the regular 'open air witness' and attended a 'lively' service in the early evening. Sundays were exhausting.

We were taught to pray at bed time. Family devotions around the dinner table consisted of a long Bible reading and an even longer extemporary prayer from my father. I quickly noticed the prayers were sermon-like, reiterating the reading, peppered with quotes of assorted texts, joined up by some aspect of what I would these days call the Christian 'meta narrative' – the broad sweep of the creation, fall, redemption and the expectation of the return of Christ. When, many years later, I asked my father about his methods, he said, 'One way or another I was determined to get it into you!' I have to say that while my later spiritual journey included a search for something more restful, I'm deeply grateful to my father. The Bible and the Christian story is part of every sinew of my body and soul.

But let me offer a brief critique. It was a form of religion that cut us off from the rest of the community. No one we knew, save perhaps members of the tiny local Pentecostal church nearby, fed their Christianity with such high-energy fuel. The Keswick strand demanded near spiritual perfection. We tended to think of ourselves as the only true Christians, even though the tiny hamlet nearest to us had three churches, all well attended. Then, it was world-denying. An obsession with refuting evolution left a somewhat threadbare doctrine of creation. The 'world' was to be avoided. No comics, no dancing, no drinking, no tobacco smoking, of course, but it went deeper than that. Here was a brand of religion that affirmed a pre-existent Christ, now risen, ascended and glorified and soon to return as judge. It was not very comfortable, however, with the doctrine of the incarnation. It could be highly imaginative in discerning allegorical 'types' of Christ in Old Testament characters, but it put little emphasis on the human Jesus of the gospels, save when he was on the stage as a teacher, as in the Sermon on the Mount. It was a faith much more comfortable with being 'a city on a hill' than 'salt and light'. It was a visible presence, occasionally addressing neighbours with a metaphorical megaphone, but less comfortable with the call to be fully part of the community, invisibly penetrating every part of society. Happily, I think, the Presbyterian side managed to keep us in touch with the general community. If the Brethrenism side had reigned supreme, I suspect we would have been even more cut off. The Brethren people we knew kept very much to themselves. Some wouldn't even consent for their wheat harvest to be sold through the local collection point, though I never worked out what they thought of the fact that it would inevitably be mixed up with other people's wheat in the hold of a ship bound for China. They lived a Sunday world where there was generous hospitality, and great love and care. It helped them to rest in preparation for the return to Monday's world, a ruthless business environment where their aim was no less than to 'slay the Amalekites'.

Inevitably this world disappeared. At fourteen, I went off to Sydney, lived with an aunt and uncle and attended the Anglican cathedral school. Being a day boy rather than a boarder was wonderful, because it suddenly widened my horizons. At fifteen, I was playing senior cricket. Visiting the homes of other boys, I found it was possible to have a Christianity that was relaxed about issues where my parents had been anything but relaxed. Here were real, compassionate Christians who approved of dancing, cinema, good wine and even a moderate intake of beer. Cathedral services and the chance to pray silently in that space signalled there was more than one way to worship. In the Prayer Book communion service, I discovered richer symbolism and sheer beauty than I'd previously encountered at the Lord's Table.

There were other challenges to come. At university, I deliberately took subjects I knew would make me think out my faith. I found philosophy hard going. More challenging, perhaps, were subjects like sociology and education where the aim of godless faculties was to impart a totally relativistic world view. Most of my peers lapped it up with glee. I owed much to the Evangelical Union, of which I eventually became president. Its custom was to hold weekly 'public lectures'. It took the university agenda seriously and debated many of the questions raised in the intellectual life of the community. It offered regular Bible expositions that built historico-grammatical-literary analysis onto what I'd already taken in under my father's influence. Alongside this, I was taking courses in New Testament under a sceptical lecturer. There I encountered, among other things, biblical criticism and the various quests for the historical Jesus. The combination was mind-blowing. Sadly, relating to my home community sometimes became painful. I no longer felt understood. With so much swirling around inside, I can well understand why.

It has taken many years to gradually bring together in harmony all these parts of me. I had to bring together the enormous love for the Bible, a hallmark of Brethrenism, with insights from modern biblical criticism; and the use of allegory in spiritual imagination drawing not only from the Scriptures but from the resources of the Christian church in all its varieties throughout all the ages. I sensed that my family's faith sought to squeeze me into a particular mould. In the Anglican Church I found a context for a faith that is eucharistic – incidentally another Brethren hallmark – evangelical, reformed, catholic, socially engaged, and where, at its best, there is space for me to be myself.

Deeper engagement in ecumenism came some years later, but it's said that I did a lot to foster ecumenical understanding as president of my university Evangelical Union. One day I took part in a forum with the very conservative Catholic chaplain, a Vincentian father named John Wilkinson. I asked him point blank: 'Do you, Father Wilkinson, recognise me, John Martin, as a fellow Christian?' He said he saw me as 'a potential Christian'.

Now Dwight, I suspect you will argue that the route I have taken on my spiritual journey was from a very particular form of faith to something that deserves the label 'catholic'. And you may want to chivvy me and say that the logical end of the journey ought to be embracing the Roman Catholic Church. I have to say that I don't find John Wilkinson's answer any more satisfactory than what the Jehovah's Witnesses offer when they knock on my door. When I ask them what assurance they can offer me of personal salvation, they say 'They that endure to the end shall be saved' (Mt. 24:13). Neither of these offer much to bank on.

There are all sorts of other issues we'll debate in the pages that follow. We will disagree quite a bit. I can't accept the authority claims of the Pope, either on the basis of history, theological necessity, or the needs of our contemporary culture. In our Western culture, the last thing the twenty-first century seeker of spiritual truth needs is hierarchies and religious pomp and circumstance. We will find we have different views on what the Scriptures are for and their place in the life of the Christian. I won't skim over some of the skeletons in the Catholic cupboard and I expect you'll give as good as you get. But I suspect our readers will be surprised at just how much agreement we find.

Assurance of salvation is my bottom line. I can't remember my answer to John Wilkinson all those years ago. I think I left it to the listening audience to make its own judgement on what he said. Today I believe, as I did then, that when I stand before my Maker, I can do so with full assurance of salvation. My plea will not be anything good that I have done, but in the work of God in Jesus in reconciling the world to himself, work in which (to use a phrase from John Henry Newman, who began as an Evangelical but embraced Roman Catholicism) I 'hope and trust most fully'.

Dwight: I'm delighted to hear more details of your evangelical childhood in Australia, since it so closely parallels my own home life in America. We're both about the same age and it's great to find somebody from the other end of the world who also came to England twenty years ago and found a home away from home.

My father's ancestors were Mennonites from the Emmenthal valley in Switzerland. The Mennonites are an Anabaptist sect – such extreme Protestants that they were persecuted by Calvin. Along with Quakers, Shakers, Moravians, Amish and other free church Christians, they came to Pennsylvania in the 1770s to find religious freedom and build a new society based on biblical principles. My mother's family was a mixture of Brethren, Mennonite and Reformed Christians. By the 1930s however, my grandfathers on both sides broke away from the religious traditions of their families. My Dad's father left the Mennonites to go to Philadelphia and learn business. For a time after his marriage he couldn't find a church he liked, so he led the family of six children in worship at home. My mother's father left the Reformed church because it was drifting toward 'liberal' ideas. He and his family joined a new independent Bible fellowship.

My own family life was much like yours. Every night Dad would lead Mom and us five kids in family devotions. We read the Bible and a little devotional booklet called *Our Daily Bread*. Sometimes we kids would mime favourite Bible stories and everybody else had to guess what the story was. The all-time Oscar winner for this biblical drama was marching in a circle around the house banging pots and pans and tooting horns. This noisy spectacle was Joshua marching around Jericho. Twice on Sunday and on Wednesday nights we went to an 'independent fundamental' Bible church where my Dad was senior deacon and taught Sunday school. The pastor was a graduate of Bob Jones university – a fundamentalist school founded by a revivalist preacher in the southern Bible Belt.

As in your home, our religion had a sectarian mentality. We were cut off from the rest of the world. Since we lived in the country this was a geographical reality too. I can remember how people outside our church were regarded as targets for conversion, and was somewhat surprised when I discovered some of my schoolmates also went to church, and one or two of their fathers were actually pastors. We never went to any of their churches. I can't remember any negative teaching, but it was assumed that they weren't really Christians. We had the same prohibitions you had – no movies, no cards, no drinking or smoking, no gambling, no dancing, little make-up for the girls. The fact that one of the local churches hosted a dance every Saturday night during the school term was a shocking confirmation of their sinfulness. As for the Catholics! They not only smoked and drank, but they had dances too. Furthermore, they gambled at their bingo sessions every Saturday. In Pennsylvania the religious divisions had an ethnic dimension too. For the most part the people of Swiss, German and English descent were Protestants. The Italians, Irish, Poles and Hispanic folks were Catholics. They had their own culture as well as their own religion.

This 'us and them' mentality extended to the preaching at our church. There was a strong element of apocalyptic teaching. Evangelists would visit who explained the fearful prophecies of Daniel and Revelation in terms of current events. With a fervent style of delivery, the preachers would warn us of the coming Armageddon, remind us of the rapture when Jesus would appear in the sky to take all the saved to glory, and exhort us to get saved before it was too late. It was assumed that all us fundamentalist Christians would get 'raptured' leaving all the wicked deluded world to perish in the aftermath.

Reflecting back on my evangelical home life I have more to be grateful for than to criticise. Like you, I'm eternally grateful for the strong Christian principles of my parents. I'm proud of my Christian heritage. For over five hundred years we can trace an extended clan that has had the courage to follow Christ in an uncompromising way. Like you, I received an education in the Scriptures which was second to none. The beautiful cadences of the Authorised Version ring through my heart and mind and I still turn to the King James Version to find verses I want because they are the words I memorised in Sunday school. I'm also grateful for the emphasis on a personal relationship with Jesus Christ. One Sunday night after church when I was five years old, I told my Mom I didn't want to go to hell and that I wanted to accept Jesus into my life. I still remember kneeling down with her and saying sorry for my sins and asking Jesus into my heart. I consider that my first experience of conversion and cherish it still. I'm also thankful for the emphasis on total commitment to Christ and the need for a holy life. On my grandmother's wall was a bit of needle-work which read, 'Only one life 'twill soon be past, Only what's done for God will last.' It may be trite, but it's true. Generations of my family lived by that vision and I never want to forget it.

Like you, this idyllic form of Christianity started to unravel a bit with higher education. Mine happened in a different way. In an attempt to preserve this pure religion, my parents sent all of us off to a fundamentalist university. They had gone there for a couple of years. My grandfather was on the board of directors and it was natural for us to go there. This was in the early seventies when American campuses were florid with the hippie movement, sex, drugs and rock and roll. A Christian university seemed a safe bet.

In retrospect, our faith might have held up better had we gone to the local state university. We were confronted with sex, drugs and rock and roll in high school and simply chose good friends and avoided the stuff. Our Christian training worked well and we chose well. At a secular college we would have been okay and our faith – because it was in a challenging situation – probably would have shone more brightly. In the extreme fundamentalist atmosphere, the religion went sour.

Our Christian home life was quiet, devotional, devout, sincere and loving. In contrast, my university was a hootin' and hollerin' hellfire and brimstone place. These are the folks who branded Billy Graham a liberal. The rules for college kids were archaic, nonsensical and absurd. Boys couldn't talk to girls before nine o'clock in the morning. If you wanted to date a girl you had to formally write her a note. Dates off campus had to be chaperoned by a staff member. Bells rang for everything from rising at seven to lights out at eleven. With its barbed wire fences and hot religion, the place was a mixture of a boot camp and a non-stop revivalist meeting. Mixed with the oppressive religion was southern racism, a hatred for Catholicism and a cynical cunning which realised how much money could be made out of religion in the deep south. This backwoods religion was strangely blended with a stream of high culture. They had a good Fine Arts department, made full length Christian movies and each year they did two Shakespeare plays and a grand opera.

Despite the oppressive religious atmosphere, I got a fairly decent education there. I did so because by this time I was genuinely interested in learning, and read everything I could get hold of. I listened to music, learned to like opera, Shakespeare, good art and English literature. I travelled to Europe and got hooked on England. While at college in America, I went to a little Anglican church which had broken away from the Episcopalians, and my Christian faith, which had withered under the constant fundamentalist harangue, was refreshed. I had discovered the religion of my heroes – everyone from John Donne and George Herbert to T S Eliot and C S Lewis. One night at Evensong in a little stone church in South Carolina I gave up my struggle and gave my life to be a priest in the Church of England. I decided I would go for the real thing – to see if I could study in England and be a country parson like George Herbert.

A year after leaving college I wrote to the evangelical Englishman James Packer and asked him to recommend some colleges in England. He kindly wrote back suggesting three. I was accepted at Wycliffe Hall, Oxford. As a devout Anglophile, Oxford was my Mecca and I was thrilled to be studying at the heart of all I considered English. Anglicanism seemed refreshing. Like you, I discovered a historic faith which had room for me and was evangelical, charismatic, catholic and socially aware all at the same time. I fell in love with the music, the buildings, the liturgy, the culture and the people of Anglicanism. Eventually I was ordained and ended up as a country parson on the Isle of Wight. It was a dream come true and I was very happy.

I'll be telling more of what brought me out of Anglicanism into the Catholic Church in the pages to follow, but I can say briefly here that I have found in the Catholic Church not a denial of the Christian faith I had before, but a fulfilment of it. Every good thing from my evangelical home, and all the good things within Anglicanism are fulfilled and completed in the Catholic Church.

I like your story of the Catholic priest who said you were a 'potential Christian'. It sounds a hard thing for him to say to you, but is it really any different than our attitude as Evangelicals towards Catholics? The Catholic priest at that time may not have regarded you as a Christian, but we fundamentalists didn't regard them as Christians either, did we? Isn't this a two-way street? After all, we heard missionaries return from Catholic countries saying how much the people there needed to be converted from the 'darkness of Catholicism' and it was considered a fact in my childhood religion that Catholics needed to 'get saved' or they were going to hell just like all the other pagans. I'm not meaning to throw stones, just pointing out that both sides at that time didn't regard the other folks as anything more than 'potential Christians'.

I can't speak for the Catholic priest who judged you a 'potential Christian', but I can tell you what the Catholic Church teaches today about non-Catholic Christians. The new Catechism of the Catholic Church is a wonderful, Scripture-based document which reformulates the age-old teaching of the Catholic Church for the twenty-first century. Firstly it recognises 'with respect and affection... all who have been justified by faith and who through baptism have been incorporated into Christ. They have a right to be called Christians and with good reason are accepted as brothers in the Lord by the children of the Catholic Church' (*Catechism of the Catholic Church* [CCC], paragraph 818)[1]. About non-Catholic Christian groups says, 'many elements of sanctification and of truth are found outside the visible confines of the Catholic Church: the

written word of God; the life of grace, faith, hope and charity
... as well as other visible elements. Christ's spirit uses these
churches and ecclesial communities as means of salvation
whose power derives from the fullness of grace and truth that
Christ has entrusted to the Catholic Church. All these blessings come from Christ and lead to him' (CCC, 819).

You then went on to speak of the assurance of salvation.
Later on I guess we'll get into the topic of 'eternal security' and
salvation, but you ended by quoting Cardinal Newman that
you 'hope and trust most fully'. Well, then you are expressing
the Catholic view. We don't hold to the Calvinist doctrine of
'eternal security' which means once saved, you can never lose
your salvation. Instead, like you we put our whole trust and
hope in God's never failing mercy and grace. We accept the
biblical promises that 'God is not willing for any to perish' (2
Pet. 3:9), and that 'his mercy endureth forever' (Ps. 136).
Trusting fully in his grace, with you we 'hope and trust most
fully', knowing that if we 'endure to the end we will be saved'
(Mt. 10:22).

John: Clearly we've established quite a bit of common ground
as far as family life was concerned and I find that fascinating.
I suspect there is a lot of similarity between the piety of
American communities with roots in Europe and the kind I
was brought up with. In both our stories, it seems that the real
watershed was moving on into higher and further education.
For me the changes stemmed as much from the widening of
aesthetic appreciation as they did from formal academic learning. I suspect my parents supported my education in the belief
that it would help complete the foundations they'd laid. I'm
not sure they bargained for a radical change in me.

What I didn't say earlier on was that one of the huge influences on my spiritual life in my late teens and early twenties
was my parents going through a bout of falling out with just
about every Christian connection they had. A capacity to fall
out has always been very characteristic of Evangelicals. The
late Archbishop Donald Coggan once bemused his hearers
when he said Evangelicals are fissiparous (the root word is fis-

sion, the tendency to divide). It is one of the explanations for the multiplication of Brethren, Baptist and other Free Evangelical churches, and perhaps even the emergence of some of the so-called New churches here in Britain. I agree with Coggan and suspect the problem grows from a confusion between loving and liking. Christ commanded Christians to love and we can sustain that if we understand that there's no corresponding injunction to like each other. The net result of my parents' various fallings-out was that they took up with people and groups who were much more extreme. Falling out leaves people lonely and sometimes in order to be accepted by a particular group, the price is subscribing to extreme doctrinal positions.

I saw my parents being stretched in all sorts of directions in this process. Those years were very traumatic and they raised very important questions for me. One was whether there were alternatives to a system of church government and administration that was like living in a goldfish bowl. What external reference points could save members of the communiy from stifling each other? What was needed to prevent members either lapsing into collective error or living in permanent disagreement over issues like end-time theories? We will return to these questions as we open up issues like authority in the church.

About your comments on what I started to say about salvation, I take at least one of your points. Certainly my parents would never have conceded that Catholics could be saved. They possessed a couple of books on cults and heresies. At least one of them included Roman Catholicism among its proscribed list. It never ceases to surprise me just how many people who are broadly evangelical appear to hold that view or something close to it.

You may be right when you say the position I have taken on salvation closely resembles a Catholic position. I would argue that in Anglicanism you have Catholicism in a reformed version, so no apologies for that. But later in the book, when we come to disuss the Reformation and the debate about justification, it will be an opportunity to examine the 'fine print' of what we mean by salvation. Among the issues for me will be

whether Catholic claims over the position of the Pope as possessor of the 'Keys of the Kingdom' touch on the issue of salvation. And there's still enough of the Calvinist in me to want
to take 'eternal security' seriously, though for me what is certain is that the way God works on these matters is bound to
trump our puny minds and imaginations

Dwight: Don't you love the English mastery of understate-
ment? Coggan's mild rebuke that Evangelicals tend to be fissiparous is a classic. As of 1981, the Oxford University Press'
World Christian Encyclopaedia[2] listed no fewer than 20,800 different Christian Protestant denominations. If you think British
and Australian Evangelicalism tends to be divisive, you ought
to try America. Over there creating new denominations is a
national pastime.

Like you, I lament this state of affairs, but the problem is
caused by more than whether we 'like' the other members of
our Christian fellowship or not. As you've suggested, the divisions are over doctrinal and moral matters which the warring
parties consider very important. Some Amish sects have
divided over whether clothes can have snaps and zips or just
pins and buttons. The fights may seem small to outsiders, but
anyone who has gone through such division knows they are
real and long-lasting with bitter condemnations on both sides.

Christ prayed passionately that all his disciples would be
one (Jn. 17:21) and he said the church was to be one flock with
one shepherd (Jn. 10:16). It seems pretty clear to me that all the
sad divisions within Protestant Christianity have their roots in
the Reformation when a single, historic and unified church
authority was abandoned. I agree with you that each new division produces a smaller and more extreme group, but it is also
true that each new extreme group is one step further from the
mainstream of historic, fundamental Christianity. I want to
press you on this a bit further in later chapters, but I bring it
up now because the need for a central authority is going to
determine my mode of discussion in our book.

I want to defend and commend the Catholic Church as that
central Christian authority which can heal the divisions in

Christ's body. I hope I will be able to make it attractive, while still admitting the terrible faults and problems within it. To do this, I am going to avoid stating my own opinion as much as possible, referring instead to the Scriptures and the Catechism of the Catholic Church. In referring to the Scriptures and the teaching of the Catholic Church, I hope to show how the Catholic understanding of the faith offers a solid rock on which to build.

I will refer to Scripture and the Catechism for a couple of other reasons. Firstly, many non-Catholic Christians still suspect the Catholic Church of being contrary to Scripture and ignorant of Scripture. I hope to show how, from the beginning, the Catholic Church has been the Bible church par excellence. Secondly, I know there are many non-Catholics who disagree with the Catholic Church, when in fact they simply disagree with what they *think* the Catholic Church teaches. By using the Catechism I hope our readers will come to understand what Catholics really believe, rather than what they think we believe.

John, in our discussion I'm going to make some pretty sharp criticisms of the Protestant position, and I'm sure you won't hesitate to point out the weaknesses of the Catholic Church. I hope none of what I say will be taken personally, and I hope all our discussions will be like one of those family pow-wows which gets a bit tense, but ends up clearing the air. Afterwards everybody has learned something and comes away from it feeling humbled but happy that through the struggle truth has found a way out.

1All quotes from the Cathechism of the Catholic Church used in this book are taken from the *Catechism of the Catholic Church*, (London: Geoffrey Chapman, 1994)

2World Christian Encyclopedia, (Oxford: Oxford University Press, 1981)

Chapter One

Only the Bible?

John:

> Read Demosthenes or Cicero; read Plato or Aristotle, or any others of that class; I grant you that you will be attracted, delighted, moved, enraptured by them in a surprising manner; but if, after reading them, you turn to the perusal of the sacred volume, whether you are willing or unwilling, it will affect you so powerfully, it will so penetrate your heart, and impress itself so strangely on your mind that, compared with its energetic influence, the beauties of the rhetoricians and philosophers will almost certainly disappear; so that it is easy to perceive something divine in the sacred Scriptures, which far surpasses the highest attainments and ornaments of human history.
>
> John Calvin, from *The Institutes 8.1.*[1]

The classical Evangelical would claim not only that the Bible is the supreme authority in all matters of faith and conduct, but that it is infused with a divine power that challenges and transforms the reader, bursting old spiritual wineskins and reshaping society. This is why Evangelicals have put a premium on Bible translation and given large sums to help found Bible societies. I am someone shaped by this heritage. In personal evangelism, for instance, I have sometimes given enquirers a copy of Mark's gospel and invited them to read it in one sitting, asking themselves the question 'What do you think of the Jesus you meet in these pages?' To my amazement, several times such people have come back to me testifying that they've met Jesus for themselves – been converted, if you like. This is a book that's greater than the sum of its parts.

An evangelical apologia for the Bible and its place in the church begins with Jesus. As a disciple of Jesus, how do I emulate his attitude to the Scriptures? From the gospels we see that Jesus gave the Old Testament Scriptures the highest place. He says 'not one jot nor tittle' would pass away. He sometimes attributes words from the Old Testament, penned by a human author, to God himself. As for the New Testament, he told the apostles that the Holy Spirit would 'bring to your remembrance the things you have learned concerning me'. So taking a cue from Jesus, I have a Bible that is utterly reliable.

Now I can feel you bursting to come in and I won't hold you up for long, but there's a further point to consider. Plenty of people will argue that the meaning of the Bible is often unclear and it's full of traps for the unwary. Even though I've done biblical criticism at university level, I can't accept that; nor have the Protestant reformers or the Evangelicals over the centuries. I would submit that there are surprisingly few verses in the Bible whose meaning is unclear, and I can think of none that would leave anyone in jeopardy over key issues such as the doctrine of salvation. William Tyndale, the great English Bible translator, taught that the Bible is perspicuous, clear enough on its own account to be understood by all. He once told a Catholic bishop that its plain meaning would not be lost even on a simple ploughboy. So taking my cue from Tyndale and the reformers, I have a Bible that I can understand in the broad sweep of things.

Dwight: I like the quote from Calvin. There's nothing there the Catholic Church would disagree with. From the beginning the Catholic Church has venerated the Bible as the supernatural word of God. The catechism says, 'In Sacred Scripture the Church constantly finds her nourishment and her strength, for she welcomes it not as a human word, but as what it really is, the word of God' (CCC, 104). Furthermore, the Catholic Church teaches the divine inspiration of Scripture: 'God inspired the human authors of the sacred books...God chose certain men who, all the while he employed them in this task, made full use of their own faculties and powers so that, though he acted in them and by them, it was as true authors that they consigned to writing whatever he wanted written and no more' (CCC, 106).

Like you, the Catholic Church recognises in the Scriptures the living and powerful word of God and so encourages us to read and study the Scriptures: 'Such is the force and power of the word of God that it can serve the Church as her support and vigour; and the children of the Church as strength for their faith, food for the soul and a pure and lasting fountain of spiritual life' (CCC,131). 'The Church forcefully and specifically exhorts all the Christian faithful to learn the surpassing knowledge of Jesus Christ (Phil. 3:8) by frequent reading of the divine Scriptures' (CCC,133), and St Jerome, that great biblical scholar and translator from the fourth century, reminds us that 'Ignorance of the Scriptures is ignorance of Christ.'

So far so good, but I'm afraid I can't buy your idea of the perspicuity of Scripture. There are two problems: first of all, if the Bible is so easy and clear to understand, why do we have over 20,000 different Protestant denominations? When I asked this question years ago, my evangelical Bible teacher said that the differences were only minor, and that we all really agreed on the basics. But the different groups don't disagree only about minor things like whether women should wear hats to church or whether you should be sprinkled, dipped or dunked for baptism. They disagree about major questions – is baptism necessary for salvation? How does a person get saved? Can you lose your salvation or not? Do good works matter? What is a sacrament? It's easy to say that the Scriptures are essentially clear, but experience doesn't bear it out because all the different Christian groups and individuals appeal to the same Scriptures to make their conflicting points. It's been this way from the beginning. In the second century some Christians said Jesus was God incarnate, others said he was not, and the problem was that the folks on both sides were good Christians and both argued their case powerfully from Scripture.

The second clear problem is what you do when Scripture doesn't present a clear teaching on some matter of crucial importance. This is especially important in our day since so many important moral questions are products of the modern age. The Bible simply doesn't discuss things like *in vitro* fertil-isation, human cloning, atomic warfare or global warming. When there are disagreements and when the Bible doesn't speak clearly, who decides? In other words, who interprets the Bible for our needs? It is either up to you and me or some authority greater than both of us.

John: I'm flattered that you seem to speak of perspicuity as my idea. You may not have meant it quite that way, but let me assure you, when I try to explain or represent my heritage of faith, I have an overwhelming feeling that I'm a pygmy who possesses a field of vision only because I sit on the shoulders of the giants of faith who have gone before. Having agreed with my quote from Calvin, I suspect you'll now want to claim that here's another Catholic position I'm taking!

Dwight: Well, it's certainly a Catholic idea that we look to the faith of our fathers for guidance. Now that I'm Catholic, I just find it rather arbitrary that Protestants look faithfully to the Christian giants from five hundred years ago, while being fairly neglectful of all the Christian giants from the first fifteen hundred years of Church history.

John: Let me take up your point about the multiplication of denominations. I think it's simplistic to suggest that the exis-tence of some 20,000 different non-Catholic denominations results from inability to agree about how the Bible is to be interpreted. Certainly it was one of the elements at stake in the sixteenth century Reformation, but even there it's not the entire story. The emergence of nationalism and the politics of northern Europe and England certainly played their part in fuelling the split with Rome. Then there are black churches around where I live, that exist in no small measure because their people didn't feel welcome in predominately white churches.

There are others, like the Adventists, Baptists, the Holiness churches or Kimbanguists, from Central Africa, who exist as a result of what they believe to be a special revelation. Others are convinced that their community is called to witness to some particular emphasis that has been lost sight of in the Christian mainstream. There is also the effect of differing God-given personality types that prefer one kind of worship over another.

My view, for what it is worth, is that the real source of the differences is that, consciously or unconsciously, we all come to the Bible with a pre-existing theological framework. The Catholic Church is no exception. Its Doctors, men like Ambrose, Augustine and Thomas Aquinas, created a theological system that fused the Hebraic and Classical thought worlds of their day. Their system has given the Catholic Church many of the tools it uses even now to resolve theological questions. But many non-Catholics cannot accept its basic theological methodology, not least because it accepts the dualistic basis of Classical thought, with its false dichotomy between the material and the spiritual. A lot of serious problems flow from this false distinction.

Is it such a big scandal that there are 20,000 different denominations? A lot of people, many Catholics included, view the multiplication of denominations as a mistake. I'm not so convinced. I see this as part of the economy of God. He glories in the sheer variety of people he's made. The emergence of new denominations, in the Protestant world, and new orders or movements, in the Catholic world, are part of God's way of seeing that issues that are neglected by the mainstream are championed. We will no doubt touch on this issue again.

Dwight: I'm prepared to admit that God has used the 20,000 different denominations to further his work in the world, but he's always in the business of pulling good out of our human sinfulness. As you've hinted, the Catholic Church values diversity, but the Catholic model is not 20,000 different denominations existing as a law unto themselves. Instead the diversity of emphasis, culture and theological approach exist within the organic unity of the Catholic Church. We have unity, but not uniformity. Sectarian religion expects uniformity and only has internal unity because it has split from everybody else.

John: Let's go back to the Bible. I need to make a couple of other points clear. One of the slogans of the Reformation was *sola Scriptura* ('Scripture alone'). It was part of a triplet, the other points being 'by grace alone' and 'through faith alone'. For a long time I believed that the brand of Christianity I followed was genuinely based on them. But what the experiences of my late teens and early twenties helped make clear was that plenty of Christians could assent to these slogans but still come to different conclusions than mine.

Dwight: That's what I mean. If *sola Scriptura* is fine and the Bible is perfectly clear, then why do all the different Protestant groups come up with such different interpretations that they have to split up all the time?

John: Let me finish. One of the possible solutions, of course, would have been joining a church whose teaching office or magisterium (the basis by which the Catholic Church makes doctrinal pronouncements) claimed to take away the problem of multiple interpretations. The Catholic Church was the obvious candidate, but I found that it, too, had feet of clay. Pope Paul VI had just enunciated his teaching on contraception. Reading Hans Kung's critique of papal infallibility reinforced my inherited Protestant scepticism.

Dwight: We'll talk about papal infallibility later.

John: Okay, but the problem is a real one and for much of my life there's been a quest for a more thought-out understanding of the place of Scripture and its authority. The basic convictions stand. The Bible is God's book and it is the Christian's final court of appeal. It will never lead me into error in matters essential to Christian living or my salvation. However, in contrast to my early days – and here is the Anglican influence – alongside I would want to affirm the place of reason (our God-given intelligence), tradition (the Creeds and the accumulated teachings of the church over two millennia) and experience (what we see around us of how God works) as tools we bring to help us to understand the Bible. There are two other considerations. First, biblical interpretation poses the challenge to 'know thyself'. I need to approach the enterprise with humility because I am apt to read the Bible through lenses coloured by my own personality type, my particular experiences, and a Western culture that doesn't naturally understand the biblical world, so that it tends to read its own world-view into the Bible. Secondly, more positively – and this is most important – I can be confident that the Holy Spirit, who inspired the Scripture and was promised in order to lead the church 'into all truth', will do just that.

Dwight: This is certainly a stronger position than the extreme evangelical one which says, 'It's just me and my Bible.' But I still want to press you on this because the basic problem still stands. Okay, you want to include reason and tradition to help interpret the Bible, but whose reason and which tradition? Just as we can prove almost anything from the Bible, so with our own agenda we can prove almost anything through reason and tradition. The Catholic Church insists that an objective, historical and universal interpretative authority is still required in order to correctly ascertain God's truth.

I take your point that the Holy Spirit is of vital importance for interpreting the Bible, but I'm afraid my own basic point still stands. We all claim the Holy Spirit's guidance for our own interpretations don't we? No doubt all 20,000 Protestant denominations all claim the Holy Spirit's work, and yet they all disagree. Was the Holy Spirit wrong? Did he lead some of them into the truth, but mislead others? In fact the Holy Spirit was given within the context of the community of faith. It is primarily the church which is the Spirit-filled body of Christ according to the New Testament, and individuals are filled with the Holy Spirit as the fruit of that. Therefore the Catholic Church teaches that only through the church can the Holy Spirit work authentically and most fully. Therefore it is only the church which can most authentically interpret Scripture.

John: You say that issues such as *in vitro* fertilisation, human cloning, atomic warfare or global warming are not directly addressed by the Bible. In one sense that's right. I would argue, however, that they can be dealt with by application of tradition, reason and experience to what the scholars call the biblical 'meta-narrative' – the broad sweep of the biblical story and the doctrinal building blocks that underlie it. The full story of God as Creator, human beings made in God's image, God's action in redeeming lost humanity, the cross and resurrection, and all the rest combine to give us guidance. But that's a subject for a book on its own.

Dwight: I agree, and the Catholic Church turns to these principles as well as competent medical and scientific authorities to help her come up with the right decisions. But at the risk of sounding like a broken record, my basic point still stands. Even with all the professional consultation and discussion in the world, somebody still needs to make the final decision. Who is best placed to make a decision on global issues like this? Who is best placed to decide the Christian position? I would argue that the best authority to decide is the one which is oldest, biggest and most universal, and therefore sees the biggest picture: in other words, the Catholic Church.

Let me pick you up on another point. You mentioned the Reformation catch-phrase *sola Scriptura*. I was brought up with this idea as well. I understand that most Evangelicals take your position that the Bible is studied along with works by competent Bible scholars, Christian teachers from the past and their own reason – all inspired by the Holy Spirit. Despite this the Bible is still the final authority. However there are two big problems with *sola Scriptura*. The first problem is logical. If the sole authority is Scripture, how do we know that is so? Evangelicals will bring out a list of verses which uphold the holiness of Scripture trying to prove *sola Scriptura* from Scripture. But this is a classic case of logical tail-chasing. It's circular reasoning. How do we know the Bible is inspired? Because it says it's inspired. But how do we know that verse is inspired? Because the Bible is inspired. And how do we know the Bible is inspired? Because the Bible says it's inspired. It makes you dizzy, but more importantly it shows that for the Bible to have any authority it needs to have another objective, historical authority to validate it.

Down through history that authority has been the church. The Scriptures were written by the church, and used by the church in worship and teaching. Then it was the church who determined over a period of time what books were to go into the Bible. The church was first and the Bible came from the church – not the other way around. The Holy Spirit inspired the church first at Pentecost, and by the leaders of the church and for the church's needs the Bible was written. Therefore the Catholic Church still says that the church is the authentic authority to interpret the Bible today.

There's another weakness with *sola Scriptura*. Let's put the circular logic objection to one side and allow that the Bible might actually teach *sola Scriptura*. When we begin to look for proof in the Bible, it's not there. We can find many verses which show the permanence, the holiness and the power of the word of God, but none which say it is the only or final authority on earth. The classic proof text for *sola Scriptura* is 2 Timothy 3:16 which says, 'All Scripture is God-breathed and is useful for teaching, rebuking, correcting and training in right-eousness.' This is a great verse and Catholics would agree on the inspiration and usefulness of Scripture; but the verse itself doesn't actually say the *only* authority is Scripture. So what is the foundational authority for our knowledge of the truth? The New Testament actually points to the church as that uni-versal authority. You say the Bible is the Christian's final authority and court of appeal, but St Paul says in Ephesians 3:10 that 'through the church the manifold wisdom of God will be made known', and in I Timothy 3:15 he says it is the *church* which is 'the pillar and foundation of the truth.'

John: I suspect our readers may be wondering why it was you, not me, who first cited 2 Timothy 3:16! You will have seen I've been careful to root the argument elsewhere, in the attitudes and example of Jesus. Even so, taken at face value this verse makes enormous claims and I don't think your circularising quite does it justice. If the Scriptures are God-breathed, then they come into a very special category of literature which I must take with enormous seriousness, leaving no stone unturned in seeking to understand their message. I find it helpful, too, that the text draws some lines about what exactly the Scriptures are there for. There are all sorts of issues and debates where I'm not obliged by this verse to look to the Scriptures for guidance or an authoritative word. I am encouraged here to look to them for 'teaching, rebuking, correcting and training in righteousness.' But I don't think I'm obliged to look there for an authoritative word on matters of history, science, sociology and so on.

I think our argument revolves around what comes first, the Scriptures or the church. Your position seems to be that the church is the primary factor, with the church defining the canon of Scripture in the first place and offering its accumulated wisdom as the authoritative interpreter. My position is that the actions of God in history, in speaking and inspiring human agents to write, come first.

Over many years a broad consensus has emerged as to which books and writings authentically bear a 'ring of truth' and the *a priori* commitment of the Christians, from the Pope downwards, should be to believe and obey what the Scriptures contain and teach in matters of faith. I may, of course, resort to reason, tradition and experience to assist me in the task.

Dwight: I'm not sure your analysis of our disagreement is quite right. The main question is not, 'Which comes first, the church or Scripture?' We don't believe either the Scriptures or the church come first. Instead Jesus comes first. The primary revelation of God to mankind is in his Son Jesus Christ, the Word made flesh. The Bible is the secondary revelation which bears witness to God's work in Christ. The book of Hebrews puts it this way, 'In many various ways God spoke of old to our fathers by the prophets, but in these last days he has spoken to us by a Son' (Heb. 1:1-2). The catechism says, 'the Christian faith is not a 'religion of the book.' Christianity is the religion of the word of God. Not a written and mute word, but incarnate and living. If the Scriptures are not to remain a dead letter, Christ the eternal word of the living God, must through the Holy Spirit open our minds to understand the Scriptures' (CCC, 108).

So God's work in and through real people's lives down through history is his primary revelation. This story is told in the inspired Scriptures and his ultimate revelation is through the word of God incarnate – his Son Jesus Christ. Jesus commanded and prophesied a church which would be his body on earth and that church produced the Scriptures which bear witness of him. That same church used the Scriptures for worship and teaching, and eventually they came to define which books were to go into the New Testament.

John: Let me make two comments. First, when it comes to the question of the canon, you've put your finger on a weakness in the armoury of many Protestants. Frankly, very few have thought deeply about it. Then I would add – to our shame – that while many of us claim to be Bible people with a high doctrine of Scripture, our standards of exegesis and interpretation don't match our claims. One of the blights of the Protestant churches is the tendency to be lazy or even downright sloppy in the way they handle Scripture. Secondly – and I think this needs to be heard by people not very familiar with the Church of Rome – when I've visited Rome, I've been enormously impressed by the seriousness with which the Catholic Church's universities and seminaries take the Bible and the depth of their scholarship. And I find that when I meet with lay Catholics to study the Bible, they tend to come to it with much less 'baggage' than their Protestant counterparts, so that the original meaning comes through quickly. It's a sign of very good spiritual health.

Dwight: I never thought of the Protestant churches as being lazy or sloppy in the way they handle Scripture, but maybe you're right. While we're admitting faults, I have to confess that I really don't think Catholics have the same level of Bible knowledge and love for the Scriptures that Evangelicals usually have. I think we're learning fast, but we could still use an awful lot more of the excellent resources and training – for both clergy and laity – which Protestant Christians have had for a long time.

John: John Stott is but one evangelical authority who's drawn attention to a gap between the evangelical zeal for the authority of Scripture and hermeneutic precision. Coming as I do from Sydney, where the Anglican Church puts a great premium on the role of the minister as teacher of the Bible, on arrival in England I was shocked at the comparative looseness of exegesis that seemed to be a characteristic of a lot of Evangelicals. Put it down to my Brethren background if you like, but few things upset me more than poor exegesis. One of the things I most applaud about the Second Vatican Council is that it challenged Catholics to read and study the Bible. Nothing but good can come of that.

Dwight: You suggested that Catholics place the church before the Bible. In a way that's true, but I think we really see the church and the Bible developing together. The ancient Scriptures and the ancient church are both alive within what we call the 'apostolic tradition'. In other words, the apostles taught the early Christians certain things. At first this tradition was an oral tradition. It consisted of the apostles' preaching and teaching. So St Peter says his divinely inspired preaching is the 'living and enduring word of God' and says that it will stand for ever (1 Pet. 1:24-25). Similarly, St Paul refers to the oral tradition when he praises the Corinthians for 'upholding the traditions which I have passed on to you' (I Cor. 11:2).

Much of the core teaching was written down in the Epistles that we now find in the New Testament, but sometimes it was only handed on orally. Paul actually refers to the authority of both his oral and written teaching. In 2 Thessalonians 2:15 he says, 'So then brothers, stand firm and hold to the traditions we passed on to you, whether by word of mouth or by letter.' He expected that his oral teachings would be handed on faithfully from generation to generation. So he says to Timothy, in 2 Timothy 1.13, 'What you heard from me keep as the pattern of sound teaching, with faith and love in Jesus Christ. Guard the good deposit which is entrusted to you.'

The Catholic Church says the oral traditions of the apostles were just as authoritative as the written word, and that the oral traditions were kept alive and passed on faithfully by the leaders of the early church. The tradition and the written word were valued equally. Eusebius, the historian of the early church, talks about one of the earliest Christian leaders called Papias who lived around the year 120. He writes, 'and Papias … acknowledges that he received the sayings of the apostles from those that followed them… he mentions them frequently by name and includes traditions of theirs in his writings.'[2]

Irenaeus is another very early witness to the value of an apostolic tradition that was both oral and written. In his work *Adversus Haereses* he says 'What if the apostles had not left writings to us? Would it not be necessary to follow the order of tradition which was handed down to those to whom they entrusted the churches?'[3] Elsewhere Irenaeus also points out how important this apostolic tradition is for people to know the full truth. 'It is possible then for everyone in every church who may wish to know the truth to contemplate the Traditions of the Apostles which has been made known throughout the whole world.'[4]

Catholics believe this apostolic tradition has been preserved from antiquity most fully within the Catholic Church. It is this body of tradition which gives us a dynamic force for interpreting the written tradition of the Scriptures with an authentic voice.

John: Thanks for helping to tease out where another of the main lines of our disagreement lies. I'm prepared to accept that underpinning the words of Scripture are traditions dating back to the apostles ('I have received from the Lord that which also I delivered unto you' as Paul told the Corinthians). But for the churches of the Reformation it is the word written that has always carried the primary authority and you haven't convinced me otherwise.

I know that Protestants and Catholics have slightly different canons of Scripture. But at least we know more or less what we are talking about when we speak of the Scriptures. What the apostolic tradition precisely consists of is less clear. The cynics have pointed out that there have been times when Rome has claimed possession of the apostolic tradition to justify all manner of whims. According to one account, when in the last century the pope, wishing to promulgate a particular piece of teaching, was cautioned by some of his Cardinals, 'Holy Father, that is not part of the tradition', he replied, 'But I am the tradition.'

Dwight: Is that story part of your oral tradition or part of your written tradition?

John: Very funny. I'm sure I saw it written somewhere, but long ago it moved into the oral domain! I do find one aspect of your critique of what I said above helpful. Of course the primary factor is the process of revelation through which God speaks, makes himself known, and is ultimately incarnate in Jesus of Nazareth. There is divine-human partnership in preservation of oral tradition and ultimately in the writing and editing of the material.

Even so I still submit – and it is here that we may ultimately have to agree to disagree – that it is the combination of the word and the sacraments that actually forms the church, rather than the other way round. And I think that this puts the claims of the Church of Rome into the correct perspective. To quote Calvin again, 'Wherever we see the word of God sincerely preached and heard, wherever we see the sacraments instituted according to the institution of Christ, there we cannot have any doubt that the Church of God has some existence since his promise cannot fail. 'Where two or three are gathered together in my name, there am I in the midst of them' (Mt. 28:20).[5]

To sum up, then. We appear to agree quite a lot. That may surprise our readers. There is a lot of clear blue water between us and the caricature often levelled against Christians who take the Bible seriously, i.e. that the Scriptures were dictated by God to human agents. We seem to share a large measure of agreement about how the Scriptures were actually formed, that underlying them is a body of oral tradition, which in the case of the Old Testament, particularly, may have existed for centuries before what we know as the Scriptures found their final form. We seem to agree that the Scriptures are a record of the sayings and actions of God who set about to redeem the human race that had become alienated from him. God makes himself known to the patriarchs and prophets. He calls a people, Israel, to be a nation through which he will fulfil his purposes, ultimately in the incarnation of Jesus. The incarnation of God in Jesus is chronicled within the context of God's many mighty acts. But the Bible goes further, offering exposition and reflection on the meaning of the gospel. And it is a book of praise and doxology as well.

We have agreed, and some may be surprised that I have conceded it, that there is much more to being a Christian than 'me and the Bible'. You have come to see the Church of Rome as best placed to give the Christian the needed authoritative guidance to understand the Scriptures and live the Christian life. For my part I see the traditions of the church as crucial, not least the doctrinal formulations of the undivided church of the first three centuries, but the Bible remains the final court of appeal. You claim that in preserving the oral sources and defining the canon that the Bible is the creature of the church. I have argued, with the Reformers, that it is the Bible that creates the church as we experience it.

The Church of Rome, you say, possesses the fullest measure of the apostolic tradition. It sounds neat, but is it as certain a bet as you've claimed? The church is an institution which Christ brought into being and it can thus be said to be of divine origin. But the church is a human institution too. There will be times when it fails to get the emphasis right. There will be times when it gets things utterly wrong. I am happy to concede that the Anglicanism I espouse is provisional. But as Paul said, for the present 'we know in part and see in part'. So it's my conviction that the Church of Rome is no less a provisional expression of the fullness of the faith.

Dwight: The Catholic Church admits to being human as well as divine, and we'll have to discuss this in more detail later. I think you've summed up where we agree and disagree pretty well. It comes down to this doesn't it? Although we both venerate the Scriptures and recognise their great authority, you want them to be the final authority and I say whoever interprets the Scriptures is the final authority. The fact remains, John, that while it's fine to read the Scriptures, we always need someone to interpret the Scriptures for us. This happens for Evangelicals when they listen to their preachers or study their commentaries. In other words they are trusting the interpretative authority of their church leaders. If they disagree with their leaders, well, then they are trusting their own personal interpretative authority. Either way whoever decides what the Bible means is the real final authority. So in fact all Christians believe in some final interpretative authority – it's just that we Catholics recognise this fact and glory in it while you guys aren't aware that it exists.

Anyhow, I like the direction this conversation is going because I think we both agree that the Bible exists within the context of the church. I want to pick at this a little more though. Just how the Bible and the church work together is something I want to challenge you with in the next chapter.

---

1 John Calvin, *The Institutes* Book 8.1, trans. Henry Beveridge, (London: James Clarke & Co, 1957), p75

2 Edgar J Goodspeed, *The Apostolic Fathers,* (London: Independent Press, 1950), p265

3 Irenaeus, *Adversus Haereses* 3:4:1, from Alexander Roberts (tr), *The Writings of Irenaeus*, (Edinburgh: T & T Clark, 1868), p264

4 Irenaeus, *Adversus Haereses* 3:3:1, as above, p260.

5 John Calvin, *The Institutes* Book 4:9, trans. Henry Beveridge, (London: James Clarke & Co, 1957), p289

Chapter Two

Apostolic Authority

Dwight: John, I'm sure that in your Sunday School in Australia you had to memorise 2 Timothy 3:16. I remember it still. It is the verse which tells us clearly that 'All Scripture is given by inspiration of God.' This is a wonderful verse, and as I mentioned in the last chapter, we Catholics affirm with you that Scripture is inspired by God. We affirm this belief, but to be precise, God doesn't inspire a book, does he? He inspires the people who write the book. This is an important point because we think the Bible always has to be placed within the context of the inspired people of God. The Old Testament is the story of God leading and guiding his people by the Holy Spirit, and the New Testament is the story of how he filled the whole church with his Holy Spirit. As you said in the last chapter, you agree with me that God's primary work of revelation is through the lives of real people in a faith community down through history and that this revelation culminates in the coming of his Son, Jesus Christ. The Scriptures are the inspired record of his self-revelation through history. What strikes me as quite wonderful is how the Scriptures are not dull academic religious studies. Instead they are the record of God's love for his people: they are the stories, the sermons, the hymns and the prophecies of the inspired people of God.

There is a detail in the Old Testament picked up in the gospels – which I find very interesting. We are told in Exodus that Moses, the one whom God inspired to record his word, is also the one who interprets the word. In Exodus 18:13 it says Moses took his seat to judge the people according to the law. When Moses pronounced his judgement he spoke 'from his seat' rather like a judge today makes a statement 'from the bench'. Now what interests me is that in Matthew 23:2 Jesus recognises that the Pharisees occupy the 'seat of Moses'. In other words, the Jews thought that their religious leaders inherited the interpretative authority of Moses. The rabbis in Jesus' time had studied the inspired law, but they were also aware of the centuries' old tradition and they were the ones authorised to apply the Scriptures to the needs of their present day. The Jewish community that gave birth to the Scriptures was also the community that interpreted the Scripture. This same biblical principle is carried over into the Catholic Church. When a Catholic bishop teaches the truth and inter-prets the Scriptures for our needs we say he speaks, *ex cathedra* which means, 'from the chair'.

Of course Jesus criticised the Pharisees because they were abusing their God-given authority, but while Jesus criticised their abuses he did not dispute that they had inherited Moses' authority. In fact, despite his harsh words against the Pharisees, Jesus still tells his disciples to obey them (Mt. 23:3). The Catholic view of apostolic succession is derived from this same biblical principle. We believe God gave Jesus his author-ity on earth (Mt. 28:18), and that Jesus shared that authority with his apostles (Jn. 20:21), and that they in turn shared the authority to know and teach the truth (Jn. 16:15; Mt. 28:20), with their successors down to the present day.

John: You've sent me scurrying for my concordance and theo-logical wordbooks. In the English Bible 'inspiration' appears only twice, in a fairly obscure section of Job 32:8 and in 2 Timothy 3:16 where a literal translation might be 'all Scriptures are God breathed' (*theopneustos*). But it's not an iso-lated idea. Inspiration belongs in a family of biblical words that cluster around the Spirit and how he operates. In the cre-ation story the breath of God brought 'the man' to life (Gen.

2:7). The Spirit of God possesses people and imparts gifts to them. In the Book of Jeremiah the Lord tells the prophet, 'I have put my words in your mouth' (Jer. 1:9). It's not easy to pin down, and in the conversation with Nicodemus Jesus enjoys a bit of word play when he says 'the wind (*pneuma*) blows where it chooses, and you hear the sound of it, but you do not know where it comes from or where it goes. So it is with everyone who is born of the Spirit (*pneuma*)' (Jn. 3:8).

So yes, God does inspire people and the classic evangelical position is that he has inspired a book. One reason why I believe I can hold this position is that I don't see any warrant for making a sharp distinction between the inspiration of people and what is created when, possessed by the Spirit of God, these people speak or write.

I'm happy to concede that the church has played its part in giving recognition to what writings should be part of the biblical library. It was achieved by a consensus that these books had a 'ring of truth' and that they had stood the test of time. What I won't concede is that this leaves the Scriptures in any way subordinate to the church. While I agree that the Bible's meaning is at times, though rarely, obscure and that it does not directly address questions of our times, I am confident that careful study will provide me with the guidance I need to live a godly life and face hard questions. The role of the church, as a classic Evangelical would contend, is to pass on and teach the tradition and offer commentary and guidance on how it may be understood. But its role is that and no more. There is good reason to think that Jesus took the same view of those who, as he put it, occupied Moses' seat.

I've read rabbinical literature of the kind that would have been very familiar in Jesus' day. I do not detect there an *ex cathedra* tone. What you have is commentary and a lot of sifting of what various great ones taught in order to discern the meaning and contemporary relevance of the Law of Moses. You have a lot of subsidiary law making. There is a famous saying: 'Moses received the law on Mount Sinai and committed it to Joshua and to the elders, and the elders to the prophets; and the Prophets committed it to the men of the

Great Synagogue. They said three things: be deliberate in judgement, raise up many disciples, and make a fence around the law.'[1] The phrase that's important here is 'make a fence round the Law'. The contention was that to break the Torah, the law of Moses, would have grave consequences. Therefore it was necessary to make all sorts of subsidiary laws so that this could never happen. It was a recipe for utter paralysis. By the way, the passage throws light on why some of Jesus' hearers were 'astonished at his doctrine because he taught as one having authority, not as the scribes' (Mt. 7:29). My contention is that the teaching office of the church cannot even be given equal status with the Scriptures. The approach you offer may solve some problems, but it simply invites a replay of the kind of confusion that abounded in Jesus' day, with the scribes constantly erecting new fences.

Dwight: I like your quote about the authority of the rabbis. It's curious that you emphasised the bit about 'putting a fence around the Law' to make your point. I thought it beautifully made my point! When the church interprets Scripture properly she 'puts a fence' around Scripture and prevents all sorts of crazy interpretations. I was also interested in the way the rabbis enjoyed the same authority to interpret the Scriptures as those who were inspired to write the Scriptures. This also illustrates the Catholic view. Just as the leaders of the Jewish community inherited authority to interpret the Scriptures from those who wrote the Scriptures, so the leaders of the Christian community inherited authority to interpret the Scriptures from those who wrote the New Testament books.

You said you cannot accept that the Scriptures are in any way subordinate to the church. Instead the church must be subordinate to Scripture. Let me stand this on its head. We think the church is subordinate to the Scriptures too, but we also think the Scriptures are subordinate to the church. The two go hand in hand, submitting to each other in a complementary relationship. The catechism puts it this way, '...the Church, to whom the transmission and interpretation of

Revelation is entrusted, does not derive her certainty about all revealed truths from the holy Scriptures alone. Both Scripture and Tradition must be accepted and honoured with equal sentiments of devotion and reverence (CCC, 82).

You want to exalt Scripture above the church, but can this be true? Didn't they develop together? In practice don't they both need one another? For the Scriptures to be dynamic they must live and work within the dynamic situation of the church, mustn't they? Use a Shakespeare play for an illustration. The director, actors and audience submit themselves to the text, but the text also submits itself to them. To live, the text has to be interpreted by the directors and actors and received by the audience. Without the actors, director and audience the text is a dead letter. Without the text, the actors have no play. It is the same thing with the church and the Scripture. For the word to be 'living and active and sharper than any two-edged sword', it has to be interpreted and applied to real situations in our lives.

You've admitted that the church was instrumental in the writing of the Scriptures and in deciding the canon. You've also said the evangelical view is that the church is there to pass on and teach the tradition and offer guidance on how it may be understood. So are you saying the church's traditions do carry some kind of interpretative authority? If so, where does that authority come from and why should I listen to one particular church's interpretation and not another's?

John: I think I'm going to start getting worried every time you say you like a quote I use!

Dwight: I'll always try to affirm what you affirm. I just can't deny what you deny.

John: So it's time for riddles is it? Anyway, that quote about the rabbis has always been one of my favourites and I'd still maintain it gets to the heart of the difference between the rabbinical method and the teaching of Jesus. If you insist I could go back to the same material and pepper you with quotes to the effect 'Rabbi so and so taught this and Rabbi so and so taught that.' You don't get very much further. If I were a Catholic apologist, I'd be wary about arguing any parallel between the rabbinical tradition and your church's own teaching authority and method.

Dwight: Who's backing off here, you or me? But I take your point. I'll be wary. I agree that you can't press this too far. I am simply interested that in this instance the Jewish ideal is very similar to the Catholic one.

Anyway, didn't you skirt my question? I said if the church has a role to play in interpreting the Scriptures, where does that authority come from and why should I listen to one particular church rather than another?

John: The reformers rejected the claims of the church to be an infallible interpreter of Scripture, insisting that scriptural authority was derived from God. To quote the evangelical theologian Herman Ridderbos, whose views helped shape my thinking on this issue many years ago, 'For whatever comes to us with the highest authority in matters of faith and life can only be dependent on God himself. Authority comes, not from below, but from above.'[2] It's here that we hit two different views as to the position of the church. You grant it inherent authority but you also say it establishes and fixes the borders of biblical authority. The church stands behind the canon and that is your guarantee that it is the word of God. The Reformers, on the other hand, made the authority of the canon dependent not on the church but on the Scriptures in themselves and their internal witness in the hearts of believers. Let me give you another quote from Calvin which I doubt you'll like: 'As to the question, how shall we be persuaded that it came from God without recurring to a decree of the Church? It is just the same as if it were asked, how shall we learn to distinguish light from darkness, white from black, sweet from bitter? Scripture bears on faith if it is clear evidence of its truth.'[3]

I'm not saying that the authority of great scholars and the spiritual giants on whose shoulders I stand are not important.

Indeed I ignore them at my peril. But they cannot be granted any kind of mandatory authority. It's my responsibility as a life-long student of the Scriptures to wrestle with their meaning and application. And when I come to the Scriptures, I trust that the Spirit will witness to them in my heart and mind so that I discern a ring of truth by which to set the compass of my life. I know you don't like the messiness involved with one church saying one thing and one saying another. I would contend that is the way of it in the economy of God. I am not scandalised by the existence of a great variety of churches. I would contend that God, evidently, has chosen to work that way.

Dwight: Okay, I admit I'm a tidy sort of guy; but it's not just that I 'don't like the messiness of one church saying one thing and one saying another'. We're talking about major differences of interpretation. We need to know the truth, but where do we turn? Who's right and why are they right? Why should I necessarily take the Baptist line or the Brethren line or the Methodist or Moravian or Anglican or Amish? They all claim biblical authority. This is not just messiness. This is chaos. If there is no objective authority to interpret Scripture then the whole thing is a matter of opinion. I guess you admit this when you say, in the end it is up to you. So you choose what you think Scripture means and I choose what I think it means. Flip a coin. No wonder modern theologians throw up their hands and say with Pontius Pilate, 'But what is truth?'

Let me pick at another problem. You say 'the reformers rejected the claims of the church to be an infallible interpreter of Scripture, insisting that scriptural authority was derived from God'. But Scripture and church aren't mutually exclusive are they? Why, if you believe in the divine authority of Scripture must you deny the divine authority of the church? Catholics believe both the Scripture and the church have been given a share in Christ's infallible authority. This is one of my grumbles about the Protestant mentality. It's always 'either-or'. Because you take an 'either-or' position you assume Catholics take the opposite 'either-or'. Thus you say only the Bible has infallible authority and assume Catholics think that only the church has infallible authority. Because you deny the church you assume we deny the Bible. In fact, the Catholic position is always 'both-and'. We believe the Bible and the church both enjoy divine authority.

I'm afraid therefore that I'm going to agree with another one of your quotes. We agree with Ridderbos that 'whatever comes to us with the highest authority in matters of faith and life can only be dependent on God himself. Authority comes, not from below, but from above.' It's just that we would apply Ridderbos' observation to the church as well as the Scripture. We accept that the Scripture's authority comes from God, but we also believe the church's authority comes from above.

The logic and the scriptural support for this is clear. It works like this: God gave Jesus Christ complete authority on heaven and earth (Mt. 28:18; I Cor. 15:27; Eph. 1:20-22). Jesus had the authority to teach the truth (Jn. 13:13). Jesus shared that same divine authority with his apostles (Jn. 17:18, Jn. 20:21). He commands them to go out with his own authority to teach the Truth (Mt. 28:20); Jesus says God will give the apostles the same truth he has given Jesus (Jn. 16:15). The apostles' teaching authority is actually from God, because Jesus says those who listen to them listen to him and therefore listen to the father (Lk. 10:16), Peter and Paul both attest that their teaching is from God himself (I Cor. 11:23; I Pet. 1:24-25). Peter says the church is to receive its teaching from the Lord through the apostles (2 Pet. 3:2). As we've agreed in the last chapter, this divinely inspired teaching of the apostles existed in both written and oral form (2 Thes. 2:15). Are you with me so far?

John: So far. But I can sense where you're heading and I'm certain I won't be going the entire journey with you. You want to claim that the Catholic Church and its leadership enjoys a continuity of authority that begins with the apostles and it carries the same weight in our present day.

Dwight: Well, not quite. We do believe the Catholic Church speaks with apostolic authority, but the bishops of the Catholic

Church don't have the same authority as the apostles. They haven't been with the historical Jesus and they can't teach anything new. What a bishop writes isn't automatically on a level with Scripture, for instance.

John: I have no problems, I trust, in ascribing huge importance to the apostles and the inspiration of their teaching, in both written and oral forms. What I won't buy is the proposition that the teaching office of a church in contemporary times can claim to be on par with them. First, there is no need for it. The New Testament record of Jesus' words and deeds, his birth, his death and resurrection, snapshots of the early apostolic preaching, Paul's teaching and all the rest, leave us with sufficient information to bring us to salvation. In other words, all the seminal information is there.

So I'm content to draw a line in the sand as far as the apostolic church is concerned, believing that the apostles' teaching is of itself sufficient in every way. I know it needs to be interpreted and I know that later it was necessary to hold councils and draft creeds in order to define the mind of the church in the face of controversy. Even here, however, I would suggest that there is no intrinsically new teaching, simply clarification of what had already come before. And the notion of making any human agency an infallible interpreter is just unacceptable. But I know that you as a Catholic have different convictions about the apostolic office and its continuing authority, and I think we need to face that one fair and square.

Dwight: I want to go off on a tangent here. You say the New Testament gives us enough information for our salvation and for the ordering of the church and sacraments. But at the risk of repeating myself *ad nauseum*, the New Testament according to whom? Some Protestants think you can lose your salvation. Others think you never can. Some think the church is a democracy, others a hierarchy, others a synod. Some think the Eucharist and baptism are mere symbols, others think they are outward signs of grace, still others think they impart grace. I still say we need an objective authority to help us interpret

Scripture. You say as much when you admit that within the first four centuries the church met to decide authoritatively certain doctrinal matters such as the incarnation and the Trinity. In other words, the church met to interpret Scripture.

Let me get back on track. I agree with you that the New Testament is seminal for helping us to understand the church, but wouldn't it make sense to ask what the first Christians actually thought the New Testament meant with regards to church order? I mean these fellows were taught by the apostles, or by the next generation after the apostles. Who do you think is a better guide to interpret the teaching of the apostles – those who were actually taught by them or the reformers fifteen hundred years later? As you know we have some of the writings from that first generation of Christians after the apostles. I'm not saying their writings have the same authority as Scripture, but they give us at least a partial picture of what the first Christians believed, don't they?

John: It's not really 'either-or'. In every generation Christians have no choice but to 'sing a new song'. It's a song whose lyrics, chords and cadences all have a contemporary tone, but it's a remix of the 'old, old story'. We all have to be interpreters and we do so in order to proclaim the gospel afresh in each generation for the sake of a world of great diversity. If we don't, no one will hear.

In that I'm helped to know about the teachings of the Catholic Church. As often as not, however, they raise as many questions as well. Witness the teaching on contraception or the legacy of the Second Vatican council. And don't tell me that this is of a different status to *ex cathedra* teaching because that will simply provide an example of the confusion I'm talking about. Then I know that in the past the Catholic Church has sometimes led the entire Christian household into grave error.

Moreover, I think you exaggerate both the extent to which the Bible is hard to understand and the extent to which the different churches disagree. On an exegetical level, for instance, as a life-long student of the Bible there are very few passages that I remain entirely fazed by. There's the stuff in early

Genesis about heavenly marriages. There's an obscure passage
in the early part of Exodus that seems to say that God tries to
kill Moses on his way to Egypt. But I don't see that such passages carry any substantial doctrinal import. Then, faced with
the Apostle's creed, few Christians would reject any part of it,
though they may decline to use it. When it comes even to key
matters of faith and order, the *Baptism, Eucharist and Ministry*
(*Lima*) document[4], for instance, shows that both Catholics and
Protestants are in broad agreement about three of the most
basic matters.

So, yes, for some it would be great to have a reliable guide
to all the possible issues on which we disagree, but alongside
having a doctrine of the church that asserts its origins in the
purposes of God, we have to assert that it's a human institution as well. As St Paul said, 'We know in part and reason in
part' and only when the kingdom comes in its fullness and
when we gather on 'that other shore' can we expect anything
else.

As an Anglican I assert what we have now as 'church' is at
best provisional. The church is not the kingdom. Occasionally,
when it's at its glorious best, it gives us a little trailer of what
the kingdom will be like. Its manifold imperfections, on the
other hand, encourage us to keep our eyes fixed elsewhere, to
the kingdom and the values it embodies. If we mistake church
for kingdom we risk utter disillusionment.

Dwight: Much of what you have said the Catholic Church
agrees with. While we believe the kingdom of God is made
visible in the Catholic Church, we believe that she is a human
as well as a divine institution. We acknowledge the human
failures of the church, and we realise that the church is not the
final realisation of the kingdom, but a glimpse of the glory to
come. Like you, we also believe that the church must speak
afresh to every age.

However, we believe the church must speak afresh to every
age in continuity with the past, not in contradiction of the past.
This goes to the heart of our belief in the apostolic succession.
We believe the bishops of the Catholic Church most fully bear

the same authority that Jesus gave to his apostles. This is not something new. The reason I alluded to the beliefs of the very first generation of Christians was because it is important to see what those first Christians believed about this vital question of authority.

From the very beginning Christians disagreed about the proper authority in the church. Their leaders said clearly that for the sake of unity there had to be a single teaching authority, and that the proper authority was handed down in succession from the apostles to the bishops of the church. The literature from the first two centuries of the church is overwhelmingly of this view.

Allow me to quote just a few examples. In the first century Clement, a leader of the Roman church, wrote these words:

> The Apostles received the gospel for us from the Lord Jesus Christ, and they went out full of confidence in the Holy Spirit...and appointed their first fruits...to be bishops and deacons. Our apostles knew there would be strife on the question of the bishop's office: therefore, they appointed these people already mentioned and later made further provision that if they should fall asleep other tested men should succeed to their ministry. (*Epistle to the Corinthians*, 42)[5]

At this very early stage, Clement believed the apostles – one of whom might still have been alive – had wished for their teaching office to be continued in the church. He upheld this authority because the unity of the church was at stake.

Ignatius of Antioch was martyred in the year 115. He was most probably a disciple of Peter and Paul themselves. On his way to martyrdom in Rome he wrote seven letters to different churches. In all of them, he encourages them to be faithful to the apostolic authority which abides in the church through the ministry of the bishops. Here are just two snippets: to the church in Tralles Ignatius says, 'You must never act independently of your bishop, also be no less submissive to your clergy and regard them as apostles of Jesus Christ.'[6] To the Magnesian Christians he writes, 'As the Lord did nothing without the

Father, either by himself or by means of his apostles, so you must do nothing without the bishop and the priests.'[7]

From another part of the ancient Christian world, Bishop Irenaeus of Lyon writes around the year 180. According to him, it is because the church leaders have inherited the apostolic authority that they can interpret Scripture properly. So he writes

> By knowledge of the truth we mean: the teaching of the Apostles; the order of the Church as established from earliest times throughout the world...preserved through the episcopal succession: for to the bishops the apostles committed the care of the church in each place which has come down to our own time safeguarded by...the most complete exposition...the reading of the Scriptures without falsification and careful and consistent exposition of them – avoiding both rashness and blasphemy. (*Adv. Her.IV*, xxiii)[8]

Catholics believe the dynamic teaching authority which Christ gave his apostles continues to live through the ministry of the Catholic bishops who have received their authority in direct line from the apostles – passed down over the last 2,000 years. Because of this direct link, Catholics believe the church has a living connection with the apostolic authority. Therefore within the living apostolic tradition of the Catholic Church we can find a rock-solid, sure, historic and unified body of teaching which illuminates and interprets the Bible without fail.

Sorry, John. I've gone on at length. I know you reject this model of apostolic succession, but as an Anglican you have bishops, and in the creed you say you believe in an 'apostolic' church. If you don't buy into the historic interpretation of this, in what way is your church apostolic?

John: Before I answer your question about Anglicans and apostolicity, may I comment on my dear friends Clement, Ignatius and Irenaeus? I agree that in their writings you find powerful apologia for a certain kind of bishop in the life of the church, but I don't draw the same conclusions as you. One reason, according to my reading, was that Ignatius' strident claims concerning the office of bishop grew from the fact that he didn't have a strong base of support for what he was proposing and his views were very much under fire. I suspect he lived among people who had never accepted this view of the office of bishop and had no intention of according bishops the authority Ignatius was claiming. It's my understanding that in the early church the line between bishops and presbyters was quite blurred and that leadership was exercised collectively. I suppose I would add that it may at times have been authoritarian in style and Anglicans and other churches of the Reformation shouldn't read our twentieth century egalitarianism back into those times. Equally, however, I'm not happy to concede that they licence the claims of the Catholic majesterium.

Now, about Anglicans and apostolicity. We share in common with you creeds that speak of 'one, holy, catholic and apostolic church'. Not a word in the creeds is wasted. When we speak of 'one', I have always taken it to mean the visible and invisible society of those who are savingly joined to Christ. 'Holy' I take to mean 'set apart' for a special calling as co-workers with God, seeking to reflect his character – 'You shall be holy, for I the Lord am holy.' 'Catholic' I take to mean not so much universal as comprehensive – composed of every culture, age, socio-economic standing and race. This is all quite familiar territory.

I would want to suggest the Anglican Church is apostolic in two ways. First, unlike a lot of the churches that have emerged since the Reformation, it claims no special or particular doctrines of its own. I have always used the hymn 'The church's one foundation' as a great example of how Anglicanism understands itself. The foundation is Christ himself. The church is his new community brought into being and sustained by word and sacrament – 'water and the word'. I could go on, but I think I've made the point. There is nothing here that isn't of the essence of the apostolic witness and teaching.

Then, secondly, an apostle is by definition 'one who is sent'. Churches exercise apostolicity in the truest sense when they discover and exercise their missionary calling. In common

with the Catholic Church, Anglicanism has a missionary calling. True, it took some time to rediscover it after the
Reformation and the closure of the monastic houses which
were the missionary societies of the medieval church. But the
missionary calling was rediscovered in Anglicanism. The
Anglican missionary movement had a dual character. Some
parts strongly adhere to the 'church' principle, seeing their
calling as planting the church in its Anglican form wherever
possible. Others strongly adhere to the 'voluntary' principle,
where the primary calling is proclamation of the gospel, with
the actual planting of the church a secondary concern. This
latter stance, particularly, left plenty of space for the newly
emerging Christian communities to draw from the soil of their
own local culture and circumstances. At best, Anglican
churches the world over have a family resemblance that draws
from what is shared in common from its apostolic heritage and
a liturgy that inherits its framework from the primitive church
but is adapted to local cadences.

Just for the record, you can find Anglicanism in over 150
countries. While it's not in the premier division on the basis of
its numbers – the most often quoted figure is 70 million
Anglicans worldwide – after the Catholic Church it's arguably
the most widely spread Christian world communion. I should
add for the benefit of people who may be tempted to think of
it as merely a product of British imperialism, that at least half
of the dioceses of the Anglican communion are found outside
the British Commonwealth of Nations.

Dwight: Wow! You can dismiss the witness of the apostolic
fathers with a magic click of your fingers! You make Ignatius
sound like an irascible old tyrant, when in fact he was a gentle
old saint on his way to being martyred.

John: I admit, he hasn't always had a sympathetic press
among Protestants and Evangelicals.

Dwight: Seriously, your point about Ignatius might hold some
water if he was lecturing his own flock about loyalty to him-

self. He wasn't. He was writing to seven other congregations beseeching them to be subject to the rightful church authority. You might be able to dismiss Ignatius if he was the only one who taught that the bishops were the successors of the apostles. But this teaching is there from the very earliest time; coming not only from one bishop in one church, but from every part of the empire: Irenaeus in France, Clement in Rome, Cyprian and Tertullian in North Africa, Ignatius in Antioch – all of these earliest church fathers are unanimous in upholding the truth which Clement expresses so clearly:

> The apostles knew there would be strife on the question of the bishop's office. Therefore, they appointed these people already mentioned and later made further provision that if they should fall asleep other tested men should succeed to their ministry. (*Epistle to the Corinthians*, 42)[9]

I am interested in your take on apostolicity. In fact, Catholics would agree with much of what you've said. Apostolicity certainly includes being faithful to the apostolic deposit of faith and being involved in the apostolic activity of proclaiming the gospel. The catechism says about the missionary mandate:

> Having been divinely sent to the nations that she might be 'the universal sacrament of salvation', the Church, in obedience to the command of her founder and because it is demanded by her own essential universality, strives to preach the Gospel to all men: 'Go therefore and make disciples of all nations, baptising them in the name of the Father and of the Son and of the Holy Spirit, teaching them to observe all that I have commanded you; and lo, I am with you always, until the close of the age' (CCC, 849).

Apostolicity is based on the fact that Jesus sent his apostles to preach the gospel, but it is also based on his promise that he would be with them always to the end of time. The catechism sums up our view like this:

> The Church is apostolic because she is founded on the apostles, in three ways:
> – she was and remains built on 'the foundation of the Apostles,' the witnesses chosen and sent on mission by Christ himself,
> – with the help of the Spirit dwelling in her, the Church keeps and hands on the teaching, the 'good deposit,' the salutary words she has heard from the apostles;
> – she continues to be taught, sanctified and guided by the apostles until Christ's return, through their successors in pastoral office: the college of bishops, 'assisted by priests, in union with the successor of Peter, the Church's supreme pastor'. (CCC, 857)

That brings us to Peter. The one who was the leader of the apostles, and whose successor we acknowledge as the focus of unity in our church. I know you'll have a few things to say about the papacy, and lucky you, it's your turn to kick off the next chapter.

John: A final word. On Ignatius, I suppose I should add a word about Protestants and Evangelicals and the period of Christian history when we meet Ignatius, Irenaeus, Cyprian and company. I suspect I'm a rare Evangelical who has actually read most of these people.

I remember an Anglican Evangelical Assembly in Britain in 1990. The theme was the role of the bishop. Several of the evangelical bishops were due to speak about their office and role. The press were there in quantity because they were looking for clues on who might emerge as candidates to be the next Archbishop of Canterbury. In a day of presentations only the most junior of the evangelical bishops so much as mentioned patristic views of the role of the bishop in the church. I remember saying to some of the veteran Evangelicals that the bishop concerned, George Carey, was the only Evangelical on show who could be Archbishop material since he was the only one who showed any historical and ecumenical understanding of the subject. They looked at me as if I'd lost my marbles. It's yet another story to exemplify how Evangelicals tend to have 'a canon within a canon' even when it comes to the whole sweep of Christian history and tend to think that nothing happened between the end of the New Testament era and the Reformation.

Another observation is that in responding to your points I can see why Evangelicals find theories of the early dating of most of the New Testament so attractive. It's much more straightforward to contend that the books of the NT were formed – if not finally recognised as an entire canon – with the close involvement of the apostles. It can be argued, thus, that this puts them in a different category from material created and classified by 'the church'. You will notice that I haven't deployed that argument because I'm not committed per se to the early dating.

As an historian I know that information from research and reflection on particular events over many years often ends up being more reliable than eyewitness accounts. If you want a modern-day example, see where eyewitness accounts of the death of President John Kennedy leave us as far as knowing for sure what happened. Thus, I'm one of those Evangelicals who's not uncomfortable with the proposition that the gospel accounts of Jesus may have been written somewhat later than many Evangelicals contend. I would argue, for the reason I've already mentioned, that this makes them no less reliable than eyewitness accounts. I have to acknowledge, however, that it has made my job in defending the evangelical position on the subject matter of this chapter somewhat harder!

---

1 Aboth 1:1ff in CK Barrett, *The New Testament Background: Selected Documents*, (London: SPCK, 1964), p139

2 Herman Ridderbos in *The Canon of the New Testament in Revelation and the Bible*, ed. Carl F Henry, (London: Tyndale, 1958), p190

3 John Calvin, *Institutes of Christian Religion*, trans. Henry Beveridge, (London: James Clarke & Co, 1957), Book 1, Chapter 7, 2

4 Baptism, Eucharist and Ministry (Lima) document, *Faith and Order Paper* No. 111, Geneva, World Council of Churches, 1982

5 Maxwell Staniforth (tr), *The Early Christian Writings*, (London: Penguin Books, 1984), pp45-46

6 Maxwell Staniforth, *The Early Christian Writings*, p95

7 Maxwell Staniforth, *The Early Christian Writings*, p60

8 Henry Bettenson, *The Early Christian Fathers*, (Oxford: Oxford University Press, 1969), p89

9 Henry Bettenson, *The Early Christian Fathers*, p33

Chapter Three

Prince Among the Apostles?

John: I begin with a reflection involving both Dwight and myself. In May 2000, we happened by coincidence to be visiting Rome at the same time. As well as sharing a few pizzas and posing outside St Peter's for a photo to use on the jacket of this book, we went together on a tour of the site that is traditionally regarded as the tomb of the apostle Peter, deep in the bowels of the earth beneath St Peter's basilica. I'd taken a similar tour some twenty years previously and at the time the young seminarian leading the tour was very gung-ho about this being without doubt the resting place of St Peter's remains. He was convinced that the container we viewed at the climax contained white slivers which were, without doubt, his authentic bones. I noticed that my latter-day guide was much more measured in the claims he made. But having left me with fewer contentious points to argue about, he helped me to a wider understanding of the significance of the crypt of St Peter's. Here is a powerful symbol of what Peter means to the Church of Rome. In one sense, it's literally built on him.

Let me offer another story. In the late 1970s I was press officer for the diocese of Sydney, Australia. One morning, somewhat out of the blue, our phones ran hot. There was a story over the wires that the official talks between the Anglicans and the Catholic Church had agreed that in a future, unified Christian church there would need to be a universal primate and that the bishop of Rome was the one Christian leader with the credentials for such a role. It happened that I was well briefed on the subject. From an Anglican point of view this was an officially authorised commission, but its powers were very limited. Any recommendations would require a wide debate. Nobody outside Australia had powers to commit our church to a particular course of action. Any decision to join with the Catholic Church on these terms, or any others, for that matter, would have to be agreed by Anglican synods the world over. Then, even if every other diocese in the world agreed to go forward into unity, Sydney would be under no compulsion to join with them. Later on, I remember wheeling out our various theologians who argued that there was neither any biblical nor historical warrant for the position taken by the Anglican-Roman Catholic International Commission (ARCIC). Nor in our day and age was there any practical necessity for a universal primacy. Eventually ARCIC and its recommendations were the subject of a stinging attack by the Archbishop of Sydney, Marcus Loane, in his presidential address to Sydney synod. In a somewhat sorrowful tone, Dr Loane criticised the attempts by minority evangelical members of ARCIC to make its position more plausible.

A decade or so later in 1988, I went to Rome as editor of *The Church of England Newspaper* to cover Archbishop Robert Runcie's official visit to the Vatican. Throughout the visit, Runcie tried to emphasise that while he, in principle, supported the idea of a universal primacy exercised by the bishop of Rome in a united Christian church, it needed to be a reformed primacy of pastoral care and compassion and not one of domination. At the time it seemed as if Runcie's message had fallen on deaf ears. Only recently has it emerged that the Vatican subsequently studied Runcie's carefully nuanced submissions with characteristic rigour.

The pope is both an ecumenical asset and liability. He is an asset as a symbol of world Christianity on the world stage. This pope knows how to play this for all it's worth in a television age. He has been instrumental in gathering leaders of other faith communities to speak up for world peace. Quietly and behind the scenes the Vatican, as a nation-state, exercises an influential role in brokering peace and international understanding. But, in my view, the office of pope is a liability because the Catholic Church wants to claim that he is more than a mere symbol. St Peter's in Rome conveys a clear message that the Church of Rome is built on St Peter and his modern-day successor is heir of Peter's role as prince of the apostles. A large statue of Peter holding the keys to the Kingdom of God says it all.

In medieval times Vatican apologists created crude forgeries, such as the infamous Donation of Constantine, a 'will' purporting to leave the temporal powers of the first Christian emperor to the bishop of Rome, to claim justification for political power even over kings and emperors. It's a liability, too, because while the Catholic Church has, since the Second Vatican council, courted other Christian communities in ecumenical dialogue, its self view has not materially changed. At times it's been saying, 'Come and let us reason together', but as the recent Vatican document *Dominus Iesus* seems to suggest, a more honest ecumenical invitation would be 'Brothers and sisters, come home!' Then it's a liability, too, because it flies so much in the face of human reality. The papacy was at a very deep 'low' in terms of prestige and power when it enunciated the doctrine of papal infallibility. In our day the human products of postmodernism place no great store by authority figures. The latest ARCIC statement, *The Gift of Authority*, is dangerously out of touch and the penny does not seem to have dropped that authority has to be accepted as well as being exercised.

Robert Runcie was very astute in his endeavours to work for a reformed papacy that had some chance of being ecumenically acceptable. Against this is the enormous weight that ballasts the self-understanding of a pope and curia who have long believed that they are the successors of Peter and the apostles, and inheritors of their authority. While they have sometimes exercised this authority with humility, too often they've done it with astonishing insensitivity and hubris.

Now try to convince me of the truth of the claims made by the Pope and that the papacy could be reformed in a manner that would benefit all Christians.

Dwight: Whew! You bring out all the big guns in your opening salvo! I certainly want to address the issues you bring up, but as it goes in the *Sound of Music*, 'Let's start at the very beginning...'

I remember that day we went down below the basilica of St Peter's together, and like that excavation into the foundations of that great church, I want to dig down to the foundations of the papacy. We say the role of the pope is built on the apostle Peter. The gospel record clearly shows how the fiery character of Peter was a natural leader. The details support this. Whenever the twelve are listed Peter comes first – and Judas last. Peter is the first apostle to whom Jesus appears after the resurrection. He is one of the small group of select apostles Jesus takes in to witness the raising of Jairus' daughter and the transfiguration. Peter is the one who declares that Jesus is the Christ, the Son of God, and Jesus says it was by special divine revelation that Peter was able to say this. With John, Peter's the one to set up the Last Supper and at that supper in Luke 22:31-32, Jesus affirms Peter's importance by telling him to hold the faith, and he gives Peter a special job to strengthen his brothers in their belief.

The most compelling New Testament evidence for Peter's leadership role is in the first chapters of the Acts of the Apostles. There, in those weeks of waiting between the resurrection and Pentecost, Peter takes charge. Then as the New Testament church is founded at Pentecost, Peter is the primary preacher. He goes on to receive special divine inspiration through a dream in which God tells him to open the gospel to Gentiles (Acts 10) and at the Council of Jerusalem (Acts 15:7), it is Peter who concludes the debate and leads them to an inspired decision.

John: Let me come in. As you are fond of saying, I can't disagree with anything you've said so far!

Dwight: Okay. Peter's leadership of the church after the resurrection was a fulfilment of a famous prophecy and command about Peter by Jesus himself. When Peter receives the divine revelation that Jesus is the Son of God – as recorded in Matthew 16:13-20 – Jesus says that this truth, which Peter confesses, is the rock on which the church will be founded. Then Jesus makes a pun on the name Peter – which means rock. Because he was able to receive this fundamental revelation from God, Peter himself will be the rock on which the church is founded. That Peter – the leader of the apostles – is the rock on which the church is founded matches up with Paul's teaching in Ephesians 2:20 where he says the church is built on the foundation stone of the prophets and apostles.

I know you'll have something to say about this passage in Matthew, but let me talk for a minute about some of the fascinating details which might escape us, but which would have been full of meaning for Jesus' hearers. It's no mistake that this conversation happened near Caesarea Philippi. At that place was a huge natural rock formation on top of which the Romans had built a temple to the pagan shepherd god Pan. So when Jesus said, 'You are Peter, and on this rock I will build my church', he and his hearers were looking at a great rocky foundation on which stood a pagan temple to a shepherd god. Jesus' meaning was clear – Peter, whose name means 'rock', was to be a great foundation for Christ's church – the church of the real Good Shepherd.

There is another detail which is worth considering. In verse nineteen, Jesus equates the church with the Kingdom of Heaven and says he is going to give Peter the keys of the Kingdom. In other words the church is like a kingdom, and Jesus is the king. But a good king has ministers and governors beneath him. Here in England, for example, the prime minister is the monarch's right hand man. The prime minister is given the authority to run the country on behalf of the monarch. It was the same in the Old Testament. The Israelite king had a prime minister, and if we look at Isaiah 22:22 we get a close-up of the relationship between the two. The prophet Isaiah recognises the prime minister of the king and describes his royal appointment to the office. Isaiah addresses the former prime minister and says, 'In that day I will summon my servant Eliakim, son of Hilkiah. [That's the prime minister.] I will clothe him with your robe [that is the king's] and fasten your sash around him and hand your authority over to him...I will place on him the keys to the house of David, what he opens no one can shut and what he shuts no one can open.'

In light of this passage, consider again what Jesus says to Peter in Matthew 16:19. 'I will give you the keys of the Kingdom of Heaven; whatever you bind on earth will be bound in heaven, and whatever you loose on earth will be loosed in heaven.' The apostles would have been completely familiar with the Old Testament. They knew the keys symbolised royal authority, they knew that Jesus was referring to the passage in Isaiah, and they understood clearly in a moment what we have to struggle to grasp – that Jesus – in granting Peter the keys to the kingdom – is appointing him as the prime minister of his kingdom. As God gave prime minister Eliakim in Isaiah the authority of the king – symbolised by the keys – so Peter was being specially appointed and chosen by Christ himself to exercise authority on earth.

As we're using big guns, allow me to quote a few Protestant scholars concerning this link between Matthew 16 and Isaiah 22. F.F. Bruce says, 'What about the keys of the kingdom? The keys of a royal or noble establishment were entrusted to the chief steward...they were a badge of the authority entrusted to him.' Bruce then refers to the passage in Isaiah 22 and says, 'So in the new community which Jesus was about to build, Peter would be, so to speak, chief steward.'[1] This link between Isaiah 22 and Matthew 16 is also attested by Anglican scholar R.T. France who writes about Matthew 16, 'Isaiah 22:22 is generally regarded as the Old Testament background to the metaphor of the keys here.'[2] Finally, J. Jeremias says, 'the keys of the Kingdom are not different from the keys of David...handing over the keys does not imply appointing a porter...handing over the keys implies appointment of full authority.'[3]

John: When I went after you with everything, I expected you would come back with compound interest! But I'm going to use your tactics again and say I agree with you. Honest exegesis of the Matthew passage compels me to conclude that the words of Jesus are quite straightforward. They are meant to leave us in no doubt: Peter is the rock and he was given the keys to the kingdom. Having said that, I'd best explain myself for Protestant readers who may have expected me to take a different line.

William Barclay has said that this passage 'is one of the storm centres of New Testament interpretation'.[4] I agree with him, too. Many non-Catholics have been unable to approach it calmly and dispassionately because of what the Catholic Church has made of it: i.e. that Peter, on whom the church is built, possesses keys that either admit or exclude people from heaven and the power to absolve or refuse to absolve people of their sins. The Catholic Church, further, has claimed that Peter, possessor of these tremendous rights, became bishop of Rome and his successors have inherited these rights, and continue to exercise them even today. It is here that we do indeed part company.

First, let me address the meaning of this passage. In Greek Peter is *Petros* and a rock is *petra*. In Aramaic Peter's name is *Kephas* and likewise in Aramaic it means rock. So in either language there's a play on words. Peter makes his great discovery and confession, Jesus praises him for his insight and courage and says to him, 'You are *Petros* and on this *petra* I will build my church.'

Now it's here that exegetes begin to disagree. St Augustine said Jesus himself was the Rock. It's not an entirely convincing position. William Barclay's free rendering of it goes like this: 'It's as if Jesus said, "You are Peter and on myself as rock I will found my church and the day will come when, as a reward for your faith, you will be great in the church."'[5] Another explanation, and I was brought up with this one, is that the rock is the truth that Jesus is the Son of the Living God. The point is true indeed. On that great truth the church stands and grows forever. Exegetically, however, this explanation glosses over the play on words at the heart of this saying of Jesus. A further possible explanation that the rock is the faith of Peter, a faith that would light a flame that has spread throughout the entire world. Again the idea has merit but it doesn't do justice to the play on words in the passage.

One of the best Protestant explanations is that Peter is the rock in a very important sense. He is not the rock on which the church is founded, for that rock is God. He is, rather, the church's inaugural foundation stone. He is the first to have understood who Jesus is, to have given expression to it and it's thus fair to say that the church is built on him. The point is given credence by arguing that in the Greek the masculine *petros* more aptly applies to stones, pebbles or flints whereas the feminine *petra* signals a large or even immense rock.

Plenty of Protestant apologists have been content to rest their case there. But in honesty, I have to acknowledge the conclusions of authorities over and beyond those you have already cited. Scholars such as Oscar Cullmann and Colin Brown argue convincingly, for example, that *petros* and *petra* come from the same root and can be used interchangeably. It could be that Jesus has used the masculine *petros* simply because Peter is male. Any real difference in meaning must be demonstrated by reference to the overall context in which *petros/petra* are used and we have very little to go on.

Dwight: Let me butt in here with another linguistic detail. Much of this discussion about the Greek words *petros* and *petra* is a red herring because Jesus spoke Aramaic and not Greek. Aramaic doesn't have two words for 'big rock' and 'little rock.' Nor does it distinguish between the masculine and feminine form. It only has one word – '*kephas*', so in Aramaic the two words are interchangeable. In the actual conversation in Aramaic Jesus had to have said, 'You are rock (*kepha*) and on this rock (*kepha*) I will build my church.'

John: Okay. You've seen that I was aware of that in what I've said. The business of translating sayings of Jesus back into Aramaic can be a bit of a poser for Evangelicals. I suspect it's why the Inter Varsity Fellowship doctrinal basis talked of the inspiration of Scripture 'as originally given'. But that's getting a bit complicated. Your point does, however, consolidate what I'm saying. D A Carson has also added the telling point that if Jesus wanted to say that Peter was a stone in contrast to Jesus the Rock, he could have made this quite plain by using *lithos*, a very common word for a stone of any size. (As an old newspaper man I remember 'cutting on the stone' – a very familiar phase in the world of lithographic printing). I have to conclude that in absence of any clear exegetical alternative, Peter is indeed the rock-foundation of the church.

The Catholic Church has endowed this passage with a huge weight of meaning. It has built this edifice on the basis of a pun. Jesus enjoyed puns, as I noted in chapter two with his reference to the Spirit in John 3. So I feel it's in order, here, to say a bit more about the use of figures of speech in New Testament exegesis. First, figures of speech need to be understood by their contexts. The New Testament writers use well-known figures of speech in different ways. Jesus was the first-born; so are Christians (Col. 1:15,18, Heb. 12:23). Jesus is the Light; so too are his disciples (Jn. 1:9, Gal. 3:26). Jesus is the Lamb of God; Christians are his sheep (Jn. 1:29, Jn. 10:8). But we need to be ultra careful about transferring the details of these metaphors across into the interpretation of passages elsewhere. There are several New Testament passages that teach about foundations in the life of the church, but to transfer across to them meaning derived from this passage in Matthew would do them exegetical violence.

Back to Matthew. I have to conclude then, in terms of this passage, that Peter has three basic roles. He is the foundation of the church/kingdom. He is the keeper of the keys of the kingdom/church. And he is the 'binder and looser' on earth. I would argue, however, that all these roles are fulfilled in Peter's actions in the second chapter of Acts. When he preaches, telling of the death and resurrection of Jesus, the One God has sent, his hearers were cut to their heart and ask 'What shall we do?' His response is to call for repentance, faith and baptism, with which comes the promise of the Holy Spirit.

Simon the Rock has announced the means of entry to the kingdom (Acts 2:38). Then in the following verse, Peter, holder of the keys, declares the opening of the kingdom 'to all whom the Lord our God will call'. He is here the earthly binder and looser of what has already been bound or loosed in heaven.

Peter, then, was the major custodian of all that Jesus taught during his earthly ministry and was thus the natural spokesman for the rest of the company. But while at the Council of Jerusalem, Peter has the final word and sums up, this is no Pope. The apostles operated as a collective and worked by consensus: 'it seemed good to the Holy Spirit and to us'. Just as God chose Abraham, Noah and Moses in ancient times for momentous tasks in furthering the history of salvation, so at one time he chose and used a Galilean fisherman called Simon whose surname is Peter. We honour him as a gigantic figure in the history of faith. We credit him with two of the greatest statements of the essence of the gospel. We are continually inspired by his zeal. As Gentiles we acknowledge that he was the first to help the fledgling Christian community to break out of the bounds of Judaism. We admire his strategic missionary thinking: to win the Roman empire for Christ you needed to establish a Christian presence in Rome. We find enormous help from the way his humanity constantly comes through – as it does in the stories of Abraham, Noah, Moses and the rest. To claim more than that, however, is pushing a biblical pun far too far.

Dwight: I'm glad you've taken this passage so seriously. It's easy for both sides to fall into polemics over this bit of Scripture and end up taking extreme positions which can't be sustained. In fact, while it's an important passage, I don't want to claim too much for these few verses on their own. The best Catholic statements take this passage at face value and say the Lord was establishing Peter as the foundation of the church, but while we believe these verses are a foundation, we do not think they're the whole edifice.

This passage is complemented by that other famous conversation between Jesus and Peter. The Old Testament spoke of God himself becoming the Shepherd of his people, (Ezek. 34:15) then in the gospel when Jesus calls himself the Good Shepherd (Jn. 10:11) he is saying this prophecy is fulfilled in him. What interests Catholics is that just as Jesus delegated his earthly authority to Peter, so he delegates his role of chief shepherd. Just before he returns to heaven, the Good Shepherd commands Peter to take charge of his flock and to feed his sheep (Jn. 21:15-17).

I agree with you that you can't take any single metaphor from the New Testament and push it too far. That's why the gospels portray Peter as both the foundation stone of the church, and the chief shepherd. The New Testament is clear that Christ is the sure foundation and the eternal Good Shepherd, but Jesus has delegated his authority to Peter as a prime minister of the kingdom, and as chief shepherd in his absence.

John, you've agreed that Peter is 'a gigantic figure in the history of faith'. About five hundred years ago some Christians started to dispute the historical fact that Peter had gone to Rome, helped establish the church, and then died there. You obviously don't take that position, so I won't bring out all the evidence for it. Suffice it to say that if people want to explore further there are a number of excellent books on this topic, which they can get from our reading list at the back of this book.

However, while you agree to Peter's fundamental influence, you want to keep it there and go no further. Allow me to challenge you further. Jesus promised to be with his apostles to the end of time (Mt. 28:18-20). What did he mean by this? Did he really just mean he would be with them to the end of their earthly lives? In the fifth chapter of I Peter, Peter refers to the elders of the church as his fellow shepherds. This indicates that Peter considered his own Christ-given pastoral ministry to be handed on to the next generation. In other words, the next generation of elders shared the ministry which Christ had given Peter. In the earliest days of the church the different elders appointed by the apostles seemed to have ruled the church as a body, but every committee needs a chairman, and it wasn't long before one elder of each city emerged as the leader of a whole group of elders. As Peter and Paul had founded the church at Rome, and Rome was the centre of the empire, the whole church very quickly came to recognise that amongst the chief shepherds of the different cities, there was one who had a primary place, and that was the bishop of Rome.

I know I tire you with my references to the apostolic fathers, but they are important because they show us just what the Christians who had been taught by the apostles believed and practised. Their writings show that the Roman church emerged very early on as a natural leader of the whole church, and that her leadership was exercised with authority over other churches. I've already mentioned a leader of the Roman church called Clement. Just thirty years after Peter's death he wrote a letter to the Corinthian church correcting their rebellion, and gently calling them to submission to their proper church authorities. He says to the Corinthians, 'you will give us great joy and gladness if you render obedience unto the things written by us through the Holy Spirit...according to the entreaty we have made for peace and concord in this letter.'[6] Ignatius of Antioch who writes about the year 115 calls the Roman church, 'the one which has the chief seat in the place of the district of the Romans...worthy in purity having the chief place in love...'[7] Through the second century there is increasing evidence which records how the different church leaders around the empire consistently consulted Rome on rulings about the faith and pastoral practice of the church. So for example, Polycarp comes to Rome to consult with Pope Anicletus about the date of Easter. Around 180 Irenaeus, a bishop in France, sums up the attitude about the Roman church:

> We will refute those who hold unauthorised assemblies...by pointing to the tradition of the greatest and oldest church, a church known to all men, which was founded and established at Rome by the most renowned Apostles Peter and Paul. This tradition the church has from the Apostles, and this faith has been proclaimed to all men, and has come down to our own

day through the succession of bishops for this church has a position of leadership and authority, and therefore every church, that is, the faithful everywhere must needs agree with the church at Rome, for in her the apostolic tradition has ever been preserved by the faithful from all parts of the world. (*Adv.Haer* 3)[8]

The witness to the primacy of the Church of Rome is universal in the very earliest years of the church, and it is always based on the fact that the leaders of the Roman church inherited their authority from Peter and Paul. From North Africa, Tertullian sums up the view, writing about the same time as Irenaeus. He says,

> Come now, if you would indulge a better curiosity…run through the apostolic Churches in which the very seats of the Apostles remain still in place; in which their own authentic writings are read, giving sound to their voices and recalling the faces of each…if you are near to Italy, you have Rome, whence also our authority derives. How happy is that Church on which the Apostles poured their whole doctrine along with their blood. (*De Praescriptione Haereticorum*, 32)'[9]

By the mid 200s Cyprian of Carthage writes,

> He [Jesus] builds his church on him [Peter], and to him he gives his sheep to be fed: and although he confers an equal power on all the Apostles, yet he has appointed one throne and by his authority has ordained the source and principle of unity…the primacy is Peter's…if a man does not hold this unity of Peter does he believe himself to hold the faith? If a man deserts the throne of Peter, on whom the Church is founded is he confident that he is in the Church. (*De Catholicae Ecclesiae Unitate*, 4-7)[10]

The Catholic Church doesn't use the passage about Peter in Matthew's gospel as its only source for claiming a universal teaching authority. From the very earliest times, we see that Christians around the world believed the Roman church exercised a primacy amongst the churches, and that the leader of the Roman church was seen as the authentic successor to Peter. This doesn't mean the early bishops of Rome were absolute monarchs or the sort of lush Renaissance Popes of the popular imagination. It simply means that from the earliest days the whole church looked to Rome for an authoritative voice of apostolic tradition.

John: I'm glad you mentioned Paul as someone standing alongside Peter in founding the church in Rome. They belong in tandem. What I said about why Peter belongs in the gallery of God's greats should apply equally to Paul. I'm aware of revisionists who've wanted to dispute the association of Peter with the founding of the church in Rome. I think it comes into the same category as the 'forced' exegesis of the 'on this rock' passage. Granted, our main source for Peter in Rome is Eusebius, who wrote in the time of Constantine. He is quite late, but I'm content that he rests firmly on other reliable sources. The late F.F. Bruce had no doubts about the link between Peter and Rome. That for me carries weight. As a Brethren, he would have had lots of friends urging him in the opposite direction!

I don't want to get into an argument with Clement, Ignatius, Irenaeus, Tertullian or Polycarp, who is incidentally one of my heroes. I will concede that they evidently accorded a very special place, even primacy, to the Roman church and its bishops. I would say that this would have been natural enough for at least two reasons: the association with Peter and Paul and Rome's position as the effective world capital. I hold these men in great respect and am one of a rare breed of lay people who actually enjoys reading them and has learned from their teachings and insights. I recognise that several of them – Tertullian, for example – have left invaluable legacies. I salute him as the father of Christian apologetics. As a writer and journalist, I delight in his ability to craft enduring sound-bites, such as 'The blood of the martyrs is the seed of the Church.' I identify with him in his wrestlings with a theology of culture: 'What has Athens to do with Jerusalem?', only to part company with his conclusions. If Tertullian ascribes a primacy to the bishop of Rome, so be it, but like everything else he did and wrote I need to subject it to all the usual theological and exegetical scrutiny.

My final argument is that the claims of Roman primacy need to be assessed according to their fruits. I'm glad that this chapter hasn't become an unedifying slanging match about the actions of popes down the centuries. But the Roman church's claim to be the successor of Peter and inheritor of the keys of the kingdom quickly gave rise to what the historians have dubbed Caesaro-papism. With the break-up of the old Roman empire, the papacy became a mighty secular power. It pursued wars, handed down legal judgements that were sometimes spurious, sentenced people to torture and death, proscribed people on the cutting edge of science and accumulated enormous wealth. Straying into corridors of temporal power often left it at odds with the Spirit of the One from whom it claimed to derive its power.

For my part, I believe it all begins on a false premise. Peter may have been given the 'the keys' by Jesus, but our Lord never gave even a hint that they were to be passed down in a line of people claiming to be his successors. In the first 300 years of the life of the church, the city of Rome was supremely important in a world where civilisation centred around the Mediterranean basin. Its leadership was crucial in the survival and propagation of Christianity over the centuries that followed, though as always endeavour of this kind brings mixed blessings. Today it is a centre of Christian excellence with involvement in education, diplomacy, aid and development, art, music, biblical scholarship and theological reflection. I can buy all that. But when Rome's bishop makes a pronouncement on a matter of faith, claims it to be infallible, and believes he has a God-appointed right to expect all Christians to adhere to that teaching more or less unquestioningly, then he is deceiving himself.

Dwight: Whoa! There is a very strong hint that Jesus intended Peter to hand on the keys to his successors. First of all, the idea

of a line of succession was central to Jesus' religious understanding because he recognised that the Pharisees were the
successors of Moses and sat in Moses' chair (Mt. 23:2). More
importantly, do you remember that the passage in Matthew
16 refers back to Isaiah 22:22 where Eliakim receives the keys
of authority to be prime minister? The Old Testament passage is one of succession. Shebna is handing over the keys to
his successor Eliakim. In the Jewish court, as well as in the
other kingdoms of the ancient Near East, the job of prime
minister or vizier was a continuing office with a vital line of
succession. The keys themselves are a symbol of the ongoing
nature of the office. When Jesus handed Peter the keys it was
understood that he was instituting a traditional, ongoing
office, and the keys were the sign that there would be a successor.

If Jesus didn't intend there to be any succession, then his
command for Peter to feed his sheep also becomes a nonsense.
Does Jesus mean Peter is to feed his sheep until the end of
Peter's life, and from then on God will leave his people without a shepherd? How could there be 'one flock and one shepherd' (Jn. 10:16), if the very shepherd Jesus appointed was not
to have a successor? Peter recognises that his immediate successors share his pastoral ministry (I Pet. 5:1), and the early
church believed it universally. This presents me with a big
problem. I hear well-meaning Evangelicals say they believe
the 'faith once delivered to the saints', but then they reject as a
part of that faith the primacy of Peter and his successors, even
when it is shown to have a biblical basis, universal acceptance
in the early church, and acceptance for the first fifteen hundred years of Christendom.

John: Sorry! I just don't see your point.

Dwight: Don't or won't?

John: Ooh, that smarts. Seriously, I just don't see the need for
the whole thing. For those of Protestant conviction, the promise of the Spirit is sufficient. I for one am satisfied that Peter

more than fulfilled this mandate in his lifetime and I just don't see even a hint from Jesus that can justify the superstructure you seem to be building on one incident.

Dwight: Your other objection is more understandable. The papacy did evolve into a power-hungry and corrupt institution. There were some very dark times indeed for the church, when it looked like the gates of hell might prevail over her after all. I don't wish to whitewash any of the papal history, and of course there are some bits I am ashamed of. I hope we will discuss this in more detail in the next chapter, but let me close by agreeing with you. You said you wish to judge the papacy by its fruits. That's fair enough; but I hope as we do this you will be able to acknowledge all the good things the papacy has brought about as well as all the terrible things. Also, if we are judging by fruits, then it is a two way street. We must also consider whether Protestant rulers ever looked to establish temporal power, whether they used that power to maim, murder and kill, and whether they too were ever corrupted by ambition, greed and lust. I think we should discuss these things openly, but we ought to tread carefully because both our territories are riddled with land mines.

John: I don't carry a brief for Protestant leaders having temporal power any more than I do Catholics. To his eternal shame Calvin, for instance, agreed to the execution of Michael Servetus and maybe others. When people today talk glowingly about the prospects for an evangelically-based Christian Peoples' Alliance becoming a force in politics, I shudderingly think of Oliver Cromwell and his failed attempt at creating a Protestant version of Christendom. That's light years from where Jesus was – or wants us to be.

Dwight: I'm glad you mentioned Cromwell and Calvin's penchant for temporal power. You mustn't forget Cranmer's alliances with Henry VIII, Luther's political manoeuvrings with the German princes, and the harsh Puritan government in the

American colonies. However, despite the abuses, I don't agree with you that the church should eschew temporal power altogether, and I hope we can discuss this further in the next chapter.

Let me finish this chapter by saying that while Peter is the rock on which the papacy is built, that we don't pretend everything all the popes have ever done has been perfect. Like Peter himself, the papacy is human and flawed, but within that flawed humanity we believe God has seen fit to work his will in the world.

---

1 F.F. Bruce, *The Hard Sayings of Jesus*, (Downers Grove: InterVarsity Press, 1983), p143-144

2 R.T. France, Matthew, Evangelist and Teacher, (Grand Rapids: Zondervan, 1989), p274

3 J. Jeremias quoting from G. Kittel and G. Friedrich, eds, Theological Dictionary of the New Testament, 10 volumes, (Grand Rapids: Eerdmans, 1968), Vol. 3 pp749-50

4 W. Barclay, The Gospel of Matthew, (Edinburgh: St Andrews Press, 1957)

5 W. Barclay, The Gospel of Matthew, (Edinburgh: St Andrews Press, 1957)

6 Maxwell Staniforth, The Early Christian Writings, (London: Penguin books, 1984), p56

7 Maxwell Staniforth, The Early Christian Writings, p103

8 Henry Bettenson, The Early Christian Fathers, (Oxford: Oxford University Press, 1969), p90

9 Henry Bettenson, The Early Christian Fathers, p139

10 Henry Bettensn, The Early Christian Fathers, pp263-264

Chapter Four

The Papacy

Dwight: I've thought a lot about our visit to the tomb of St Peter in Rome. At one level you are underground, beneath the basilica, standing within a first century cemetery next to the traditional site of Peter's tomb. From there you can look up and see the floor level of the church built by Constantine in the early fourth century. On top of that is the floor level of the present church and the base of the centrally placed altar on which only the pope himself can celebrate the Eucharist. Then the whole thing is crowned by Michelangelo's great dome, around which are inscribed in letters seven feet tall, 'You are Peter, and on this Rock I will build my church.' What a visual aid!

Having that experience made me consider again just how important Catholics believe the pope really is. We don't think he is just another church leader with slightly better credentials than the others. We really do believe God has set up an earthly system for us to know the truth, and to do this he has used real human beings as his instruments. I admit, in this chapter I am going to have to grasp some nettles. You will want to talk about bad popes and the abuse of the papacy, and I know you will have a problem with papal infallibility. I am happy to answer your questions, but before I do, I'd like to begin at the foundations like I've done before. I'd like to discuss just how God does work in human history, and show that, in principle anyway, you don't have any objections to the idea of a sinful human becoming God's channel of infallible truth.

From the beginning of the whole Judeo-Christian story God has communicated with his people through particular individuals. What strikes me about the Bible stories is how little whitewash there is. God doesn't choose perfect people, he chooses people with faith. The individuals with whom God establishes relationships are always deeply flawed. Abraham was a man of faith, but he disobeyed God when he took his wife's handmaid to bed. Jacob cheated his brother, Joseph was arrogant and ambitious. The later heroes of the Old Testament story were even more flawed. Moses murdered a man to defend the honour of his fellow Jew. David committed adultery, then ordered the husband to be killed in battle, Jonah was a rebel and Solomon a powerful and greedy philanderer. The same deep flaws are there in the characters of the New Testament as well. Paul persecuted the Christians and colluded in Stephen's death while Peter denied his Lord three times. All these characters were channels for God's revelation in the world, and many of them, such as Moses, David, Peter and Paul, were actually the inspired authors of his written word.

As an Evangelical I was brought up to believe that the Scriptures were inerrant or infallible. The precise definition of this varies among Evangelicals. Some think every word of the Bible has to be true historically, scientifically and theologically. Others think the word of God is infallible because it does not fail when it teaches all things necessary to salvation. Like me, I expect you go for the second definition, and would agree with Catholics that the Scriptures are infallible in that sense. Evangelicals agree that if the Scriptures are to be authoritative, they need to be infallible. So we can trust the truth, we declare the source of truth to be without fail.

If the Scriptures are infallible, and they have been written by sinful men like Moses, David, Peter and Paul, then anyone who believes in the infallibility of the Bible will have to admit that God used very flawed human individuals to communicate his infallible word. Now at this point, I'm not pushing things too far. I'm simply trying to establish the principle that we can agree on. The principle is that a flawed and sinful person can be the channel for God's infallible truth. Is this something you can go along with?

John: I like the way you describe the various layers under the dome of St Peter's and the way they all combine in a massive statement of the self understanding of the Catholic Church. But let me give it to you straight and unvarnished: I just don't buy it. I don't buy it because it runs so counter to the spirit of what Jesus was on about. And I don't buy it because if Jesus was at all interested in creating a 'succession' it was a succession that is quite different from that propounded by people of a more 'catholic' outlook.

Let me backtrack and respond to your comments about individuals whom God has used. I don't have any quarrel with what you say. The great thing about the Bible is that it's full of encouragement for people like myself who know only too well that I'm flawed and I'm human. I remember we had a family friend of whom it was said he was the kind of person 'that only God could use', but use him God did. But if you mean to use that to start building a platform to get some of the more notorious popes off the hook for their misdeeds, then be careful. It does no good to relativize sin. On the day of reckoning the only shoes I will have to stand in will be my own. At least the present Pope's millennial *'mea culpas'* suggests he understands that shortcomings of his predecessors need to be faced head on.

Let's talk about this business of succession. In the last chapter you claimed that Jesus clearly had in mind the creation of a succession and you cite the post-resurrection encounter with Peter and the call to 'feed my sheep' in support. I can see from this particular passage that Jesus is entrusting a special responsibility to Peter, but I see nothing to support the idea that Jesus is here conferring something to be passed down to a series of successors.

The historian Eusebius records that there was a succession in Jerusalem carried on by Jesus' own family: James the Just, Judah and then Simeon. Here, surely, are credentials as good or even better than that of the family Bar Jonah. And if you take into account Jerusalem's association with Abraham and David in the history of salvation, then the case for whoever is the rightful successor to James as leader of the Christian community of Jerusalem is surely as good or better than the case for our man in Rome. May I hasten to say that I'm not seriously advocating a case for a universal primate based in Jerusalem but I think the case in a relative sense is even stronger than any claim Rome could put forward.

Let me come back to my key points. I contend that so much of what is encapsulated by the pomp and circumstance of the Roman curia is light years from anything Jesus could have intended. Jesus does not fit at all under the dome at St Peter's. Then as to succession, the deposit handed on is the gospel itself. I judge Christian leaders not by virtue of the office they hold but by their faithfulness in word and deed to that gospel.

Dwight: You've made some interesting points. Let me take up two of them. Firstly, you quote Eusebius that there was a succession in Jerusalem. This supports my view, doesn't it? It shows that the ancient cities all looked to apostolic succession as their source of authority. Jerusalem may have had a claim to primacy, but so might Antioch because Peter was a church leader there. Indeed the Antiochene Christians claim Peter was bishop of Antioch before he was bishop of Rome. Despite this strong claim, to my knowledge, the Antiochenes have never claimed primacy over Rome. As I have tried to demonstrate, history shows us that from a very early stage it was the Roman church that was recognised as the primary seat of authority. It couldn't have been Jerusalem because after the destruction of the city in 70AD, both Christians and Jews were pretty much routed.

Second, you say that my argument for succession is based on one incident – Jesus' conversation with Peter after his resurrection. Sorry, but I didn't base it only on that. The strongest evidence is in the meaning of the keys which Jesus gives Peter in Matthew 16. I showed how the keys represented the authority of an Old Testament office, and that since the keys were always handed on, they represented a successive office. In giving Peter the keys of the prime ministerial office in his kingdom, Jesus is giving him an authority, which he expects will be passed on. Succession is part of the meaning of the keys. Catholics agree with you that it is the deposit of the gospel which is handed on, but we also say that without the authority to define and defend that gospel, it cannot be handed on faithfully.

My essential point was a modest one. It was simply to demonstrate that all of us believe God uses sinful men and women to communicate his word to the world. In fact, as you've said, we believe this to be true in our own lives. Despite our human failures, we believe God will still use us as his instruments. When it comes to declaring, defining and defending the faith, God does this through human instruments in various ways. Looking at Peter's ministry in the New Testament gives us an excellent picture of how God uses an ordinary human being to communicate his word.

He does so in four basic ways. First of all he inspires that person. Peter received direct divine inspiration on three occasions: when he recognised Jesus as the Son of God (Mt. 16:17), at Pentecost (Acts 2), and when he had the vision in which God commanded him to take the gospel to the Gentiles (Acts 10). Secondly, Peter is empowered to preach the gospel. Throughout the Acts of the Apostles he preaches the gospel in the power of the Holy Spirit. Thirdly, in the power of the Spirit Peter exercises the authority to interpret the gospel, even if that means endorsing a revolutionary development in the church's understanding of the gospel. This is clear from his handling of the Gentile question. The apostles understood wrongly that the gospel was only for the Jews. Peter is given the inspiration to expand the scope of the gospel message, and it is through Peter (Acts 11:2-18; 15:7-21) that this expanded understanding is authorised and accepted by the church. Fourth, Peter is inspired and empowered by the Holy Spirit to write down his teachings, and those written teachings are eventually recognised as holy Scripture.

I don't know if you would agree with me, but I believe all Christians enjoy a certain amount of this inspiration. All of us are empowered by the Holy Spirit first to understand and accept the gospel, and then to proclaim it with our words and works. However, most of us recognise another level of authority which the church gives to trained and ordained ministers. No matter what our denomination, we believe the ordained ministers have a special role of studying, preaching and interpreting the word of God for us. For historical reasons Catholics simply take this a bit further. We believe the chief shepherds, the bishops, have a greater burden of leadership. Because they are the leaders they bear a heavier responsibility to faithfully proclaim and defend the gospel inheritance. The shepherd who bears the greatest responsibility to define, defend and declare the unchanging gospel is the successor of Peter.

John: When I was a youngster my Dad's library contained a blue volume titled *Halley's Bible Handbook*. I believe it's still in print, though successive editions have gradually toned down its highly inflammatory chapter on the history of the papacy. I can't remember many of the lurid details, but lurid they were. I read it in the late 1950s and what I do remember most of all is the chapter's finale, which went something like: 'Now we come to the present Pope, John XXIII. Readers will note that there was another John XXIII (see page such and such). We wonder.' The Catholic Encyclopaedia doesn't own to an earlier John XXIII but Halley records, with great gusto, a profane and lust-driven criminal who enriched himself, robbed pilgrims and violated nuns. What that tells me is that, as with martyr stories, there are different versions of the history of the popes, and their tone and texture depends on where you start from in your journey of faith and understanding. Search the World Wide Web and you quickly see this reality remains alive and well in our day. Search under 'Bad popes' and beside fanzines for a pop group I hadn't heard of before, you'll find there are many sites which will tell you the sins of the popes. Alongside these are sites by Catholic apologists who don't duck charges of wrongdoing, but maintain that among the ranks of 265 popes, there were only relatively few bad eggs.

Bad eggs there were, of course. Protestants are most familiar with some of the more notorious popes who lived around the Reformation era. Commenting on Leo X (1513-21), the Pope who dealt with Martin Luther, the Lutheran historian Roland Bainton says he was 'an elegant dilettante, a patron of artists, a gambler, hunter and composer of elegant, im- promptu Latin orations, a man who, according to a modern Catholic historian, would not have been deemed fit to be a housekeeper in the house of the Lord had he lived in the days of the apostles.' But Leo X would not rank among the worst. Political corruption and immorality in the Vatican probably reached its zenith under the infamous Roderigo Borgia who became Pope Alexander VI (1492-1503). Following him was Giuliano Rovere, Julius II (1503-13), the patron of Bramante, Raphael and Michelangelo. His attempts to secure the secular powers of the Vatican state led him to wage a series of disastrous wars which prompted the Dutch humanist Desiderius Erasmus to pen the satire *Julius Excluded from Heaven*. It pictures the 'warrior Pope' swaggering up to the gates of heaven, where to his mortifica- tion he encounters his predecessor St Peter, who refuses him entry. It was Rovere's vision for Renaissance Rome that gave rise to the need for novel approaches to fund-raising. When Albert of Hohenzollern, already holder of two bishoprics, appealed to the pope to be made bishop of Mainz and effec- tively primate of Germany, the pope demanded an installation fee of 12,000 ducats, for the twelve apostles. Albert's counter bid was 7,000 for the seven deadly sins. When they finally set- tled on 10,000 it was agreed that Albert should be granted an indulgence for his territories, to be split fifty-fifty with the pope for the building of St Peter's. Very soon unseemliness in high places was being mirrored by the activities of Tetzel, the most notorious of all the indulgence sellers whose ditty, 'As soon as the coin in the coffer rings, the soul from purgatory springs' so provoked Luther. In the passage in Matthew 16 about the keys, Jesus speaks of Peter binding and loosing things bound and loosed in heaven. By the time of the Reformation popes, or at least their agents, were claiming power to bind or loose quite independently of any action on the part of heaven.

It needs to be said that the early sixteenth century was not the only time when the papacy reached a low ebb. One such era was that leading to the Great Schism between the Eastern and Western churches when in 1054 a papal legate excommunicated the Patriarch of Constantinople on the basis of a papal Bull that was riddled with flaws. It was an era when the Western church had become notorious for abuses such as simony and clerical concubinage. And yet there arose Gregory VII, a reformer, who set the errant monastic houses in order and ushered in a new missionary era.

Where the papacy has always fared worst has been at times when its secular power was threatened or in decline. Under the leadership of medieval popes such as Gregory VII, Innocent III and Boniface VIII there developed a doctrine that became known as *plentitudo potestatis* – the fullness of power. To papal apologists this gave the popes supreme authority over the church. Quickly, however, the claim was extended. Not only did popes claim to be the vicar of Christ on earth but also supreme administrator, lawgiver and judge. There arose the doctrine of 'the two swords' which asserted papal supremacy in secular as well as spiritual matters. It led to a long, drawn out wrestling match with the medieval emperors. It left the papacy weakened. It ushered in a period (1307-77) when the popes resided in Avignon, southern France, more or less under the control of the kings of France. There were rival claimants to the papacy and later Luther labelled this era as 'the Babylonian Captivity of the Church'.

All humans have weaknesses and all institutions have their ups and downs and that is why if our readers want a feast of lurid stories about popes doing their worst they should visit the Protestant Reformation Society or surf the World Wide Web. I want to go a different route and suggest that it is the system, not individuals, that gives rise to problems of the kind I've identified. In the case of the papacy, it's a system that begins on false premises both about the mission Jesus gave Peter and about the claim that he should have a succession.

Now let me come back to the points you make. First this business about the succession in Jerusalem. I suppose what I was hinting at was that if any church has any right to claim primacy it is surely Jerusalem. The fact is, however, that no-one regards this proposition with any seriousness. All I can suggest is that God's providence was at work in this. And if we were to look around Jerusalem today for a church to carry the mantle of primacy there would be a bewildering number of rival candidates.

I've already offered a scenario about the meaning of the keys. I've said, Jesus gave Peter the keys of the kingdom, but what are we to make of that? I've suggested that it was fulfilled in Peter's role on the Day of Pentecost. Most of the episodes in the gospels are there to make a single point and it's dangerous to build a huge doctrinal edifice on a single incident. Getting an isolated text or incident out of proportion is often a gateway to sectarianism and I think that here the Catholic Church is in danger of such in this matter. Where are the exegetical steps that take you from Peter at first-century Caesarea Philippi to Karol Wotilya in Vatican city at the beginning of the third millennium? Where is the warrant for the successor to a Galilean peasant to become someone who, in his name, became a temporal ruler, waged wars, claimed the right to crown and depose kings, amassed fabulous wealth, sanctioned the Inquisition and claimed infallibility as a teacher of the faith? Whatever Jesus had in mind, I cannot believe that it was this.

What I would want to say is that Karol Wotilya in our day does indeed exercise significant authority as a Christian leader. No honest person can deny it. I would contend, however, that such authority is derived not by virtue of anything passed on by a ceremony of the laying on of hands, but from what he is, says and does being congruent with the gospel. Authentic apostolic succession is succession in truth and love. Some of the predecessors to Karol Wotilya have exercised this nobly and well within the limitations of the accretions that have gradually been added to their office. Some have never even been in the frame.

Dwight: I mustn't be flippant, but you forgot the particularly juicy story about Pope Stephen IV who dug up the corpse of one of his predecessors in the year 897. He dressed the mummified cadaver in pontifical robes and put it on trial for perjury and other crimes before hacking it up and chucking it in the Tiber. It's a true story, and I tell it not only because it's gruesomely interesting, but to show that I agree with you one hundred percent that there have been wicked popes, and that their shocking example has done terrible harm to the body of Christ. I also agree with you that when popes clutched temporal power they were far from the gospel teaching that the greatest is the one who serves. You probably know that the old catchphrase about absolute power corrupting absolutely was first applied to the popes.

I suppose I could answer your charges by giving a list of saintly popes. I could recount the intelligent, sensitive and dynamic popes. I could explain how one of the most loved and ancient titles for the pope is 'the servant of the servants of God'. I could explain that while many popes were weak or misguided, there were very few who were absolutely wicked. Alternatively, I could take the rather immature tack and begin dishing the dirt on all sorts of Protestant leaders from Calvin and Cromwell to the cultists and tele-evangelists. But I think all these forms of argument miss the point. They miss the point for the same reason that I think your arguments miss the point. They miss the point because they equate moral goodness with the ability to teach the objective truth.

The essence of your argument is that for a person to teach the truth faithfully he has to be a good person. You say John Paul II speaks with authority because he is a moral and spiritual giant. It is true that his authority is strengthened by his moral, intellectual and spiritual greatness, but a person's ability to speak the truth cannot rest on his ability to live that truth or none of us would dare to speak at all. Of course when those who preach also practise what they preach, the message is stronger and more believable, but a person doesn't have to live the truth to be able to speak the truth, does he? An imbecile can speak the truth and a murderer might preach a very effective sermon on the wickedness of murder.

This takes us to the heart of what we claim for the popes. The Catholic Church doesn't claim that every successor of Peter will be an intelligent, prayerful, dynamic and holy man. We don't claim that every pope will be a saint; on the contrary, we insist that every pope is a sinner. However, what we do claim is so that we might have a sure foundation for our faith: God has granted to Peter and his successors an authority to teach the truth in matters of doctrine and morals without error; and this gift is not dependent on their personal morality. In other words, certain popes may not have lived like Jesus, but they never taught that Jesus wasn't God. Popes may have been liars and murderers and thieves, but they have never taught that lying, murdering and theft were good. The amazing thing is, that when you read back through the history of the papacy you may find scoundrels, but you will not find any pope who has formally taught heresy. This is not to whitewash the popes' misdeeds or to pretend they do not matter. It is simply to re-state my first point that personal sin is not necessarily a bar from a person's ability to speak the truth. The truth I preach is still true even if I'm a hypocrite.

Now that we've got to this troublesome belief in papal infallibility, allow me to explain just what we believe it means. To do that let me first say what it does not mean. It does not mean we believe the pope to be morally perfect. He is a sinful man. It does not mean we believe the pope is historically, scientifically and socially correct in his every utterance. It doesn't even mean that every theological and moral statement of the pope is automatically without error. Instead 'papal infallibility' is a belief that in matters pertaining to salvation and morals, and under certain strict conditions, the pope may teach without error. Even then, what he has said may not be the final word and the complete and total truth, it is simply that what he has said is reliable, trustworthy and true. This belief is based on Jesus' promise that he would build his church on Peter the Rock and the gates of hell will not prevail against it. It is also based on Jesus' words in Luke 22:32 that he has prayed for Peter that his faith will not fail, and that he is to strengthen the faith of his brethren.

Here is what the Catechism says about infallibility:

> In order to preserve the Church in the purity of the faith handed on by the apostles, Christ who is the truth willed to confer on her a share in his own infallibility…The Roman Pontiff, head of the college of bishops, enjoys this infallibility in virtue of his office, when, as supreme pastor and teacher of all the faithful – who confirms his brethren in the faith – he proclaims by a definitive act a doctrine pertaining to faith or morals.. The infallibility promised to the Church is also present in the body of bishops when, together with Peter's successor, they exercise the supreme Magisterium, above all in an Ecumenical Council. (CCC, 889, 891)

The Catechism is clear that the infallibility is Christ's, and that through the Holy Spirit he has granted a measure of that infallibility to his church. Christ's infallibility, present in the church, is exercised by the bishops, and expressed by the leader of the bishops – the pope. Notice that the infallibility rests on the office of the papacy, not on the individual. It is also present when the bishops of the church come to formal agreements within a church council. The precedent for this is in Acts 15 when the decisions of that first council were considered to be led by the Spirit, and therefore without error.

You have brought up another point which I'd like to address. Several times you have said that the pomp and circumstance, the temporal power and the mighty institution of the Catholic Church is light years from the simple gospel of Jesus Christ. There are two answers to this criticism. First of all, while the church is a large international institution, the Catholic Church is also local. In its essence, the large institution is seen as a grouping of local churches. The reality of the kingdom is lived out primarily in the local churches and dioceses, and the centralised church is there to serve the local church. Yes, the Catholic Church has a great centre of unity in the Vatican, but the real Catholic Church is best found on the next street corner where ordinary Catholics meet to worship and live out their faith. You have fairly criticised the corrupt and ostentatious papacy as being far from the spirit of Christ. But the church is not made up only of popes, cardinals and cathedrals. If you are going to be fair you have to set beside them the lowly thatched church in the barrios of Brazil, the Missionary of Charity on her knees at five o'clock in the morning in the heat of Calcutta, as well as the wonderful Catholic saints in every age who have shown the spirit of Christ in all their radiant zeal. These elements are also part of the Catholic Church. If we recognise the power and the glory of the kingdom through the grandeur of the papacy, we also recognise that the real power and glory springs from the lives of the saints in imitation of Christ.

To be sure, the history of the Catholic Church is a history of both saints and sinners. But doesn't that make it feel authentic and real to you? Would you really trust any church whose history was a spotless tale of pure unrelenting holiness and goodness? Wouldn't you smell a rat? There is plenty of blood and thunder in the history of the church, but to my mind that makes it like the history of the Jewish people in the Old Testament. There is lust, murder, mayhem, disobedience and rebellion, but there is also tenderness, love, forgiveness, and the abiding presence of a God who leads his people through the presence of the Holy Spirit. One of my favourite images of the church from Vatican II is the church as the pilgrim people of God. As Catholics we admit the failures of our leaders in the past, but while we're concerned about where we've been, we're also concerned about where we're going. We don't profess to have always got it right, one hundred percent of the time. We're a pilgrim people, and that is all the more reason to cling to Christ's promise that despite corruption within and persecution without, the gates of hell will never prevail against his church.

John: You say that teaching the objective truth can somehow be separated from the moral character of the teacher. Surely it can never be as simple as that. Jesus said, 'By their fruits you will know them' (Mt. 7:16). You will know that as a parent. Remember the saying, 'I can't hear what you're saying because your actions are shouting so loud.' There is nothing more likely to prompt teenagers to reject the moral guidance of their parents than an inconsistent example. Here is a point where the dualistic Aristotelian theological roots of the Catholic Church puts it at odds with the more holistic Hebraic mindset. Christian leaders have no let-out from the Divine admonition, 'You are to be holy, for I the Lord am holy' (Lev. 20:26).

Yes, there are plenty of skeletons in the closet of non-Catholic leaders. I know about the shadow-sides of Luther, Cromwell, Calvin, the henchmen of the English Reformation as well as the fallen idols of tele-evangelism. They have to be judged by the standards they have set for themselves. The claim to be the successor of Peter, invoking powers to bind and loose what heaven binds and looses, is awesome. It puts the office of the papacy and its incumbents in a category of their own, and the standards against which they are judged will be very high indeed.

Dwight: Let me come in here to agree with you that the popes will be judged accordingly. At the last judgement two texts immediately come to mind when I think of the bad popes. The first is, 'to whom much is given much shall be required', and the second is the one about it being better for a millstone to be hung around the neck and the person thrown into the sea rather than to cause a little one to stumble. Of course it is better for parents and preachers and popes to practise what they preach, but my basic point still stands that despite our imperfections we might still proclaim the truth of God authentically.

John: Okay. I guess we're chasing our tails on this one a little. I am thankful for your exposition of infallibility. May I urge our Protestant readers to take careful note because it's far more nuanced than the way it is often caricatured by opponents. I fear I don't find it a lot of help in the end. I don't think I'm alone in having problems over distinguishing exactly which utterances of popes are supposed to be infallible and which are not. I understand, for example, that *Humane Vitae,* which includes Pope Paul VI's teaching on contraception, does not actually come under the category of 'infallible' teaching. But how many Catholics actually appreciate that, and where does it leave them in practice? I know Catholic priests who tell their flock that if they use artificial contraception they cannot come to communion. That seems to be according huge importance to this bit of papal teaching. In the end, it seems to me that what you outline here doesn't win appreciably more points for perspicuity than what I have offered in relation to the authority of the Bible.

Then you say that there are no examples of popes who were scoundrels actually leading people astray in matters of faith. Luther was unequivocal on that one. Popes have erred, he said, and so too have councils. I think he might have added that scoundrels and non-scoundrels alike have erred. By billing its contemporary teaching as 'apostolic', the Catholic Church is apt to debase the currency. As I read, for example, the utterances of the Council of Trent or the First Vatican Council, I sense I am reading material that is different and inferior to material from the first century – or even the first three centuries for that matter.

Then we have a long-standing phenomenon of papal over-reaction to external events and (alleged) non-reaction when some sort of clear initiative was called for. I don't want to get into detail on the latter, but you get the sense on reading the utterances of Pope Pius XII, during the course of World War II, that here was someone whose convictions about the eternal nature of the church seemed to consign events in Europe to something in the nature of a temporary glitch. As for over-reaction, it interests me that the doctrine of papal infallibility is a relatively recent innovation and was launched at a time when the political status of the popes had reached its lowest ebb. Garibaldi was at the gates of Rome. The pope's temporal power was evaporating all around. In my view this strident piece of teaching is a serious over-reaction in the same order as the utterances of the infamous Boniface VIII (1294-1303) who, having fallen out with Kings Edward I of England and Philip IV of France, declared that no human beings, including kings, could be saved unless they were subject to the pope. It hardly needs to be said that both this particular pope and the office of the papacy were the ultimate losers.

To conclude may I offer one more comment and that's to do with the whole business of what a pope stands for. Part of the difference between you and me, Dwight, is one of temperament. You've said you like to think of yourself as a tidy sort of guy. That's not me. Witness my work den. I sometimes think I invented the chaos theory! Some temperaments are happy to suspend individual judgement and accept the words of a priest, patriarch or pope. Others are dead opposite, though not necessarily consistent in their thinking. Of one thing I'm certain: the cultural tide is running in a direction where increasingly people will not take the word of popes, or anyone else, on the basis of their office. Witness how in the field of healthcare, 'Trust me I'm a doctor' no longer cuts much ice. The way the church expresses authority in such a culture is full of traps. Rather than making statements to assert its authority, the church would be wise to offer its teaching in humility and leave it to the faithful to drawn their own conclusions about both the message and the messenger.

Dwight: Three points quickly. You say it is unclear which teaching of the Catholic Church is infallible and which isn't. That's fair enough. The church does have a hierarchy of teaching. Certain core truths are deemed infallible. There is a second level which the faithful should hold to 'with faithful assent'. There is a very wide third level of church teaching which is authoritative, but debatable. But while these gradations exist, to focus on them is missing the Catholic spirit. As I understand it, Catholics are to subject themselves in faithful obedience to *all* the church's teaching. This doesn't mean we may not think or question the teaching – but that we are to question in a spirit of 'faith seeking understanding'. In other words, it is not a Catholic mindset to say, 'I think this bit might be infallible, but I don't like that bit so I don't think it is infallible.' Catholics are not cafeteria Christians.

Secondly, you claim popes have over-reacted or under-reacted to current events. I'm sure you're right that certain popes have made decrees under pressure of circumstances that have, with hindsight, proved foolish or incorrect. But none of these edicts have had anything to do with the infallible core of Christian teaching. Though Luther may have claimed popes have erred, I have yet to find an example of any pope formally teaching heresy. If we had more time I'd challenge you to uncover one.

Finally, you suggest that our disagreement may have more to do with personality type than anything else. Maybe you're right up to a point, but on the other hand it can't be the whole answer because there are plenty of tidy Protestants and an awful lot of messy Catholics. Instead I think you've hit on a central dividing point not only between us, but between Catholics and Protestants generally. Protestants simply don't believe that God has established a continuing earthly authority by which we can know his saving truth reliably. Catholics do. As a result of this the Protestant and the Catholic have very different centres of focus. The Protestant will always look to his opinion and his interpretation of the Bible. The Catholic's basic instinct, on the other hand, is to submit himself to the One, Holy, Catholic and Apostolic church.

I know this sounds superior. I don't mean it that way at all. In fact I have found this submission to the church to be both humbling and terrifically liberating. I feel, as the psalmist says, that my feet have been placed in a large room. I no longer have to make it up as I go along, and it seems like an amazing grace that God has seen fit to bring me into this church which is far more universal, ancient and beautiful than I ever could have imagined.

John: You've summed up well. If pressed, I don't think I'd put our differences down merely to personality type or even failed communication. I don't buy the view expressed by the Anglican-Roman Catholic International Commission that the Reformation debate about justification was all a misunderstanding. At the same time I'd never under-estimate psychological or sociological forces. If these forces counted for nothing, how is it that that the two great historical rifts which divided the church were east versus west, producing the Great Schism, and southern Europe versus northern Europe, producing the Reformation. But you've got it right. Protestants just don't buy this notion of continuity in any atomic sense. It's an unseen continuity that is the work of the Spirit that blows where it wills. In terms of definition, we therefore have different visions of God's amazing grace. I'd hope and expect, however, that we'd both agree that God's grace is truly amazing!

Chapter Five

Channels of Grace

John: One of the most illuminating bits of information about the early Christians and their worship is to be found in the letters of Pliny. He was sent by the Roman Emperor Trajan to Bithynia (c.112) with a mandate to reorganise a province that had become an administrative shambles. Pliny's letters reveal a bit of a duffer who is almost totally unable to think for himself, but as a result his letters go into great detail about the issues that vexed him. One such issue concerned how Rome's administrative and legal arm should deal with Christians. Courtesy of Pliny, we have what are some of the earliest independent accounts of Christian worship and community life. Pliny reports that 'it was their habit on a fixed day to assemble before daybreak and recite by turns a form of words to Christ as a god; and that they bound themselves with an oath not for any crime, but not to commit theft or robbery or adultery, not to break their word, and not to deny a deposit when demanded. After this was done, their custom was to depart, and to meet again to take food, but ordinary and harmless food...'

I start here because when I was in my formative years, the Christian community to which we belonged believed their life and worship mirrored the life of the early church. If Pliny's account is anything to go by, I think they had a point. Clearly there was some form of liturgy, although Pliny offers few clues as to what it contained. There was mutual exhortation to high standards of moral and ethical behaviour. Then, there was a culture of simple hospitality, a lifestyle that traced its origins to Jesus who put a great premium on what the scholars have called 'table fellowship'. All this was in the context of a community that knew it needed to keep its head down. Even though the horrors of the persecutions under Nero and Domitian were behind them, second century Christians understood only too well that the authorities were paranoid about secret societies, especially those who might constitute a challenge to the cult of the Emperor.

The Christian community in which I spent my early years was highly suspicious of Anglican and Roman Catholic worship, which they dismissed as 'ritualism'. The common belief was that such churches had added all kinds of unnecessary accretions to the simple worship style of the early church. Our worship was indeed simple. There was an introit, a bidding prayer, a rousing hymn, a psalm mostly read antiphonally, another hymn, a long extemporary prayer, a further Scripture reading which was at least the starting point for a long sermon that followed after another hymn. Then came a short prayer, a closing hymn and a benediction. Most of the worshippers would have insisted that they had no liturgy at all and that this was Christianity spontaneously expressed. Read prayers were eschewed. Few realised that to help his congregation feel uplifted in prayer, the minister worked very hard to craft a prayer that contained substance but seemed conversational.

In my mother's Brethren background was the tradition of celebrating the Lord's Supper every Lord's Day. My father's Presbyterianism had a tradition of the quarterly communion service. The pattern became a service of communion once every one or two months. Again the liturgy was simple: the minister as president surrounded by the church elders. There was a reading either of a gospel account of the Last Supper or St Paul's account from I Corinthians. Otherwise there were few preliminaries other than one lay person offering a prayer of thanksgiving for the bread, symbol of Christ's body broken for us, and for the cup (but note, not the non-alcoholic wine).

Celebrating communion infrequently, if anything, kept it special as far as I was concerned.

There was a special emphasis that is largely missing in Anglican worship, what the theologians have labelled *anamesis*. In the Lord's supper we remembered, or 'kept a memorial' of Jesus' death until that great day when we eat and drink the new wine of the kingdom in the company of all those who love Jesus. To make the point, the front of what was a simple communion table bore the words 'Till he come'. And although I wonder if these folks would have ever articulated it, the idea of *anamnesis* seemed to be echoed in many other aspects of their life together. For if the liturgy was somewhat threadbare, with enormous effort required to serve up something that seemed fresh each week, the strength of the community was its commitment to table fellowship. On Sundays everyone brought a picnic lunch, joining together around trestle tables in the local park. If the weather was inclement they would repair to the church hall. Many years on, I was pleased to see that the World Council of Churches-sponsored multi-lateral ecumenical conversations culminating in the *Baptism, Eucharist and Ministry* report (1982) affirmed *anamnesis*. Here, it said, was a valued insight, cherished by some Christians but neglected by others, especially those whose liturgies trace their origins through the Catholic Mass back to the great liturgies of the early church.

Later on, of course, I was to discover Anglican liturgy and with it many new dimensions of worship. As a teenager going to school nearby, I began to relish the chance to slip into Sydney cathedral and sit in silence. Silence was rarely a hallmark of the worship I'd been brought up on. While the Christian community of my early years claimed they were more 'biblical' than other churches, I found that more Scripture was actually heard in the course of an Anglican liturgy and the worship was pregnant with biblical allusions. Then I found in the Prayer Book words that summed up my spiritual longings far more eloquently than I could have unaided: it is a blessing in itself to ask the Lord to 'pour on us the continual dew of thy blessing.'

At the end of Matthew's gospel, Jesus promises that he would be with his church until the end. Throughout my years I have found the church to be both generous and mean, uplifting and depressing, glorious and flawed, humble and pompous. But Christ always keeps his word and the promise that he will be present whenever two or three gather in his name rings true in great cathedrals, parish churches and even when a small group of his people go to the local park to share their sandwiches, tea and cakes.

Dwight: Our early religious background was virtually identical. In our independent Bible church in Pennsylvania, we had the same mixture of hymns, prayers, readings and a long Bible sermon. I thank God for my foundation in the Christian faith in such a church. I still love those old hymns, and because the Bible we used was the Authorised Version, I actually memorised the Bible passages in the beautiful cadences of the finest English ever written. We also had church suppers, Sunday school picnics, and fellowship outings. I agree with you that the Lord was there are in the midst of our fellowship. He was there in our worship, in our intimate prayer meetings, and in our home Bible studies.

Jesus Christ is certainly present wherever two or three of his disciples are gathered in his name. This beautiful principle is at the very heart of what it means to belong to the church. I think it is no exaggeration to say that the idea of being a completely solitary Christian is a contradiction in terms. By very definition, to be a Christian means we belong to the body of Christ. What it means to belong to the body of Christ is expressed with a great richness in the Catholic tradition. The interesting word in the term 'Body of Christ' is the word 'body'. The word applies to the congregation of believers, which are sometimes called the 'body of believers'. Paul used this image of the church in a very physical way in his first letter to the Corinthians.

I think the word 'body' is important for another reason as well. It reminds us that our faith is physical. You have a body. I have a body. This is the way God made us, and it's no mistake. Some people think the body is merely the container for our mind and soul; but this is not fully Christian. Instead, like the Hebrews before us, we believe our minds, souls and bodies are one. Therefore, what we do with one aspect of ourselves influences the rest. Recent research has confirmed that if we pray and meditate, if we read the Scriptures regularly, then we will tend to be healthier physically as well. On the other hand, if we have over-eaten, or not taken exercise, we will find it more difficult to pray. So the term the 'body of Christ' is something very physical for me. I want my faith to be physical as well as spiritual and mental. I want all of me to be saved, not just my heart and mind. While I am grateful for my Bible church background, I would criticise it on this count. I think the Bible-only Christians tend to neglect the physical dimension to the faith.

I wonder if you agree with me that in coming to the Anglican Church, you have experienced a physical and historical dimension to the faith that was lacking in your earlier experience? I know when I became an Anglican in my early twenties I enjoyed the physical-ness of the faith. The candles, the vestments, the grand architecture, the stained glass windows, the beautiful music and the words of the liturgy gave my faith much more physical expression. As I moved towards Catholicism, I began to understand that none of this was a mistake, and to grasp why the church ministers to us in sacraments. The sacraments are simply powerful physical channels through which God's grace can flow. I can remember being quite excited when I realised how the sacraments reflected the truth of the incarnation. God himself took flesh in Jesus Christ. That's the way he expressed his truth and goodness to the world. It seemed perfectly reasonable to me that he should continue expressing his love through the physical means of sacraments.

Despite all the differences between Christians, I find it encouraging that the vast majority of believers celebrate some form of sacraments. They might not call them sacraments; they might deny that sacraments do anything; they might insist that there are only two sacraments and not seven, but they still have them. Christians everywhere are baptised. In almost every denomination they gather to celebrate the Lord's Supper. All Christians recognise their marriages are sacred. They select special people to lead the congregation, then train and ordain them. Most denominations anoint the sick with oil for healing. Many denominations seal baptismal vows with confirmation. All Christians believe confession of sins is vital, and some agree that serious sins should be confessed to a Christian brother or sister.

Over the years, the Catholic Church has developed these practices into a system which helps ordinary believers make regular, powerful contact with the living Lord. We believe that through the sacraments, God seals his love to us in a sure and certain way. To have a sure hope of salvation we need to participate in these sacraments, which take us into union with Christ himself. This brings us back to the necessity of the church, because we cannot administer the sacraments to ourselves. Instead it is the body of Christ – the church which administers them. One of the most important beliefs of the Catholic Church is that it is Christ himself who administers the sacraments to us through his body the church. Can we agree on much of this, or is there something here on which you want to challenge me?

John: We seem to be in danger of getting a bit too matey! You've said a lot I agree with. The theme of the body is crucial to how we are to understand the church. As to the point about the physical body, of course, it's not only Anglicans and Catholics who helped people discover the body in all its dimensions. I always thought that the ecstatic aspects of charismatic and pentecostal worship did likewise, and we all stand to learn something from that.

But you've given me some issues to bite onto. One of them is the idea of sacraments. Back to the understanding of the Lord's Supper which I was brought up with. I can't remember the whole hymn, but one line sums up a very different outlook to the Catholic one: 'Too soon we rise, the symbols disappear…' For Catholics I know the bread and wine of the

Eucharist are much more than 'symbols'. I remember Catholic children coming back from Mass telling how they'd been taught to swallow whole rather than bite a communion wafer – indication that here was more than a symbol. I remember a young former Catholic coming to our church and sharing communion. When the bread was passed round she said she was in great turmoil. What would happen if she bit into it, but how would she get it down if she didn't. You might want to explain to me a bit more about popular Catholic devotion on a point like this, and suggest whether she'd been well taught.

But you have made one point that I can't allow to pass. You say, 'To have a sure hope of salvation we need to participate in these sacraments, which take us into union with Christ himself.' Now I need to be careful not to misrepresent you, but we're back to the 'bottom line' I delineated in the first chapter. I will pay the notion that the Eucharist may, by some mystery that I don't understand, strengthen my soul. But I find myself in alien territory on two counts. I can't accept that any work I do – and that includes faithfully participating in the Eucharist – will actually affect my salvation. On the other hand violating it has enormous consequences. But we probably begin at different starting points. I was brought up to believe that the Eucharist is for the person who already senses assurance of salvation. And the converse is that, as Paul says in I Corinthians 11:27, those who eat and drink unworthily 'eat and drink damnation to themselves'.

May I ask another question? Catholics insist that only priests may baptise or preside at communion. Now coming, as I do, from the Diocese of Sydney, a champion for the cause of lay presidency, I'd be interested to get a Catholic slant on the issue. In my early years, in absence of clergy, lay men (not women, as I recall) did preside at communion. I suspect there was a different underlying view both of communion and ordination! And, by the way, is there a distinction between routine church order and emergencies in this matter?

Dwight: So what's wrong with being matey? What do I think about the little girl who was told not to bite the communion bread? Well, maybe she and her teachers were being a little bit fussy. It reminds me of the Baptists I knew who used to get themselves all in a twist over whether a person should be baptised by immersion, sprinkling, or pouring. It's a case of people with good intentions becoming too worried about the particulars, isn't it?

You seem to have a problem with the idea that the sacraments are necessary to our salvation. It worries you that the sacraments are something you do, and you quite rightly want to avoid any appearance of salvation by works. We'll have to discuss the whole question of salvation, faith and works in another chapter; but here let it suffice to say that the sacraments are not something we do. Each sacrament is something which Christ does through his body, the church. All we do is receive a gift which he gives. For a Catholic, participating in the sacraments is a way to receive God's grace. When I was a teenager, I went to evangelistic rallies where we were encouraged to come forward and accept Jesus into our hearts. No one suggested that going forward was a way of earning our salvation.

John: In my later reflections, of course, I think I've come to the conclusion that treading the sawdust trail according to a particular prescribed formula probably comes into the category of 'works'.

Dwight: Billy Graham's catch-phrase was, 'I want you to get up from your seats…' Treading the sawdust trail may well be an authentic response to the gospel. If through that act of faith we repent of our sins and turn to Jesus, then we are obeying his commands. As you've hinted, to participate in the sacraments is also one of the primary ways of obeying the commands of Jesus. He commanded his apostles to baptise, and to celebrate the Lord's Supper. When we participate in the sacraments we are sharing in mysterious way in his life, death and resurrection.

May I correct you on a little detail? You said that we insist that only priests may baptise and celebrate communion. This is not strictly true. In fact any person may baptise. In most situations it will be the priest who administers baptism, but in an emergency anyone may baptise. All they need is water, an intention to do what the church does, and to baptise in the name of the Trinity. For celebration of communion to be a valid Catholic celebration, the person presiding must be a priest. That the ordained church leader presides at communion is a discipline shared by most Christian denominations, isn't it? I know some people are pushing for a lay presidency, but even then, only lay people who are properly authorised may celebrate. Every church that I know of expects a high level of discipline in this area.

From the very earliest days of the church, it was necessary to limit the leadership role at communion to those who held the leadership role in the church. In the New Testament Peter, Paul and John all rebuke false teachers very soundly. Those who did not teach the fullness of the Christian faith were barred from Christian leadership. Only those who bore the authentic apostolic authority were permitted to teach, act as pastors and express their leadership by presiding at the Lord's Supper. The other reason to have a recognised leadership was to promote church unity. For the sake of solidarity, each congregation had one pastor who acted in solidarity with his bishop. This unity was a sign of authenticity; remembering Jesus' words, that the unity of the church would be a sign to the whole world. To show how early this discipline was in the history of the church, allow me to quote from Ignatius of Antioch who wrote around the year 114. In his letter to the church at Smyrna he writes,

> Shun divisions, as the beginning of evils. All of you follow the bishop, as Jesus Christ followed the Father, and the presbytery as the apostles...let no one do anything that pertains to the church apart from the bishop. Let it be considered a valid Eucharist which is under the bishop or one whom he has delegated...it is not permitted to hold the love feast independently of the bishop...That all your acts may be sure and valid.[1]

The Catholic pattern of ministry is actually based on the New Testament. As you know, the New Testament church had two types of leaders chosen by the apostles: elders – called presbyters, from which we get the English word priest – and deacons. The New Testament sometimes calls the presbyters 'overseers' (the word is *episcopos* – from which we get the word 'episcopal', which refers to bishops). In the early church there was an elder over each congregation. Before too long, the Christian congregation in a particular city had split into many smaller congregations, with their own local elders. The senior elder in the city became known as the bishop, or overseer. The elders of the other congregations were considered to be like his fingers. They exercised apostolic authority on his behalf. They worked in solidarity with him, and their unity as priests together was an expression of the unity of the whole church. This same pattern continues today, despite the huge expansion of the Catholic Church. The priest of every parish works in solidarity with his bishop, and every bishop works in solidarity with the top bishop – the bishop of Rome. Call me a tidy guy, but I like this. The structure is not only scriptural, but it is basically simple, yet flexible enough to meet the needs of a world-wide church. Are you Anglican enough to appreciate priests and bishops, or do you view the whole structure as a necessary evil?

John: I'm glad you put me on the spot here. I argue that all our church structures are at best 'provisional', not least because as humans on this side of heaven 'we know in part and reason in part'. Language itself is an exercise in the use of symbolism, and this carries over into how we approach theological formulation.

Dwight: John, you're going all fuzzy and Anglican on me.

John: If I try to expound the meaning of the cross, for example, I have to operate in the world of symbolism and metaphor. I can never sum up every facet of its meaning, nor can I exhaust its poetry and its power.

Dwight: Of course, Christ's action on the cross is an eternal mystery. Church structures, however, are a bit more practical, aren't they?

John: I would say of our church structures that there are aspects where, if I were to start from scratch, I would not start with what we have now. To take one example from Church of England practice: whatever would first century Roman Christians worshipping in the catacombs, or the writer of the Book of Revelation have said if I proposed that the King or government should chose the bishops of the church?

Dwight: Is there anybody out there who doesn't think that more than a little bit odd?

John: Yet on the other hand I sense that the vision of Anglican Divines, like Richard Hooker, for a Christian commonwealth was a noble one. Even today, removal of few of the threads of Anglican establishment may have unforeseen and bad consequences for the social cohesion of the English nation. We have inherited some features which are good, some which are bad, and some which are indifferent. We have a style of priesthood which is in some ways a liability, but starting from the principles that God calls and God equips with charisms, God-given gifts that add extra dimensions to a person's normal human powers, I believe in ordination and the setting apart of certain people to teach the people of God and embody Christ-likeness. From being part of one or two Christian communities that fought to a standstill about doctrinal inessentials, I believe in the system of episcopal oversight. I do so, not because I think someone should dictate what should be done, but because we need a presence that reminds local Christian communities that they are part of something bigger. I believe that the ministry of oversight is a divine calling and that God equips sometimes the most unlikely in the exercise of this office.

I would suggest that there are other strong reasons for the ordained ministry, not least because I put a premium on their being people set aside in the Christian community to devote themselves to studying and teaching the faith. As an occasional preacher in my parish church, I know just how much effort is involved in maintaining consistently high standards of preparation and presentation. With the best will in the world,

I think there will always be limits on what the laity can contribute in ministry and mission without a full time enabler. And from my neck of the woods in inner east London, I appreciate the value to the community of having a resident professional who is a generalist, who knows the people and can relate across all the different institutions and agencies that touch their lives.

I have no theological objections that would constitute a barrier to lay people – under certain conditions – presiding at the Eucharist. I would oppose 'open season' for any lay person to do so. I think lay presidents would need to be widely recognised as natural leaders of their local Christian community and should be well instructed in the faith. Having said that, if I were a synod member I doubt I would vote for it, not least because there are far more important issues that we need to address in the life of the church. Moreover, I think it poses a threat to unity in Anglicanism that we can do without. Having said all the above, I think we can deduce from that a system somewhat like the one you describe for the administration of the local church community and its oversight. I think most of this was in place before the end of the New Testament era.

But now let me lob one back at you. Priesthood (in both its Anglican and Catholic forms) carries all sorts of accretions, like strange clothes whose origins aren't Christian at all. Octavian, the adopted son of Julius Caesar, gave himself the title Augustus (meaning 'the Reverend'). And based on such doubtful underpinnings priests conduct 'confessions', prescribe penances and tell people their sins are forgiven – when we know, don't we, that Christ is the only mediator and that the living Lord constantly makes intercession for us. What say you?

Dwight: I always used to squirm when I was an Anglican vicar and had to read that gospel passage which says something like, 'Beware the scribes and Pharisees, they love to wear long robes and be seen sitting in the best seats of the temple.' There I was all dressed in my cassock, surplice, hood, scarf and preaching tabs; and seated on a raised platform at the front of the church in the rector's stall! It's true that fancy religious clothes can give the wrong image, but so can a tele-evangelists's three thousand dollar suit. In any society people in authority wear a uniform. Clerical dress and priestly vestments are worn to show that the priest is set apart for the service of God. The same is true of the titles which clergy use. Like the terms 'Doctor' or 'Professor', clerical titles are a mark of respect and a signal of professional status. I know some non-Catholics also object to the fact that we call our priests 'father'. They think it contradicts Jesus' command to 'call no one father' (Mt: 23.9) However, in the verse before that Jesus also says his disciples should not be called 'teacher', but no one objects to using that term for those in a teaching position.

You've challenged me on a more important and controversial point however. It is true that Catholics are expected to confess their sins to a priest. It is also true that the priest declares our sins forgiven, and gives us a prayer or good action to do to help us make amends. I know this sacrament can be easily misunderstood, but on the other hand, it is this sacrament which, after baptism and Eucharist, is closest to our Lord's commands. In the gospels everyone is amazed because Jesus takes the authority to forgive sins. In several places he delegates that authority quite clearly to his apostles. The clearest reference to this is John 20:22-23 which says, 'With that he breathed on them and said, 'Receive the Holy Spirit. If you forgive anyone his sins, they are forgiven; if you do not forgive them, they are not forgiven.''' A picture of the early church practice is found in the epistle of James where the believers are expected to 'call the elders of the church... and confess their sins to one another' so they might be healed (Jas. 5:14-16). Very early in the church's tradition, this public confession of sin developed into private confession to the church leader.

The gospel shows how Jesus shared his authority to forgive sins with his apostles, and we believe this authority is passed on to priests through their ordination. Remember, as in all the sacraments, it is Christ who is acting; not the priest himself. The priest does not forgive our sins, Jesus does. Because of Christ's work on the cross the priest has the power to solemnly declare Christ's forgiveness to us. This answers your other challenge about Christ being 'the only mediator between God and man'. This is scriptural, and Catholics also embrace this truth. At the end of every confession the priest says, 'Go in peace and remember to pray for me too, who am also a sinner.' So when we go to a priest for confession we are not going to him instead of going to Jesus. We are going to Jesus along with him.

While the Catholic Church teaches that the faithful should go to confession regularly, I should add that we also believe Christians can confess straight to Jesus in private. I think the main objection people have to the sacrament of confession is that it seems so embarrassing. It's not too hard for me to confess my sins in private to Jesus, but it is rather daunting to tell another person the darkest secrets of my life. However, I can say from experience, that while confession to a priest is difficult, it is also one of the most blessed and Spirit-filled moments of my spiritual life. Catholics are sometimes criticised for not having a 'personal and intimate relationship with Jesus.' But let me tell you, once I'd been to confession and really told everything, and then received the assurance of Christ's forgiveness, I felt a personal relationship with him more powerfully than I could have imagined before.

John: One of the more cringe-making hymns of my youth was one that began, 'I come to the garden alone, while the dew is still on the roses...' and the chorus (talking of Jesus) went:

> And he walks with me and he talks with me,
> And he tells me I am his own.
> And the joy we share
> As we tarry there
> None other has ever known.

Dwight: If you'd let me I could have finished the chorus for you. We had the same hymn. Maybe we should open our radio programme with the two of us singing it as a duet.

John: A lot of the more pious Evangelicals talk at length about having a personal relationship with Jesus. And as with this example, some of the more popular attempts to celebrate it get somewhat sugary. Evangelicals can learn a lot from Catholics about devotional disciplines, not least the mystics like St John of the Cross, and many are doing so. I'd add that the Puritans likewise knew a lot about the practice of the presence of God, though their methods are less in fashion in our day than Catholic ones. At the heart of it, Evangelicals are somewhat more comfortable with the pre-existent, now risen, ascended, glorified Christ than they are with the human Jesus. I suspect that the church as a whole is in the same boat, although those traditions that put great store on incarnational theology cope with it better. From an evangelical point of view, it's something that Philip Yancey picks up in what I think is a ground-breaking book at popular level, *The Jesus I Never Knew*. He imagined what it would have been like to follow Jesus about during his earthly life and ministry. The Jesus who emerges isn't terribly cosy and the people who found his company and teaching attractive were not particularly the respectable kinds of people who we might find in evangelical churches today! It's very challenging for those of us whose spirituality is a self-conscious quest to be like Jesus. A person who is Jesus-like isn't necessarily a comfortable companion, nor could such a person be relied on to always keep the best of company.

There is another evangelical tradition, and it's most often seen in missionary experience, where Jesus reveals himself directly. I've heard a lot of examples of this from Islamic countries, often from places where there's no Christian church presence. Not that it's evangelically inspired, but the novelist Susan Howatch includes an example of a Christ experience in her book *The High Flyer* where the heroine runs for her life through the streets of London and gradually senses a protecting 'presence'.

What I'm saying, then, is that I very much believe in the quest for a personal relationship with Jesus. I am willing to accept that some evangelical conversions are direct Christ experiences. I'm willing to venture that personal relationships with Christ are capable of taking forms we don't expect. More importantly, however, the whole idea is very challenging. I have never had a Christ experience, so for me the quest is to seek to be a life-long disciple based on the biblical and historical data that we have. It's no easy quest, and the calls on you can sometimes be very awkward and challenging, not least when it comes to being Jesus-like in challenging the social consensus and popular wisdoms of our day.

As a footnote I'd add that I think certain Evangelicals make the mistake of thinking that if they do or believe certain things, then a relationship with Jesus will follow. It's not necessarily so. As in Old Testament times, there are periods when it seems as if the Word of God is 'scarce'. In just the same way, at times our prayer life seems to bring us to the very throne of grace while at other times the Lord seems silent and far removed. I suspect that one of the reasons why Evangelicals are adamant about assurance of salvation, and tend to relegate sacramental celebration to a lower division, is precisely this point: they wholeheartedly believe that like Paul they can 'know Christ, and the power of his resurrection.'

Dwight: It is always a challenge for us to try to get in touch with the Lord Jesus. I'd like to read Philip Yancey's book. From what you've said, it sounds a bit like the spiritual exercises of St Ignatius. The spiritual exercises are an attempt to use the imagination to re-experience the gospel stories and apply them on a deep level to our own lives. Like you, I'm sure there are many valid personal experiences of the Lord. From the evangelical experience of 'getting saved', through to the human experiences of beauty, truth and love, we may in fact meet Jesus Christ. However, while acknowledging the goodness of these experiences, the Catholic Church wants to go further. While various forms of subjective experience *may* be authentic, it's also true that we may be fooled by our subjective experience. Spiritual experience is a flighty thing. Our 'spiritual' experiences may have more to do with the fact that the weather has been good or that we have just had a very good dinner.

Furthermore, we have to be careful that subjective spiritual experiences of a particular sort do not become the criteria for authentic membership of the body of Christ. I've met quite a few evangelical Christians, who having been brought up in a good Christian home, agonise over the fact that they had never had a 'born again experience'. This is one area where I challenge Evangelicals quite strongly. To demand a particular type of religious experience is grossly unfair. Very often, religious experiences are determined by personality type. For example, an informal, hands up, screaming and fainting charismatic service doesn't do much for me at all. And yet I can see that for many people this sort of religious experience is fantastic. On the other hand, I can be transported to the seventh heaven when the Catholic liturgy is celebrated with restraint, dignity and silences which hum with the music of eternity. I'm sure there is another whole class of Christian, who has hardly ever had an emotional response to their faith at all. They worship faithfully, they say their prayers, they live a quiet life of love, and yet perhaps they have never experienced what they would call a profound religious experience. Their faith is also valid, and in the long run maybe of more value than the superficial types of fireworks religion.

Because of the fickle nature of personal religious experience, the Catholic Church has put great emphasis on the reliability of the sacraments. We believe that the sacraments are not only symbolic, but effective. In other words, they effect what they signify. So for us, baptism does not simply signify our immersion into the death and resurrection of Jesus, it really does make this happen. The Eucharist is not just a symbolic memorial of Christ's death. It is a real sharing in the body and blood of Christ. Through the sacraments there is a powerful, personal transaction whether we feel the emotion of it or not. I find this exciting, because it transcends the pressure for anyone to experience religion in a particular way. Jesus comes to us through baptism and in the Eucharist, whether we are charismatic and happy clappy or fond of smells, bells and fine liturgy. Jesus comes to us through the sacraments whether we are in a good mood or a bad mood, whether we are elated at the birth of a son, or bereaved at the death of a husband.

I sensed in your words above that while you are enthusiastic about the 'quest for the personal Christ experience' you sense that this may be a bit like the quest for the Holy Grail. That is to say, it is an important quest, but you remain a little bit sceptical about the possibility of finding the 'real Jesus.' I admit that I used to share this scepticism. I believed such a meeting with Christ was possible, and thought it had sometimes happened to me. But despite my evangelical teaching on eternal security, the actual experience remained elusive. This is where the Catholic teaching on the objective reliability of the sacraments becomes so important. Neither is this simply a theological theory. When I became a Catholic, I experienced a new reality in my faith. Through the sacraments I met Jesus in a way I never could have imagined. Suddenly there was a solidity, and concrete-ness which I find difficult to explain to non-Catholics. Before I was a Catholic my experiences of Jesus Christ were shadowy, subjective and often emotional. Now when I go to Mass, I meet with my Lord in a way which I can only describe as profoundly down to earth, historic, solid, and eternally dependable. It has given a whole new dimension to those poignant words of the psalmist, 'the Lord is my rock and salvation, of whom then shall I be afraid?'

---

1 Henry Bettenson, *The Early Christian Fathers*, (Oxford: Oxford University Press, 1969), p59

Chapter Six

The Real Presence

Dwight: In the last chapter you described the worship in the church where you grew up. The communion service you spoke about reminded me of how we used to celebrate the Lord's Supper in our independent Bible church. On the first Sunday of the month, after the main worship service was over, the pastor and about a dozen deacons would go to the front of the church. The table in front of the pulpit was covered with a crisp white tablecloth. Two piles of round interlocking trays were placed on the table. The trays contained broken pieces of unleavened bread which resembled the sort of biscuits you might eat with cheese. The other trays held tiny glasses filled with grape juice. The pastor and deacons sat with their backs to us; the pastor read various passages of Scripture to help us meditate on the death of Jesus. Then the deacons would distribute the bread and wine and we would all hold the bread and wine until everyone had received. Then after a pause for silence we would eat together at the same moment. The service was treated with solemnity and dignity. Furthermore, the formality of it along with the repeated words and actions turned the worship into a simple form of liturgy.

As I moved through the Anglican Church to become a Catholic, I have often remembered that simple biblical communion service. I was impressed with the fact that even in the most non-liturgical church communities, there seems to be an instinct to turn the Eucharist into a ritual. With set roles for each person to play, with a set form, and traditional words, and significant actions, the pastor and twelve deacons re-enacted the Last Supper. By participating we were there with them. This is the way liturgy works. The word 'liturgy' means 'work of the people' and I think it is a beautiful thing that even there, in an independent Bible church, God's people were working out their worship by 'doing liturgy'. By re-enacting the Last Supper, we were doing more then simply remembering it together. In a way, we were reliving it together. We were entering into the saving events of Jesus' last week on earth. As a result, what we experienced there was a simple and faithful memorial of the death and resurrection of Jesus.

While I can see all of this significance and meaning within that simple communion service, I can never remember anyone teaching us that this is what we were doing. If we were taught anything at all about the communion, it was that it was an optional extra. It took place after the main worship only once a month. Somewhere along the line I was also told what the communion service meant and did not mean, and the emphasis was always on what it did *not* mean. Our communion service was a 'commemoration of our Lord's death until he comes again'. Despite the solemnity of the service, we were clear that the bread was still bread, and the wine was still wine. Now that I'm a Catholic, I can recognise that this memorial service was good as far as it went; but the gospel actually goes further than that.

At the Last Supper Jesus says, 'This is my body. Do this in remembrance of me.' In the Bible church, we were strong on the phrase 'do this in remembrance of me'; but we overlooked the other phrase, 'This is my body.' Now as a Catholic I embrace *both* phrases. Catholics believe the Eucharist is a commemoration of our Lord's death until he comes again, but we also believe Jesus' words that the bread is his body and the wine is his blood.

This is an area where I would like to challenge you quite strongly, John. As Catholics we accept the clear meaning of the gospel. In Luke 22 we have the account of the Passover meal which Jesus shared with his apostles just before his death. Luke tells us that it was the feast of Unleavened Bread – one of the feasts during Passover week. Jesus gathers with his apostles to celebrate the Passover ceremony together. As he takes the unleavened bread he holds it up and says solemnly, 'This is my body which is given for you. Do this in remembrance of me.' Then he takes the cup and says, 'This is the blood of the new covenant which is poured out for you.' In John 6 Jesus teaches about the bread of heaven and then goes on to say that he is the bread of heaven. He says that this bread is his flesh which he gives for the life of the world. He then says that unless people eat his flesh and drink his blood they cannot have life within them. In 1 Corinthians, St Paul states the teachings of the early church. He says that the bread of communion is 'a sharing in the body of Christ'. That the bread and wine become the body and blood of Christ in the communion service is the unbroken teaching of the early church. It was not until the twelfth century that this belief was challenged, and it wasn't explicitly denied for another three or four hundred years. At the Reformation, however, this belief was overturned. Various theories were put forward by the different reformers as to the meaning and effect of the communion service, but they were united in their common rejection of the simple gospel truth that the bread and the wine are the body and blood of Christ.

I expect you'll want to challenge me about some aspects of the Catholic Church's teaching and practice when it comes to the Eucharist, or what we call the Mass. But as this book is called *Challenging Catholics*, allow this Catholic to challenge you. Jesus says the bread and the wine are his body and blood. That the bread and wine become the body and blood of Christ in the communion service, was the universal belief of Christians for the first 1500 years. So why do Protestant Christians insist on rejecting this simple gospel-based teaching?

John:

Transubstantiation (or the change of the substance of Bread and Wine) in the Supper of the Lord, cannot be proved by holy Writ;

but is repugnant to the plain words of Scripture, overthroweth the nature of the Sacrament, and hath given occasion to many superstitions. The Body of Christ is given, taken, and eaten, only after a heavenly and spiritual manner. And the mean whereby the Body of Christ is received and eaten in the Supper is Faith. (From Article 28, The Articles of Religion).[1]

You seem to be turning up the temperature, so I must respond with a blunt answer. What you have called 'simple gospel based teaching' is simply not so. Or, to answer in terms that are more Anglican, the Catholic teaching as you set it out, cannot be defended, on the grounds either of Scripture, tradition or reason.

You will remember from earlier on a story about the Catholic chaplain at my university. Your comments have brought him to mind. I recall another dialogue meeting where he, with characteristic Irish-Australian bluntness, made most of the points you have made. His words were something like: 'There's no mistaking it. The Scriptures are utterly plain. Christ said, `This is my body" and there's no more to be said.' Catholic apologists have been using this line ever since Luther's famous Reformation debate where a Catholic opponent just kept repeating the words, 'This is my body.' It reduced Luther to a quivering rage but, frankly, didn't do the Catholic Church any real service either.

Let's go back to the night of the Last Supper. Jesus is present here in human form – flesh and blood. So when he speaks about something on the table he cannot have been pointing to objects that were one and the same as his flesh and blood. He is using symbolic language. To say that this bread and wine are literally his body and blood represents a kind of literalism that I would expect from a fundamentalist academy, but not from a learned source. And when we look at the earliest account of the Lord's Supper (1 Cor. 11:28ff) it is not 'my blood' that Jesus signifies, but 'the new covenant in my blood'.

Then the other big play Catholic apologists make revolves around the meaning of the verb 'is'. What we need to bear in mind is that Jesus would have spoken in Aramaic where the mindset is quite different from the Aristotelian form of definition that underpins Catholic teaching in this matter. The Catholic Church reads 'this is' as if it carried the force of a classical definition. That is not the Hebraic mindset. I could give you a heap of references where Jesus uses metaphor revolving around use of verbs like 'is' or 'am' – 'the door', 'the true vine', 'good shepherd' and we do it without any sense that we need to press the metaphor to the limits.

I suggest, further, that the historical record doesn't point to 1,500 years of the uniform interpretation leaving the position you offer unmodified throughout. Yes, the early church fathers spoke of the bread and wine as Christ's body and blood, as was their right because our Lord did likewise. But they understood instinctively the place of metaphor and there is no crude literalism. Ignatius (circa 102) spoke of it as 'the heavenly bread, the bread of life'.[2] 'Christ is our Bread, because Christ is life and bread is life' wrote Tertullian.[3] Clement of Alexandria said 'The flesh figuratively represents to us the Holy Spirit; for the flesh was created by him. The blood indicates to us the Word, for as rich blood from the Word has been infused into life.'[4] St Augustine (fourth century) turned the whole idea on its head: 'If you want to know what is the Body of Christ, hear what the Apostle [Paul] tells believers: `You are Christ's body and his members' (1 Cor. 12:27). If, then, you are Christ's body and his members, it is your symbol that lies on the altar – what you receive is a symbol of yourself.'[5] One Augustinian scholar, F Ivan de Meer, has said that in hundreds of extant sermons on the meaning of the Lord's Supper, Augustine 'does not speak of a real presence'.[6] I have to conclude that it is only later with Thomas Aquinas' syntheses of Western Christian theology and the philosophical method of Aristotle that we come to something like what you are saying.

On this foundation a whole range of bizarre teaching and acts enter the scene: insistence that only priests may preside at the Lord's Supper, amid increasing pomp and ceremony; the idea that somehow a priest is given the power to consecrate, pronouncing 'magic words' that transforms wine and wafer; the idea of an eucharistic sacrifice where, (as I understand it) the Mass is a re-enactment; all sorts of unhealthy or plain crazy rituals surrounding the 'host'.

What is at stake is that the Catholic Church, at its official level at least, lacks an adequate understanding of what the body of Christ is. For if I read 1 Corinthians, in which the earliest account of the Lord's Supper is set, the overwhelming understanding of the 'body' of Christ is of a human community, where the eye and the hand understand their complementary functions and where if one part suffers, all suffer. So when I assist with the chalice at my church, as I am licensed to do, I view the body of Christ not in the communion elements but among the people who come forward to partake as one body.

Dwight: Okay, I admit I was lighting a fuse in my opening statement. You've responded well with some of the fireworks I thought might be the result. I just hope I haven't got you into a 'quivering rage' like a latter-day Luther!

Let me try to answer some of your points. First, I think we should agree with the Irish priest you debated with at college, that the gospel teaching is plain. Jesus does say, 'This is my body.' In John 6 he does say, 'Unless you eat of my flesh and drink of my blood you do not have life within you.' This is the gospel teaching, and it is simple. Where we disagree is over what that teaching means. You are right that the early church fathers speak of the bread and wine in symbolic terms, but you are also right when you admit that the early church fathers always refer to the bread and wine as the body and blood of Christ. I don't think Catholics have a problem with the idea that there is a symbolic dimension to the Eucharist. However, we insist that there is a real and corporeal presence of Christ as well. We are both/and. In other words, we admit both the symbol *and* the real presence of Christ's body and blood. Those who hold that it is *only* a symbol and deny the real presence of Christ's body and blood are denying one aspect of historic Christian belief in this area, and have to do verbal linguistics to get around the simplicity of Jesus' words. You quoted my friend Ignatius of Antioch. Well, he also had this to say about some early heretics called Docetists: 'They do not admit that the Eucharist is the flesh of our Saviour Jesus Christ which suffered for our sins.'[7] This is interesting to me because the Docetists said Jesus only *seemed* to be God. Likewise I guess they argued that the bread and wine only seem to be Christ's body and blood. The early church teachers insisted that the truth was more than that. Christ's presence was not just symbolic, but real and corporeal. They also insisted that what you believed about the Eucharist reflected your beliefs about the incarnation.

Let me address one or two of your finer points. You said that at the Last Supper, Jesus could not have meant that the bread and wine were his flesh and blood because his real, historical flesh and blood were standing there. But this is precisely the basis for our whole eucharistic belief. Through the miracle of the incarnation, God came to us in flesh and blood. Because he was flesh and blood, Jesus could institute that miracle in which ordinary bread and wine become his flesh and blood. This link between the incarnation, and the eucharistic miracle is reflected in the language we use about the Eucharist. To explain what I mean, let me try to explain this complicated term, 'transubstantiation'.

Transubstantiation literally means 'substance across'. This word 'substance' is confusing because the medieval philosophical definition is almost the exact opposite of our modern ordinary definition. When we say something is 'substantial' we mean it is solid, physical and real. But when the theologians of the thirteenth century spoke of 'substance' they did not mean the physical nature, but the invisible underlying reality of a thing. Your 'substance' is that 'John-ness' in you which remained the same when you were a toothless newborn, and will be the same when you are a toothless old man on your deathbed. Although Aquinas used this terminology he didn't invent it. This term 'substance' had a long philosophical and theological history before the thirteenth century, dating right back to the New Testament and beyond. The Greek form of the Latin Word *substantia* is *hypostasis*. The word is actually used in Hebrews 1:3 when discussing Jesus' relationship to God; and as you know, this word *hypostasis* was used to discuss and define the nature of Christ's union with God. The early church said that Christ was of the same 'substance' with God. Therefore our use of the term 'substance' to discuss the Eucharist links in with our understanding of the incarnation itself.

We use the word 'transubstantiation' to try to explain philosophically what happens at the Eucharist. Catholics do not believe that the bread and wine become human flesh and blood in a chemical way. Instead, we believe that the 'substance' of the bread and wine is miraculously transformed into the body and blood of Christ. In other words, the 'bread-ness' of the bread and the 'wine-ness' of the wine become Christ's body and blood. I should add that all Catholic theologians stress that transubstantiation is not a complete explanation of the mystery. The mystery of Christ's constant and real presence with us can never be explained. Transubstantiation is simply a philosophical attempt to explain what we believe happens. As an explanation it is good as far as it goes, but there is much more to it than that. After the explanations are finished and the clever philosophers have shut up we are called to simply become one with Christ by eating his body and drinking his blood (Jn. 6:56).

Let me address another question of yours. You said Jesus was simply speaking metaphorically when he said, 'This is my body.' It is true, of course, that Jesus used metaphors to make his point. He said, 'I am the way' and 'I am the Good Shepherd.' He said, 'I am the door' and he said, 'I am the bread of life.' However, his later references to bread, wine, flesh and blood are of a very different order. With this one metaphor about bread, Jesus went much further than with any other figure of speech. He not only said, 'I am the bread of life', but later he took real bread and broke it and said, 'This is my body which is broken for you. Eat it.' You can't get much more literal than that. He never did that with a door, or a shepherd, or a road.

In John 6, Jesus realises that his words are upsetting. The Jews begin to argue with him (Jn. 6:52). But Jesus doesn't say,

'You misunderstood, I was only speaking symbolically.'
Instead, he makes his point even more strongly. He uses his
solemn method of speaking and says,

> I tell you the truth, unless you can eat the flesh of the Son of
> Man and drink his blood you have no life in you. Whoever eats
> my flesh and drinks my blood has eternal life and I will raise
> him up at the last day. For my flesh is real food and my blood
> is real drink. Whoever eats my flesh and drinks my blood
> remains in me and I in him. (Jn. 6:53-56)

At this point, many of his disciples left him in confusion and
disgust (Jn. 6:60, 66) but he doesn't call them back and say,
'Wait a minute fellas, it was only a figure of speech!' He simply says to his remaining apostles, 'Will you leave me too?'
When taken altogether, Jesus' words about bread, wine, flesh
and blood are much stronger than any other metaphor.

I'll let you carry on in just a minute about magic words,
priests and sacrifices because we need to discuss these issues.
But let me finish with a brief word answering your criticism
that Catholics do not appreciate the real meaning of 'the body
of Christ'. I recommend an excellent document prepared a
couple of years ago by the Catholic bishops of England and
Wales. It is called, *One Bread One Body*, and it discusses the
unity we see between the church and the Eucharist. The whole
document is an extended meditation on the text you quoted in
which St Paul refers to both the church, and the eucharistic
bread, as the body of Christ. We believe this is no mistake, and
that the true unity of the church is expressed in the full communion of the church as we participate together in the
Eucharist. There, we believe, is a mystical unity between the
individual, the church and Christ because there he draws us
together to his own body and blood under the forms of bread
and wine.

John: I'm appreciative of your account of transubstantiation
and real presence. Again I would encourage our more
Protestant readers to study what you have said very carefully. I

say that because it's too easy for people unfamiliar with it to dismiss Catholic thought as superficial. That's neither fair nor true.

What you offer is interesting and internally logical, but I keep saying 'Whoa there! You are investing a simple though profound metaphor with a world of meaning that for the life of me I cannot trace back to Jesus. My contention is that it emerged when the doctors of the church embarked on the project of synthesising the Christian faith with classical thought, in particular that of the Greek philosopher Aristotle. The enterprise was important. It presented Christianity as a hard-minded alternative to the 'old religion' of the late Roman empire. It brought the church into the thought world of educated people. It gave it a language with which to discuss and debate with that world.

Dwight: I wouldn't dispute the philosophical background of Christian theology. But Bible-believing Christians shouldn't have a problem with this method of formulating their beliefs, should they? After all, this same integration of Christianity with Greek thought was going on in the New Testament. St Paul was happy debating on the terms of the Greek philosophers in Athens (Acts 17) and was confident using Greek philosophical terms in his formulation of Christian truth. Likewise, St John was happy to use the Greek philosophical concept of *logos* to explain the incarnation. So there is nothing wrong with using Greek philosophical concepts *per se*.

John: Okay, let's discuss a philosophical detail which troubles me. Catholic apologists tell us that at the Eucharist, in the act of consecration of the bread and wine, the *substance* of the elements change while their *appearance* remains unchanged. You could suggest, for example, that it's possible for H_2O to appear in two forms or 'accidents', ice and water. That sounds quite plausible until you push right back to what I believe to be theological basics. Here the classical tradition hinges on a fundamental dualism: that there is an ultimate distinction between spirit and matter. The Hebraic worldview, in contrast, asserts the basic unity of all things in God. In my view, all kinds of mistakes grow up when you make a false distinction between spirit and matter or the soul and the body. I hasten to add, for example, that Evangelicals and Protestants have just as readily got this wrong by putting a premium on saving souls over against asserting the need to care for the whole person. Likewise it has sometimes left Christianity open to the charge that didn't give due care to the environment, a point I don't necessarily buy.

I'm reluctant to engage point by point with the arguments you offer about what and what does not happen to the eucharistic bread and wine. What I'm contending is that your arguments are based on a framework of thought that was not there, either in the upper room or even in the minds of those who wrote down what we now have as the biblical accounts of what happened. You accuse me of failure to affirm something that's simple and straightforward. I'd want to come back and insist that it's the Catholics who've taken what is a very simple gospel act and invested it with a body of meaning that it was never supposed to have. On the surface the formulation you offer sounds simple. A lot of people will be content with that, but press the questions a bit and the answers become very complicated and outside the thought world of the Galileans who first uttered and heard them and passed them on. I'm content to say that when Jesus said 'This is my body' he was using metaphorical language that is full of meaning but in the end incomprehensible. I'll fall into error if I'm over-reductionist: it won't do to say it's nothing more than a metaphor. Likewise I'll fall into error, or at least get things out of balance, if I over-invest and try to extract every last bit of meaning.

Dwight: Fair enough. But this clash you see between the spiritual order and the natural order is not so extreme as you might think. Catholic thinkers from the earliest days of the church have confronted this same question. Thus St Ambrose says about this conversion of bread and wine,

> Be convinced that this is not what nature has formed, but what the blessing has consecrated. The power of the blessing prevails

over that of nature, because by the blessing nature itself is changed... Could not Christ's word, which can make from nothing what did not exist, change existing things into what they were not before? It is no less a feat to give things their original nature than to change their nature.

But I agree with you that the philosophical definitions go further than the mindset of first century Galilean fishermen. There might be a problem with that if we were proposing transubstantiation as the one, only, full and final explanation of the eucharistic mystery. We don't. While we think transubstantiation is a valuable way of explaining what happens, we conclude that transubstantiation is still only a philosophical explanation for what we believe happens, and that the communion itself remains a profound, simple and inexplicable mystery. As a result we also use poetic explanations, theological explanations and personal experience to further illuminate the mystery.

John: I need to come back to some of the other points you make. Yes, Jesus does put a great premium on the Eucharist. I'm not quite sure just how much weight to put on the saying you quote from John 6. For instance, I wouldn't want to build a doctrine from it that said 'no communion, no salvation'. And what I've said about the body would shift my emphasis slightly, to value being part of the community of the church as a Christian essential without insisting that without it I would be excluded from heaven.

I do think that people of a more Protestant temperament need to take the Eucharist more seriously. Those who operate solely in an *anamnesis* (memorial) frame often don't appreciate how the Eucharist imparts comfort and strength in some indefinable way. Then I hasten to point to the profound truth about how I am personally involved with the death of Christ. One of my favourite verses, and a favourite of a huge number of Evangelicals, is Galatians 2:20, where Paul says, 'I have been crucified with Christ; it is no longer I who live, but Christ lives in me; and the life I now live in the flesh I live by faith in the

Son of God, who loved me and gave himself for me.' Think of it: Christ 'loved *me* and gave himself for *me*.' That's something that invites an eternity of wonder and doxology. In a very special way it is the continued celebration of the Eucharist that tries to sum this up in a tangible way for the here and now.

Getting the Eucharist absolutely right in the life of the church, however, is a challenge. For example, I don't think it should be the centrepiece of the main service of worship every week. In my experience that truncates the role of preaching and teaching. Moreover, it fosters an inward focus among congregations who should be active in mission. Why this is so I'm less sure. It's clear from sources like Justin Martyr that the Eucharist was the centrepiece of worship in the early church and this in no way inhibited evangelistic mission as the expansion of the church indicates.

But let me try to move the conversation on. I would want to contend that the way the Catholic Church defined and practised its eucharistic theology invites serious practical problems. By the time of the Reformation the Eucharist was surrounded with a plethora of superstitions and downright abuses. They still lurk. Then alongside it stalks an unhelpful edifice that noisy Protestantism labels 'priest craft'. I will want to address these issues more, among them a question that has vexed Anglicans since the Reformation – the idea of the Eucharist as sacrifice. Meanwhile you may want to take a cue from me and say more on a personal level on what the death of Christ means to you, and how the Eucharist witnesses to it in your life and strengthens you for day to day living.

Dwight: I hear what you're saying about superstition and 'priest-craft'. Let me repeat that we believe the miracle of the sacrament is performed by Christ – not the priest. Again, this is affirmed from the earliest days in the church. So St. John Chrysostom writes: 'It is not man that causes the things offered to become the Body and Blood of Christ, but he who was crucified for us, Christ himself. The priest, in the role of Christ, pronounces these words, but their power and grace are God's' (CCC, 1375).

I want to affirm with you the necessity of preaching the gospel, and I admit that Catholics have sometimes been weak on preaching and teaching, but I don't think there's any necessary clash between a frequent celebration of the Eucharist and faithful preaching and teaching. The New Testament says that the celebration is, in fact, a form of preaching the word. St Paul says, 'For as often as you eat this bread and drink the cup, you proclaim the Lord's death until he comes' (1 Cor. 11:26).

Much of this actually links in with our understanding of that important word *anamnesis*. It sounds like you consider this 'memorial' idea inadequate, and sometimes Evangelicals think Catholics don't see the Mass as a memorial at all. We do. It's just that our idea of what a memorial or *anamnesis* is, is very different than simply a visual aid or a memory prompt. Our understanding of *anamnesis* or 'ritual remembering' goes back to the Hebrew understanding of the Passover feast. Every year when the Jews celebrated the Passover, they re-enacted the Passover in a ritual manner and through this believed they were sort of transported in time. It was like that first Passover was being brought into the present moment and they were participants in that powerful act of God's salvation. Through the annual Passover celebration the moment of salvation continued to live within the experience of the Jewish people, and through the ritual remembering they could become a part of it.

When Jesus instituted the Eucharist at Passover time he was instituting the Christian replacement for the Passover feast. The early church believed this and therefore they understood what happened at the Eucharist as the same kind of transaction. *Anamnesis* or the 'ritual remembering' was a way to bring the saving event of the cross into the present moment. This is part of what Paul means when he says the Eucharist is a way to proclaim the Lord's death. Through the Eucharist we 'preach Christ crucified'. In the Eucharist the Lord's timeless act of salvation on the cross is brought into the present moment and applied to us and our needs.

This concept also explains what we mean by the phrase the 'sacrifice of the Mass'. Many Bible Christians have been taught that Catholics sacrifice Christ afresh every time they say Mass.

They quote the verses from Hebrews which say clearly that daily sacrifices are no longer required. But this is a misunderstanding of the Catholic belief. The Council of Trent and the Catechism of the Catholic Church are quite clear that we do not sacrifice Christ afresh at every Mass. Instead, through the action of the Eucharist, the once for all sacrifice of Christ is brought into the present moment and applied to our needs. The Catechism (quoting Trent) puts it this way:

> The Eucharist is thus a sacrifice because it re-presents (makes present) the sacrifice of the cross, because it is its memorial, and because it applies its fruit:
>
> [Christ], our Lord and God, was once and for all to offer himself to God the Father by his death on the altar of the cross, to accomplish there an everlasting redemption. But because his priesthood was not to end with his death, at the Last Supper 'on the night when he was betrayed,' [he wanted] to leave to his beloved spouse the Church a visible sacrifice (as the nature of man demands) by which the bloody sacrifice which he was to accomplish once for all on the cross would be re-presented, its memory perpetuated until the end of the world, and its salutary power be applied to the forgiveness of the sins we daily commit.
>
> The sacrifice of Christ and the sacrifice of the Eucharist are one single sacrifice : 'The victim is one and the same: the same now offers through the ministry of priests, who then offered himself on the cross; only the manner of offering is different.' (CCC, 1366-67)

Like the Passover, the sacrifice of Christ is in time and it is also eternal. We believe Christ gave us this regular ritual remembering to bring his eternal sacrifice into our present moment. Because of this dynamic understanding, I can begin to explain the wonderful effect going to Mass has for me. When I go to Mass I am taken to the foot of the cross. At every Mass I am brought into that timeless moment, and through the mystery of Christ's presence I am brought physically, mentally and spiritually into a participation in the death of Christ. The wonderful passage you quoted from Galatians 2 about 'I have been crucified with Christ...' therefore comes true most powerfully for me when I share in the death of Christ at Mass.

John: Let me sum up. This chapter has been a very difficult one as far as I'm concerned. The big reason is that here the traditional disagreement between Catholics and the rest are at their sharpest. In a discussion like this, we are most likely to lose sight of what it's really about because we focus on our differences instead of what the Eucharist proclaims and celebrates.

I'm helped by your comment that while transubstantiation is a valuable way of explaining what's at the centre of the Eucharist, it's 'still only a philosophical explanation for what we believe happens and that the communion itself remains a profound and inexplicable mystery.' How I wish the tone of the Council of Trent, at the time of the Reformation had been as humble and honest. It might have saved a lot of anguish and bloodshed. But I write this on the anniversary of the birth of Galileo. That reminds me that while humility was always one of Jesus' most lovely attributes, it hasn't always rubbed off on his followers, especially the institutional church, and I don't want to single out the Catholic Church as the only one deserving blame for that.

Let me turn the conversation towards the future. If you come to my church it would be theoretically possible for you to take communion, although for conscientious reasons I suspect you might not. If, on the other hand, I come to your church, it's definitely unlawful for me to take communion. It's the sharing and receiving of eucharistic hospitality that is the strongest indicator of where we are up to in the ecumenical journey and that tells us that there's some way to go yet. Now official talks like the RC-Lutheran and Anglican-RC theological conversations have made great strides in clearing away misunderstandings. So have dialogues fostered by the World Council of Churches and published in the document *Baptism, Eucharist and Ministry*.

That such a measure of agreement exists, at least in theory, leaves me wondering why eucharistic hospitality is so long in coming. Having said that, I strongly disagree with those who would seek to shortcut the ecumenical progress by taking matters into their own hands. I prefer to live with the pain of division that these church rules cause until such time as they're formally abolished.

---

1 Article 28, The 39 Articles of Religion, *The Book of Common Prayer* 1662

2 Ignatius, *Letter to the Romans*, Chapter 7, section 50, in *The Ante Nicene Fathers*, Volume One

3 Tertullian, *On Prayer*, Chapter 6, section 39, in *The Ante Nicene Fathers*, Volume Three

4 Clement of Alexandria, *The Instructor*, Chapter 6, section 89, in *The Ante Nicene Fathers*, Volume Two

5 St Augustine, Sermon 272

6 F. de Meer, *Augustine the Bishop*, trans by B Battershaw and G.R. Lamb, (London: Sheed & Ward, 1961), p284

7 Henry Bettenson, *The Early Christian Fathers* (Oxford: Oxford University Press, 1969) p49

Chapter Seven

Brother Are You Saved?

John: 'The God who made you without you, without you does not make you just' – St Augustine.[1]

Scene: the Palace Theatre, Parkes, western New South Wales in rural Australia. The year: 1959. Over a thousand people had crowded to hear evangelist Billy Graham via landline relay from the Sydney showground. As the address drew to a close, Billy issued his customary 'invitation'. 'I'm going to ask you to get up out of your seat and come out to the front .... '
The landline meetings had been going on for over a week without a single response, but on this hot April Sunday afternoon a well-dressed man in his early thirties quickly got up and walked determinedly to the front. He'd made his actual 'decision' a couple of nights earlier. Going forward was the public acknowledgement. It was a culmination of an inner process stretching over some months. From that day Toby Priestley became a firm friend of my family, particularly my father, who for many years mentored him in faith.

Toby was brought up a Catholic. There were few signs that the Catholic schools he'd attended managed to cram much religion or learning into his head, though he nursed vivid memories of lavish use of the strap by teaching staff, most of them members of religious orders. He left school without qualifications and 'put up' his age to join the army in the latter stages of World War Two. A few weeks after he married

Heather, an Anglican, the local Catholic priest came round and told the couple they weren't married because they hadn't had a Catholic nuptial mass. Toby, in something of a state of inebriation, was so riled that his first reflex was to use his fists to teach the priest a lesson – he was a more than useful boxer – but an inner voice warned him to keep his fists to himself. As years went by, he slipped deeper and deeper into alcoholism and a pattern of domestic violence emerged that once left Heather with a broken nose.

I tell this story because Toby was the first person I knew to have a classic evangelical conversion. I believe, further, that it brought nothing less than salvation, both for Toby and the Priestley household. As far as I'm aware, he never touched another drop of alcohol. He became an enormous encouragement to the little Christian community that enfolded him and his family with care and friendship. When we first knew him he was practically illiterate. Reading the Bible became a gateway to education and a better life.

I tell the story, too, because it illustrates some of the difficulties I see with the way both Catholics and Evangelicals understand salvation at a popular level. For the Catholic Church that the young Toby Priestley knew, it seemed sufficient that he was baptised and attended Mass regularly. There seemed to be no emphasis on making worship accessible and no notion whatever of fellowship or on-going nurture. For the church he joined it was important that services were lively and 'helpful' and accompanied by good 'fellowship'. Understanding the faith was deemed very important and one of the main arguments proffered against infant baptism – and even speaking in tongues – was that there was no 'understanding' on the part of the main participant.

Since that time, I have known many other persons who have similarly come forward to receive Christ. Among the first were people who did so directly under Toby's influence, although few had a testimony as dramatic as his. But what surprised me as a youngster was the very high proportion who didn't last the distance in their journey of faith and lapsed back into their old lifestyle. It's been an issue for reflection over many years.

Let me try to identify the theological issues at play in this story. I believe they are much the same as the main issues from Reformation times, and that these issues still produce a great divide between Catholics and Evangelicals. One concerns the meaning of personal faith. In what sense can an individual be confident of his or her final salvation? Is there any merit in the evangelical slogan 'once saved, always saved'? Many of the players in the story I've told would have said that the act of 'going forward' was an outward act that signalled the receiving of salvation.

This brings us to consider the huge theme of justification, how it is to be understood, and how it relates to other major doctrines such as righteousness and justice. Here was one of the flashpoints that triggered the fracture of the Western church in the sixteenth century. With it went a huge debate over the value of 'good works' and different emphases on works in God's plan of salvation. For Martin Luther and the Reformers we were saved by 'faith alone'. While there was no direct Anglican involvement in those particular debates, *sola fide* became part of its inheritance as a church of the Reformation. Then we have the place of the church in salvation – with Catholics suspicious that other traditions relegated its ministry and sacraments to a back seat.

I suspect that one of the ways by which people who knew him maintained certainty on the question of Toby's salvation was that it was accompanied by a much changed life, and that he was such an inspiring witness to his faith. What I found increasingly less convincing was how Toby and the Evangelicals surrounding him accounted for the failure of many of the other new converts to continue in their new-found faith, and here I think neither Catholics nor Evangelicals get it right in their traditional formulations. I've come to see that there is more to leaving or cleaving than remaining confident in belief (the main evangelical concern) or regular sacramental discipline (the main Catholic one). I believe people 'cleave' to faith because a particular experience of relating to a community of believers meets the combination of their spiritual, social and emotional needs. Toby persevered because he had people like my Dad and others who gave him an enormous amount of their time and encouragement. I suspect there was less time available for mentoring the people to whom he witnessed and brought to a 'decision'. More important, however, is that along with many other people brought up as Evangelicals, I've also come to see that for most people coming to faith is a process rather than a crucial moment. Stories like Paul's Damascus Road experience or John Wesley's account of his heart being 'strangely warmed' are wonderful and few evangelists can resist using them. But to speak of salvation only in terms of conversion stories has been an error on the part of a lot of Evangelicals.

I've tried to get at the subject through a story. You may have stories you could share. But for the benefit of readers whose understanding of the Catholic Church's view of salvation may be 'frozen' around Reformation events, you may want to address the questions I raise: justification (to which I think I need to return), assurance, the balance between faith and works, and the part that the sacraments and belonging to the Church plays for the Catholic Christian.

Dwight: I don't doubt Toby's real conversion experience. I remember how my father led a young soldier named Greg to Christ. Like your Dad, he befriended Greg and nurtured his faith, and Greg is a vibrant Christian even now. My own first step in the Christian faith was a similar 'born again' experience. At the age of five I came home from our Bible church one Sunday evening and told my mother I wanted to accept Jesus into my heart. We knelt by the bedside and I told Jesus I was sorry for my sins and wanted to accept him as my personal saviour.

This is a cherished memory, but as you've hinted, there are a few holes in the evangelical theory of 'getting saved'. While we all rejoice at Toby and Greg's very real conversion I am troubled, as you are, about all those evangelical converts who simply fall away after a time. Were they really saved or not?

Once we start to press matters it becomes even more complicated. What do we do with all those cradle Evangelicals who
profess to be Christians, but who can never point to a born
again experience? They say they can never remember a time
when they weren't followers of Christ and profess allegiance
to him every day of their life. They haven't had a born again
experience so are they saved? What about those who have
been born again but have fallen into terrible sin? Do they need
to be saved again? Can they be saved again? The highly individualistic born again experience is a fairly recent phenomenon in church history. What do we do about all those non-
evangelical Christians both now and down through the ages
who have never heard of a born again experience, but who
were devoted disciples of Jesus? Were they saved or lost?

Many evangelistic messages are based on a very subjective,
highly emotional appeal. With moving music, powerful, rousing preaching and a fever pitch of mass emotion the individual is motivated to receive Jesus. This may be all well and
good, but what about all the people for whom this approach
simply doesn't work? Many people are moved by big meetings, emotional music and powerful preaching, but many others are not. Can they be saved, or must they grit their teeth and
go through a highly public, emotional experience to be saved?
Even more profoundly, can a highly emotional response be
trusted? Do we make our best decisions in life in the heat of
emotion? Passion and high emotions are wonderful, but they
are also fickle. If people make a decision for Christ based on
emotion, is it any wonder they soon dwindle and die? The
passionate commitment is great, but shouldn't it have a more
solid foundation?

Common sense tells us that validating salvation by one particular type of religious experience just doesn't work. There
are too many questions still to be answered. But common
sense also tells us that we want to know who is Christian and
who is not. Therefore the Catholic Church uses very objective
criteria to establish a kind of bottom line. The bottom line is
this: if a person is baptised, they are members of the body of
Christ. St Paul says this in Galatians 3:27: 'As many of you as

have been baptised into Christ have put on Christ.' So our bottom line is baptism. Baptism needs to be accompanied by personal faith. Confirmation is the sacrament where the Christian confirms or makes sure his baptism. At confirmation he studies the faith and decides for himself.

Every effort is made within the Catholic system for the baptised child to come to a full understanding of the faith and to make an educated and inspired personal decision to repent and follow Christ. It's true that many people like Toby still fall through the net, but if you're honest, wouldn't you agree that many people brought up in evangelical churches also fall through the net? It isn't because either the Catholic Church or the evangelical churches haven't educated their children and brought them up to love and fear the Lord. It's simply that for many complicated reasons the children simply don't 'get it' or else they choose to go their own way.

The main point I'm trying to establish is that the Catholic Church doesn't use subjective, emotional criteria for saying who is Christian and who is not. We use very objective, unemotional criteria. We believe the sacraments work. If a person is baptised he is received into the body of Christ. That's that. This sounds like we take an automatic or magical approach and that we have no time for personal experiences of Jesus in our lives. This isn't true either. Over and over again, in a multitude of ways the Catholic Church encourages us to make our baptism real. The church expects us to go through a period of instruction to be confirmed. We are called to reaffirm our baptismal vows annually. We are called to regular confession where we repent of our sins and ask for Jesus' forgiveness in a very personal and intimate way. We are encouraged to pray daily. We are called to weekly communion with Him in the Eucharist. So while we base our salvation experience on something very objective and hard and real, we are constantly called to participate in the gift we have been given and to meet our Lord face to face. The objective gift is received in the sacraments, but our subjective meeting with the Lord also comes to us through the sacraments. The church administers the sacraments, and we cannot have them without the church.

Therefore a Catholic's whole salvation experience is tied up with being a member of the church. This makes unified sense to us because to be a Christian is to be in Christ and Christ's body is his church.

One of the other flash points between Catholics and Evangelicals is this question of justification by faith alone versus justification by works. Instead of addressing this one directly, let me shove it back to you. As an evangelical Anglican do you believe in *sola fide* or salvation by faith alone? Do you think Catholics believe in salvation by works?

John: Thanks for sharing your personal story about receiving Christ. For those of us who've had such an experience and who've persevered in faith, such stories tend to be indelible in the memory bank. It's one of the witnesses in your life to the love and grace of God. At the same time, the combination of experience, years and theological learning tends to leave us somewhat critical of what happened. I often say that even as a tiny boy I had a sense of the spiritual and of knowing God. Even so it didn't stop a lot of earnest Evangelicals in our network pressing me to 'make a decision for Christ'. I still get irritated when my memory throws up instances of being subjected to all kinds of preachers' tricks designed to encourage me in that direction. They knew how to spot vulnerable bits in the psyche, like the guilt youngsters brought up evangelical feel when as adolescents they find themselves in conflict with their parents. Would that they had put their energies into preaching to people outside the church, instead of making what were essentially Christian kids feel guilty.

Many Evangelicals I knew in my early days would contend that having made a 'decision', they are saved. You have identified some of the problems with that and the story I told shows I sympathise with much of what you say. You say that for the Catholic Church baptism is the tangible sign of salvation, with confirmation playing a part alongside. I've become more sympathetic to that position than I once would have been. It's very neat and tidy. In practice, however, it still doesn't offer cast-iron guarantees. For many, confirmation often marks a point where young people cease attending church.

Dwight: That's right. Confirmation is the service where they confirm the fact that they don't have to go to church anymore.

John: You cynic! But about baptism and confirmation – I'm certain, and I'm equally certain that you'll disagree with this statement – that the practices with which both Evangelicals and Catholics surround initiation into the church are not the same as salvation itself.

As I began to study the Bible to try to get beyond what the evangelists said about salvation, I began to come to a tentative conclusion that here again, the Western way of thinking, formed as it is with reference to Aristotelian logic, leaves both Evangelicals and Catholics with a problem. There's a shared mindset that doesn't serve them well in the matter. Aristotelian thinking encourages us to think in hard and fast terms. You are either 'in' or you are 'out', you either have been baptised or not, you have 'gone forward' or not. In the face of these, my being wants to shout 'But do any of these constitute knowing, loving and serving the invisible God?'

A biblical word study of 'salvation' and its associated words offers some challenging data for both sides of the traditional divide. In New Testament Greek the word salvation is translated from *sozo*, 'to make whole'. It appears in various forms: *sozomai* ('I am being saved'), *sesosmae* ('I have been saved or am in the position of being saved') and *esosemae* ('at some stage I was saved and this process is single and complete').

I believe we need new categories for our thinking and we can achieve this by recovering the Hebraic dimensions of the biblical theme of salvation. In the Old Testament, for example, various acts of God in the here and now are deemed to be his 'salvation'. The best example is events surrounding the Exodus. As the people contemplate death at the hands of Pharaoh's army, Moses tells them to 'Stand still and see the salvation of the Lord.' I submit that, in the gospels, salvation is also an event, the coming of Jesus. Simeon in the Benedictus gives thanks for the baby Jesus, declaring that 'my eyes have seen your salvation.'

The Anglican scholar N.T. Wright has argued persuasively that Jesus understood himself to be unveiling the new Exodus. It is no accident that the core of the early apostolic preaching was summed up as 'Jesus is Lord' and this became the first Christian creed. I would want to submit that to be saved, to embrace God's salvation, is a matter of affirming and living by this creed. By making that affirmation I put myself under the rule of God and enter his new community (the new Exodus, if you like). Living by that creed will manifest itself in personal holiness, regular worship, and Christ-like love of neighbour, in the full sense of what this means. Accompanying this is an inner process whereby through God's grace I am kept and preserved to eternal life.

Interestingly enough, the scholars tell me that it's not just the Protestant/Catholic debate that has suffered from being set up in terms of unhelpful Aristotelian categories. The same applies in relations between Christianity and Islam. Islamic scholarship was deeply influenced by Aristotle. Indeed he was largely lost to the West but reintroduced via contacts with Islamic philosophers. It was the Anglican mission historian Bishop Stephen Neill who once said, 'The Christian has no other message for the Muslim than Jesus Christ himself.'[2]

So then, I'm arguing that the debate between Catholics and Protestants over salvation, the meaning of justification and its relation to sanctification, needs to burst the old wineskins. I am suggesting that it needs to centre around a better understanding of Jesus, his life, teachings, and death. Back to your question. Do I subscribe to *sola fide* (salvation by faith alone)? I've been trying to take you to where my thinking and study is leading. *Sola fide* is as much as anything a slogan, a rallying point. It's attracted much more heat than light on the subject. The same can be said of other Reformation slogans such as the priesthood of all believers. On the latter, the Bible doesn't actually use the phrase, the closest it gets to it being 'a kingdom of priests'. I suggest that *sola fide* falls well short of a nuanced understanding of how the Bible deals with salvation.

Now, then, do I think Catholics believe in salvation by works? The short answer is that in history it has sometimes erred in that direction. Moreover, I would say that I discern this tendency in some popular contemporary devotional practices. But I'm satisfied from reading the fruits of ecumenical discussions, not least the mountain of books that have flowed from the official Catholic-Lutheran dialogue, that your best Catholic theologians are well aware of the points that the Reformation rightly queried about Catholic beliefs and practice. The only trouble was that the bulldozing tone of, for example, the Council of Trent or the wording of the excommunication of Queen Elizabeth I, painted your church into a corner. So it finds itself wishing to embrace other Christians, but with one hand firmly tied behind its back.

Dwight: I like what you've said about salvation, I'm glad you've scooted around the landmine of *sola fide* and I agree with you that it is an unfortunate and crude slogan. Does even the most fervent Protestant really believe good works are totally irrelevant? If they do they contradict the New Testament which says 'Faith without works is dead' (Jas. 2:17).

You assumed I would disagree with what you've said. In fact, the position you've expressed is very Catholic. I have to remind Evangelicals that we don't actually believe in the Calvinist doctrine of eternal security – that teaching that says 'Once saved always saved, and you can know for sure that you are going to heaven.' Like you, we don't think there can be cast iron guarantees. We trust utterly in the saving work of Christ, but we believe no one can know for sure if they are saved eternally because God alone is our judge. As a result, our understanding of salvation is very close to what you've expressed. We repent of our sins, we accept Christ as our Saviour, we accept the grace God gives through the sacraments of the church. Based on this grace we express a sure and confident hope of finally going to heaven, but we never proclaim that once and done certainty which a certain type of Evangelical proposes.

You've expressed salvation as a process of living in Jesus as Lord. This is a very Catholic view. Like you, we see salvation as a life-long, faith-full process. We are baptised as infants, then day by day, week by week, year by year we need to grow in grace. We need to live the life of faith. We need to receive the sacraments which confirm and consolidate the life of Christ within us. Furthermore, we believe it is possible for a person, once he has accepted Jesus Christ, to turn away from him and reject the salvation he once embraced. Hebrews 12:15-17 talks about Esau, who turned away and was unable to repent. I think we agree with this passage from Hebrews that faith also needs endurance:

> Therefore do not throw away your confidence, which has a great reward. For you have need of endurance, so that you may do the will of God and receive what is promised. For yet a little while, and the coming one shall come and shall not tarry; but my righteous one shall live by faith, and if he shrinks back, my soul has no pleasure in him. But we are not of those who shrink back and are destroyed, but of those who have faith and keep their souls (Heb. 10:36-39).

You mentioned the Council of Trent in a somewhat disparaging way; I heard a sub-text that the Council of Trent was this great anti-Protestant event. But have you read the documents of the Council of Trent? I was surprised when I read them how mild they were. To be sure, there are formal anathemas pronounced against heretics, but this has been the apostolic role of the church from New Testament times. Peter, Paul and John were all very outspoken in their condemnation of false teachers. But what interested me most in reading the anathemas of Trent was that I heard Protestants complaining only about Justification Canon 19 which condemns anyone who holds to salvation by faith alone. What they didn't say is that the first Canon on Justification condemns anyone who teaches that salvation is by works. The Catholic Church condemned the idea of salvation by works when it first appeared as the Pelagian heresy in the fifth century. It may be true that certain Catholic devotions and customs look like people are working hard to earn their salvation, but that criticism can be levelled at any Christian group who are involved in good works, can't it? A study of history shows that the Catholic Church has never taught salvation by works, and always soundly condemned such teaching.

If you haven't done so, I recommend you to hop on the internet, do a search for the Council of Trent and then read the Council's teaching on justification. I guarantee you will agree with most of it. What I find most exciting in recent years is the Catholic-Lutheran dialogue. After many years of patient discussion, our church signed a document with the leaders of the Lutheran Church in which we have basically agreed that 'justification is by grace alone through faith'.[3] The implications of this agreement are profound. The agreement on this should ripple down through the whole Catholic Church, and from the Lutheran Church to all Evangelicals. The message is: 'We've solved this one. We all agree that salvation is by grace through faith, and that faith must be lived out through the Christian life.' This is an exciting step forward and I reject your comment that we have gone into the whole thing with 'one hand tied behind our back.' I admit that we go into ecumenical discussions with a grave sense of reality and an awareness that big problems need to be solved. Don't you agree that's better than an overdose of sentimentality and false optimism?

I'm glad we agree substantially on the need for both faith and a life of faith. But to be clear about Catholic teaching, I should point out a subtle point of difference between an evangelical understanding of good works and the Catholic view. As an Evangelical I was taught that because of original sin I was totally depraved. I was utterly unable to do any good work. When God justified me, he saw Jesus – not me. It was as if he covered my sin with Jesus' saving blood. I think Martin Luther used the analogy of 'a dungheap covered with snow.' This is not the Catholic view. We believe in original sin, but not in total depravity. Following St Augustine, we believe original sin wounds God's image in us. In other words, we need to be healed. Christ's work on the cross restores us and enables us to co-operate with God's grace in our lives. Catholics believe that justification is not just something put over us like a cover. Instead we believe justification is at work within us, changing us and transforming us into the image of Christ.

As an Evangelical, I got the impression that even after I was saved I couldn't do anything good. Now, as a Catholic, I am told that it is my responsibility to co-operate with God's grace by doing good, and that my salvation depends on it. I know this sounds very close to salvation by works, and I can see how some people misunderstand. But I should make it clear that we always say that any good works we do are impossible without God's grace empowering us. Again, it is by grace that we have faith, and it is by grace that we are able to live the faith-full life. I guess you can sum up the Catholic view with this little riddle: 'Good works can never save you, but you can never be saved without good works.'

John: I promise you I'll re-read the Council of Trent. I assure you I have read it but, sadly, what sticks in my memory are the anathemas and the hubris that makes a human institution think it can pronounce on such matters as the standing of other human beings with God. To be fair, I would hasten to add that I've seen people from the other side of the divide expressing themselves in similarly awful ways.

Let me comment on a couple of points you raise. It's helpful to be reminded about the Catholic Church's condemnation of Pelagianism. I agree, this is indeed evidence that it doesn't propound salvation by works in the way it's often caricatured as doing. It might be helpful for our readers, though, to unpack this just a little. Pelagius was the first English heretic, a fourth century monk. His least favourite Bible verse would have been 'All our righteousness is as filthy rags' (Isa. 64:6). He reacted to the sombre view of humanity that inevitably grows out of the doctrines of the fall and original sin, and was optimistic about human nature. When people today talk of 'a spark of divinity' in the human soul they are indulging a dash of Pelagianism. But it all goes wrong when it encourages people to believe their personal goodness will enable them to escape God's judgement and condemnation. I suspect Pelagianism remains one of the great British practical heresies to this day. How often do you hear people say, 'I know I'm no saint, but I'm a good and reasonable chap, so why would a good God condemn me?'

On balance I agree that Athanasius, Augustine and company left a legacy that has laid Christianity open to accusations that it has an unnecessarily low view of human nature. Your Luther quote is probably the daddy of them all, but some of the Puritans weren't far behind. About twenty years ago a group of writers, including Harry Williams, did us a service by analysing the Anglican liturgy in terms of the psychological damage caused by over-emphasis on human wretchedness, like Cranmer's 'We are not worthy so much as to gather up the crumbs under your table.' We need to strike a balance. Being made in the image of God we bear his likeness, but there is no part of us that isn't marred or spoiled by our sinfulness. We therefore need God's mercy, forgiveness and enabling in order to live 'a righteous and sober life' as the old liturgy puts it.

Sin isn't a very fashionable subject these days but I will offer a comment on Catholic teaching about mortal and venial sins. I've come to the conclusion that it can be helpful to warn people that there are actions and attitudes that will kill the soul. However, while I can see what the Catholic Church is trying to get at, I don't think the categories 'mortal' and 'venial' help very much. The emphasis should lie not on the fact that I commit sins, but that I *sin* because I am a *sinner*. Then I need to understand that even if I commit what might be called a 'venial' sin in order to prevent committing one that's 'mortal', I must regardless seek God's mercy and forgiveness.

Dwight: I think you've missed the point here. Because we categorise some sins as mortal and some as venial, it doesn't mean the venial sins don't matter. Neither are we permitted to commit a venial sin to avoid a mortal sin. We are told not to sin at all and that both mortal and venial sins displease God and need to be forgiven. The categories of mortal and venial sin are established in Scripture (I Jn. 5:16-17). The church has taught that this simply means some sins, by their very nature, separate us from God eternally whereas 'lesser' sins like sins of omission or sins against charity, do not necessarily separate us from God.

John: We've agreed a lot in this chapter, more than many might have expected. The point where you leave me troubled, however, is your dismissal of 'eternal security'. As with many of the great issues in the life of faith, at the centre of the doctrine of salvation is a profound mystery. I'm somewhat helped by the way some of the more modern-day Calvinists approach it by reference to the twin themes of perseverance and preservation. If I have been savingly joined to Christ I am kept and preserved to eternal life. If I persevere in faith it's a sign that I've been savingly joined to Christ. If I turn my back on the faith of Christ it's a signal that I may not have been savingly joined to Christ in the first place. Now I think that is hardly cut and dried in the way that the 'eternal security' slogan makes out. It's not so much a definition of what happens as some pointers by which I can examine my actions and motives. God alone will judge in the matter of my salvation and yours but we're not kept entirely in the dark as to how this will turn out because we have the witness of the Holy Spirit in the life of the believer.

Dwight: Well, maybe we're not too far apart on this question either. The Catholic Church teaches that we should have every confidence and hope of our salvation, but that God alone is the judge. Like you, we believe that because of our baptism and faith we are part of the body of Christ, but that we need to persevere to the end to be saved.

John: Writing my contribution to this chapter has been a huge challenge but one I've enjoyed very much. One of the great benefits of the official ecumenical dialogues with the Catholic Church, in particular the Anglican and Lutheran dialogues, is that it has forced us to get behind the slogans of the sixteenth century and go to the Bible itself and the experience of the entire church throughout the ages. It was interesting that the Anglican-RC dialogue, pressed very hard by Anglican Evangelicals to face head-on the issue of justification, finally produced a statement that focused on the far more defining issues of salvation and the place of the church in it.

In this chapter I'm satisfied that we've got close to agreement about salvation. For my part, though, I doubt that the same can be said about the church part. The Catholic Church, in my view, has always tried to claim too much for itself as an arbiter of who's 'in' and who's 'out'. We have its understanding of Peter and the keys and the anathemas of the Council of Trent. Then we have my old friend John Wilkinson who saw me as a 'potential' Christian: not, I suspect as you suggested, because he had a definition of salvation that put everyone in a provisional category, but because he saw the Catholic Church as the only sure route to salvation – being careful in his choice of words not to give the impression that he thought it the only route. A sensitive understanding of general revelation, the idea that God is knowable in all sorts of ways, among them nature and the things he has made, is an important corrective to ecclesial hubris. So too, I think, is the recent official Catholic teaching on mission (*ad gentes* and other key statements). And we have a warning from Jesus himself which could as much apply to church people as his original Jewish hearers: 'Many will come from the east and the west and eat with Abraham, Isaac and Jacob in the Kingdom of Heaven, while the heirs of the Kingdom will be thrown into outer darkness...' (Mt. 8:11). Am I right?

Dwight: Of course you're right that lots of church people, Catholics included, will be surprised to find themselves outside the heavenly gates. Catholics have always believed this – witness those delicious medieval paintings of the Last Judgement with lots of corrupt cardinals and bishops being thrown into hell.

You have a problem about the Catholic Church deciding 'who's in and who's out'. But didn't Jesus give his church precisely this power? In the passage where he establishes the church he says to Peter, 'Whatever you bind on earth will be bound in heaven and whatever you loose on earth will be loosed in heaven' (Mt. 16:19). This is backed up by his gift of the Holy Spirit in John 20:23 in which Jesus gives his apostles the power to forgive or not to forgive sins in his name. I know it's galling to imagine that the church has this power to say 'who's in and who's out' but what else could the gospel words possibly mean?

It's true we have a clear formula to decide if a person is formally a Christian or not. We also have a clear formula as to who are Catholics and who are not. It's also true that we have worked out that there are some heroes of the faith who we believe are most certainly in God's presence. Likewise we decide that there are some people who follow false teachings, and despite their claim to be Christian, are not Christian at all. All denominations do this, don't they? Furthermore, in my experience, the anathemas and judgements that emanate from conservative Evangelicalism are far more narrow and exclusive than they've ever been in Catholicism. But you are an Anglican, and Anglicans pride themselves on their comprehensiveness and tolerance. Therefore I know you find the Catholic Church's dogma and definitions particularly annoying. But as I've said before, from New Testament times onward part of the church's apostolic role has been to define the truth and expose error. I realise that the Catholic Church's continued ministry in this area is offensive, but that too is nothing new.

But in affirming this, it doesn't mean we are doing God's judging for him. Making formal definitions based on external, objective criteria is a fair exercise for any religion. However, this is not the same thing as declaring an eternal judgement on individual souls. We can ascertain if a person is baptised or not. We can determine if a person is living openly in sin or not. We can determine if a person formally denies the faith or not. Based on this the church may predict the direction their soul seems to be going, but what we *cannot* do is determine the thoughts and intents of their hearts or the eternal destiny of their soul. That is always the task of God, who alone is the judge of all our hearts. And that's why judgement day is going to be so very full of surprises.

---

1 St Augustine Sermons 169, 13

2 Bishop S. Neill, *Crises of Belief*, (London: Hodder & Stoughton, 1984), p89

3 *Joint Declaration on the Doctrine of Justification*, Annex, Para. 2, London, Catholic Truth Society

Chapter Eight

Heaven, Hell and Purgatory

Dwight: John, being brought up in a conservative evangelical home, did you ever worry about the millions of 'unsaved' people who were going to hell because they had never accepted Jesus as their personal saviour? I can remember coming home from church one Sunday night and asking my father what would happen to all the people who had never heard about Jesus. My father is a gentle man, and I can't imagine his answer was too harsh, but certainly the teaching we received at church was pretty uncompromising about the fate of the 'unsaved'.

From the evangelical position it is a tough one to resolve. After all, the Bible does say that God is not willing for any to perish, so it seems a bit hard that everyone who hasn't had a 'born again' experience is damned. But then again, the gospel is clear that Jesus is 'the Way, the Truth and the Life and that no one comes to the Father except through him'. As you suggested in the last chapter you have problems with Catholic exclusivity, so presumably you have problems with the even stricter exclusiveness of much of Evangelicalism. If Catholics declare some people outside the fold, aren't Evangelicals even harsher in their judgement?

As I moved from Evangelicalism through Anglicanism, Catholicism's common sense and compassion in this area increasingly impressed me. While we insist there is a fullness

of the Christian faith within the Catholic Church we're also
clear that there are worthy Christians outside that full communion. The catechism says

> The Church is joined in many ways to the baptised who are
> honoured by the name of Christian, but do not profess the
> Catholic faith in its entirety or have not preserved unity or com-
> munion under the successor of Peter. Those who believe in
> Christ and have been properly baptised are put in a certain,
> although imperfect, communion with the Catholic Church
> (CCC, 838).

Furthermore, we recognise that God's love and mercy can
flow through non-Christian religions in some cases. Chief
among these are the other monotheistic religions of Judaism
and Islam. There is also good among the other religions, and
God may draw people to himself through them as well. So the
catechism states

> The Catholic Church recognises in other religions that search,
> among shadows and images, for the God who is unknown yet
> near since he gives life and breath and all things, and wants all
> men to be saved. Thus, the Church considers all goodness and
> truth found in these religions as a preparation for the Gospel,
> and given by him who enlightens all men that they may at
> length have life (CCC, 843).

I have a feeling you will be broadly sympathetic with this
position, but as you would expect, it has been heavily criticised as 'too liberal' by many conservative Evangelicals. One
of the reasons Catholics allow this openness is because we
have a different view of the after life than Protestants. For the
classic Evangelical a person either accepts Jesus in this life and
goes to Heaven, or he rejects Jesus and goes to hell. We think
it's not as easy as that. It's not that easy because it is clear from
our human experience that many of those who profess the
name of Christ still have a lot to learn about being Christlike.
Similarly, there are many people who may seem to reject the

Jesus of organised religion, but who accept the ultimate truths that are found within the Christian faith. A bad Christian and a good pagan both have a lot to learn. The gospel says salvation is always through Christ. Perhaps when those who never knew Christ or rejected him through no fault of their own get to the other side they will see Christ as he really is for the first time, and say, 'Of course. He is the Love, the Truth, the Beauty and the Goodness I have always sought.'

Catholics believe in Heaven and hell, but we also believe Heaven has a kind of waiting room where souls can continue to learn about God's love. The traditional name for this place of realisation and spiritual growth is purgatory. This simply means a place of cleansing. The best book about purgatory, Heaven and hell has to be C.S. Lewis' fantasy story called *The Great Divorce*. There he explains how our choices on earth become final and real once we have died. Purgatory is the place where the uncertainties are cleared up, the old sins are purged away and where we are scrubbed up and prepared to enter into God's presence. This process is hinted at in the gospels when Jesus speaks of a situation in the afterlife where a reckoning will have to be made. In a parable about the judgement he encourages his hearers to take heed lest they be put into a prison not to be released 'until the last penny is paid' (Mt. 5:26). I Peter 3:19 says after his death Jesus went to 'preach to the spirits in prison.' So this prison or 'reform school' we call purgatory is based on scriptural hints, although the doctrine itself developed as the church reflected on these matters.

Lewis suggests that purgatory is not a third place distinct from Heaven and hell, but is actually an antechamber of Heaven. As a result, while purgatory is a place of difficulty and learning, it is also a place of great joy because everyone there is destined for Heaven. In his poem about purgatory the poet Dante captures this sense of grace and hopeful hardship beautifully. I believe in purgatory not only because it has been church teaching from time immemorial, but because it provides a compassionate and common sense answer to the burning question I had as a child. Does the idea of purgatory make sense to you too?

John: I liked your reference to C S Lewis' *The Great Divorce*. It belongs among my all-time favourites. It helped articulate for me something I think I always understood intuitively – that 'the life everlasting', even more than this mortal life, will be one in which we can – and will – grow spiritually. Now while Lewis has made the best case I've ever read for something like purgatory, I remain unconvinced about it. I would simply suggest that in the life to come, we will have an advanced capacity to have and participate in the things we wanted most in this life. On that basis there is no need for a heavenly antechamber. God simply kits us out based on the values, attitudes and spiritual insights and skills we have acquired in this life and brought with us into eternity. In his mercy and grace God will start with us where we are. As C S Lewis put it, 'The hills and valleys of Heaven will be close to those you now experience, not as a copy of the original, nor as a substitute for the genuine article, but as the flower to the root or the diamond to the coal.' In the afterlife God will lead us into new paths, as we grow into the likeness of Christ. For many, this may mean it will gradually dawn on them that there is a bigger world of experience beyond their self-made spiritual reality. As they move on, the experience will be baffling sometimes, even painful.

That takes me to my second point. What I have said above is largely down to my imagination. We have no real way of knowing what Heaven is like. 'No eye has seen, nor ear heard, nor the human heart conceived, what God has prepared for those who love him' (1 Cor. 2:9 NRSV). And yet the Bible is full of images of the life of Heaven and they've inspired countless Christian classics and hymns. So there's no shortage of ways to help us focus our minds on Heaven. But I've become utterly convinced that Heaven will be far bigger than what either the standard Catholic or evangelical formation generally allows for.

I say this for two reasons. First, one part of the Bible I'm prepared to take literally is the vision of Heaven in Revelation (7:9) as containing a crowd 'that no-one can number'. Then, secondly, I've come to the view that, for me at least, it's inconceivable that the first Adam should lead more people to destruction than Christ, the second Adam, will lead to glory. God made the human race to be in relationship with him. I do not know how God will bring this about. I don't think it's helpful to speculate. Nor would I want to frame a theory that would in any way give the impression that God's grace is cheap or that humans can be cavalier about the gospel. We become part of God's eternal future through Christ and we fit ourselves for it by becoming more and more like him. Let me add immediately that nothing I have said above rules out hell as a reality. If in eternity we have an advanced capacity for the things we want most, God is not going to force people to share his presence if they don't want to do so.

In this chapter I want to take up the themes of Heaven and hell in more depth. But let me explain what's brought me to the vision of Heaven I've shared. For many years my Mum and Dad were Evangelicals, fairly much in the pietistic tradition. Then they went through a process of falling out with the people with whom they'd gone to church for over a decade. In the process they tentatively linked up with various groups as they sought another way to 'do church'. One such group labelled themselves as 'reformed', and this meant they sought a doctrinally 'pure' faith based on the doctrines of the Reformation. Part of the baggage was their doctrine of 'limited atonement'. To explain it they offered a form of syllogism, something like this. 1. For whom did Christ die? 2. If he died for the whole world, how is it that some are not saved? 3. Clearly then, he died not for the whole world but for those elected to be saved. Here we have an expression of the biblical themes of predestination and election in extreme legalistic terms. The conclusion had to be that God had elected some for damnation.

I was affronted. What sort of God was this? How does it square with what we know of God in Jesus? That invited me to explore further the question of God's ultimate purposes. My conclusion: it is to reconcile the world to himself in Christ. One possible implication was that God's work with each individual to that goal might not necessarily end at the time of physical death. But for those who continue to resist God's love and grace the ultimate fate is what the Bible calls 'the second death'. Now have I got your heresy bells ringing?

Dwight: You haven't rung any heresy bells for me, but I can see that some conservative Evangelicals will brand you as a wishy-washy liberal. I agree with you in finding extreme Calvinism a harsh and legalistic religion. I expect, like me, you had to memorise John 3:16. I can remember when the full meaning of the next verse hit me between the eyes. I was struggling with this total depravity, double predestination stuff at theological college and in one of those clearly Spirit-led moments the words of John 3:17 shot like an arrow to my heart. 'God did not send his Son in to the world to condemn the world, but that the world through him might be saved.' The whole gospel suddenly shouted this message, ' He came to save the world – not to condemn it!'

As I've outlined above, the Catholic view makes room not only for a very wide range of Christians, but we also allow that God may also see fit to save those of non-Christian religions who, through no fault of their own, have either not heard of Christ or have rejected a false image of Christ. Notice that we do not say God *will* save them – only that he may save them. Christian missions are an absolute imperative because for us too, hell is a reality and we believe many people will choose to be there rather than be forced into Heaven. While we admit God may save some who have sought goodness and truth within non-Christian religions it is our duty to work with Christ to 'seek and save that which is lost.'

We've agreed on pretty much everything so far in this chapter, but let me push you a little more. While we're talking about Heaven, how do you see the relationship between those of us who are still here below and those who have died? As you know, we Catholics believe it is a good and proper thing to continue praying for our loved ones who have died. If they are still learning and growing, as you've said, then we believe our prayers here on earth can help them in that process. Our belief that this is a wholesome thing is based on 2 Maccabees 12:46 which says, 'It is therefore a good and wholesome thing to pray for the dead, that they may be loosed from their sins.' Are you happy with this too, or is this where we part company?

John: Wishy-washy liberal? One of the authorities I could cite for the ideas I shared about Heaven and its population is John Stott, and if he's not mainstream Evangelical, who is? I don't think anything I offered lacks for biblical warrant. I was very careful to say that my capacity to grow spiritually later is down to the spiritual resources I cultivate in the here and now. And if in the afterlife you have an advanced capacity for what you want most now, then there will be those whose fate is the second death. Put that way, I'm back to my basic evangelical instincts to go out with utmost urgency into the highways and hedges and plead with people to listen to the gospel!

Dwight: I wasn't name-calling. Just predicting that some of our brothers and sisters might think our view on who is going to be saved might be too close to Universalism for comfort.

John: Fine. I've recounted a growing point in my faith bred out of adversity, with all that stuff about limited atonement. Another growing point for me – and this was much happier – was a series of biblical expositions on Hebrews 11 given by one of my greatest mentors, the Reverend Dr Howard Guinness, founder of the Inter Varsity Fellowship in Australia. It happened at the end of my first year at university. Guinness helped unlock for me how 'seekers' who lived many years before the coming of Christ were exercising what the writer of Hebrews saw as something with the same cash value in God's eternal economy as faith in Christ. In the final verse (Heb. 11:40) the writer more than hints that they participate with us in the salvation offered through Christ. It's not hard to speculate from there – and Guinness did – that people from right outside the Judaeo-Christian world might also receive Christ's salvation. I've become less and less willing to rule this out, not least from hearing stories, for example, of Muslims with practically no information about Christ, meeting him direct in dreams. My bottom line here is that it is through Christ that salvation is to be found, for there is 'no other name' (Acts 4:12). How this works out in practice, how one day 'every knee will bow and every tongue confess that Jesus Christ is Lord' (Phil. 2:10) is more God's business than mine. What I offered in the last chapter was the suggestion that what we mortals see are some of the visible and outward signs, and so we see good works, perseverance, being part of the visible body of Christ. Alongside is the invisible work of God's grace. So I am saying that I think there is clear Scripture that propels me to think Heaven may have a much bigger population than my evangelical background might have allowed. But I'm loath to go much further than that because I don't have much scriptural data to go on and in the end who gets to Heaven and who doesn't is in God's hands, not human hands.

Dwight: I'm on your side here. As I understand it, what you're proposing is congruent with Catholic teaching on the subject.

John: Before we agree too much, let me pick you up on prayers for the dead. I'm glad you mentioned that notorious passage from Maccabees. For the thorough-going Protestant it alone is sufficient reason for the non-inclusion of the Apocrypha in the biblical canon! This is one of those issues where Evangelicals tend to get very nervous. These days the Evangelicals in the General Synod of the Church of England are quite a diverse bunch. This, however, is one issue where they show great solidarity. Influential Evangelicals on Synod take great pains to oppose and eradicate every nuance that might even hint of praying for the dead in Anglican liturgies. They would contend that even a hint of a possibility that someone's eternal destiny might change from damnation to salvation following death is to embark on a slippery slope. It's not a debate that exercises me greatly. I offer a comment along similar lines to what I would say to proponents of extreme interpretations of predestination and election: from a human perspective no speculation about the actions of God should ever excuse me from the task of evangelism. I feel the same, therefore, about praying for the dead.

Dwight: It's getting off the point, but Catholics want to challenge you a bit on just why you folks felt it necessary to discard the books of the Apocrypha from the Scriptures. The earliest church fathers were unanimous in accepting these books as Scripture, and they were included in all the most ancient canons of Scripture. I admit there was some doubt about their validity in some circles, but no Christians rejected them utterly until the Reformation. Considering that Luther wanted to exclude the book of James from the New Testament, it all sounds a bit too much like your guys were picking and choosing according to what they liked or disliked.

But even if, for the sake of argument, we say the Book of Maccabees is not part of Scripture, the verse still shows that prayer for the dead was a venerable Jewish custom from very early times. As such Jesus must have known of it and it must have been accepted by the early church. Remember there is that curious verse (I Cor. 15:29) which shows that the early Christians baptised on behalf of the dead. They must have believed that prayers for the dead were both desirable and effective. Indeed, the archaeological evidence at the catacombs in Rome show that Eucharists for the dead and prayers for the dead are some of the best attested facts about early Christian worship. So once again, why did the Reformers chuck out something which was universal Christian practice up to their time?

John: Probably because the practice was being so abused – which brings me to a fresh point. Another traditional flashpoint between Catholics and Protestants has to do with indulgences. The indulgences controversy in Wittenberg triggered Martin Luther's 95 Theses and the sixteenth century Reformation. For a long time I'd thought indulgences were a dead letter and that the Catholic Church found them a bit of an embarrassment. Why, then, did Pope John Paul II recently issue fresh instructions about their place and use in the

Catholic Church? Is he an out of touch reactionary, or is there something I've missed all these years?

Dwight: You're right that indulgences are linked with our belief that it is beneficial to pray for the dead. I have to admit that indulgences were one of the things I found difficult to accept about Catholicism. Let me try to explain the logic of it however. First of all, we believe that the forgiveness of sin and the punishment for sin are two different things. Our sins are forgiven by Christ's atoning work on the cross. Through the victory won there we also have the power to overcome sin. Although the sin is forgiven forever we still have to share in the consequences of our sin. If my son breaks the neighbour's window we might all forgive him, but somebody still has to pay for the window to be repaired.

An indulgence is a legal framework set up by the church so we can feel confident that our prayers and faithful loving actions are helping to put right what we've done wrong. This is not earning salvation or earning forgiveness. Salvation is a free gift. It is taking responsibility for our actions and taking the rap. Because we believe that Christ gave the church power to bind and loose, and to forgive sins, we also believe the church can recognize that the temporal punishment for sin is taken care of. So when the church grants an indulgence for, let's say, going on pilgrimage, visiting the sick, or fasting and praying, the church is giving us a little reward for the effort we've made. In cultures where the people are illiterate and need precise guidance, indulgences may help them focus their Christian lives towards further faithful acts of love and prayer. One of the traditional times for Catholics to make pilgrimage is during a Jubilee year. This is why the present Pope explained again how indulgences work – so that the millions of pilgrims in the year 2000 might understand how their prayers and faithful good works might be eternally beneficial.

If these prayers and good works can help to put right what we've done wrong, and if our prayers for others are beneficial, then somebody came up with the logical idea that we can apply the benefits of our prayers and loving actions for others

– both living and dead. This is why, from the very earliest days, Catholics ask for the Eucharist to be celebrated for their dead loved ones. This is a way of focusing their prayers on that person. But this idea that we may pray and do loving actions for others is also where the abuse of indulgences came in. One of the acts of mercy has always been giving money to the poor. Corrupt churchmen became very legalistic and said 'Giving x amount of money to the poor can earn you or your loved ones x amount of time out of purgatory.' It wasn't too much of a jump to see that this little trick could become a big earner for the church, and it was this greedy abuse of indulgences that the Reformers were right to criticise.

I must admit that while I understand indulgences, I don't find them particularly exciting. There's something too pat about it all – too legalistic. But you don't have to love everything Catholic to be a Catholic. I'm happy to accept them and leave it at that. But what interests me more is how corrupt religious leaders so often fall into the honey trap. Let's be honest. The Catholic leadership of the sixteenth century was pretty greedy and corrupt. But I was brought up in the kind of evangelical religion which sometimes taught the 'prosperity gospel'. If you tithed ten percent of your income to the church God would bless you many times over. What's more corrupt – getting the faithful to cough up their cash to win the spiritual benefit of their loved ones, which is what the abuse of indulgences amounted to, or getting the faithful to cough up their cash because they'll get lots more cash in the future if they do? Both are terrible abuses, but at least indulgences have a measure of altruism in their theory.

Sorry, I didn't want to get into stone throwing. Neither do I want to discourage the proper kind of sacrificial giving. I simply want to make the point that corruption and greed rears its ugly head in many ways, times, forms and places. Christ's church is always broken and shamed by it no matter where it occurs.

John: I don't doubt your last comment. I'm glad that at least some Catholics are a bit sheepish about indulgences: history says they ought to be. But I hasten to add that some of the shenanigans of American TV preachers in the last decade or so belong right up there with the indulgences controversy of the sixteenth century among the serious blots on Christianity.

By now some of our readers may be wondering whether one or other of us will ever get round to broaching the subject of hell. You've said that the Catholic Church teaches that there is a hell. I've spoken of it already, using the term 'the second death', from the Book of Revelation, to sum up how I understand it. It's there in Jewish tradition and in the Old Testament. The gospels leave us in little doubt that Jesus believed in hell. You referred to Dante earlier – and this is where I sense a point of departure.

I suspect that the popular Christian understanding of hell owes more to Dante than a careful reading of the Scriptures! I can't square Dante and the image of God as an eternal torturer with the God whom Jesus revealed. Nor does it square with what the New Testament actually says. As with talk of Heaven, we have little choice to resort to imagery. Jesus does that. He called it *gehenna*, which in fact was the name of the garbage dump outside the city of Jerusalem whose fires never went out. The Book of Revelation likewise calls hell the lake of fire. And yet Jesus also speaks of it as a place of 'darkness'. The two images can't be harmonised. Fire creates light. So I think we need to look for a deeper meaning and I think the theme of the second death in Revelation gets us there.

A lot of Evangelicals are fond of saying that hell is 'separation from God'. I can see why it's an attractive turn of phrase, not least because it's a way around gruesome Dantesque literalism. Over the years, however, I've subjected the logic of it to a bit more scrutiny. To speak of separation from God is simply another way of saying 'non-being'. If I'm separated from God, I'm cut off from the source of life. That sounds like something that's terminal and not some kind of lingering state of being.

Let's try to sum up. I think that discussion between Catholics and Protestants about salvation gets into difficulties because, as I've suggested, we sometimes confuse salvation with the different approaches our churches take to the question of Christian initiation. Evangelicals have insisted on personal conversion, with various rites and traditions that help people to publicly lay claim to Jesus' promise that 'to as many as received him, to them he gave the power to become the sons of God'. Catholics have put their emphasis on baptism as the sign of joining the church. There used to be quite a gulf between the two, but as we've seen it need not be as great as we once thought. Evangelicals take great encouragement from the stories of the changed lives of people who have had personal conversions: Catholic devotion has a different genre of people stories and they tend to serve a slightly different purpose, but Catholics, of course, do possess some cracking conversion stories as well.

What is certain is that Jesus taught that we can jump through all the various ritualistic and theological hoops, be they Catholic or Protestant, and may even call Jesus 'Lord', but still not enter the Kingdom. This is a vital piece of grit in the oyster for those of us who feel very much at home with religion and with all its beauty and its fascinating theological intricacies.

We religious people need to be constantly reminded that God's primary interest is not religion: God is primarily interested in life, of which he is the Creator and sustaining force. As Jesus made very plain, on the day of reckoning, what will loom large in God's deliberations in sorting the sheep from the goats will not be whether we are Catholic or Protestant, believers in limited atonement or whatever. His questions will be about what we did for hungry, naked, homeless or displaced people, or those who are in prison. Jesus taught that those who ignore the practical needs of these people, who he called his 'family', do so at their eternal peril.

Let me end on a more positive note. As I get older I'm finding that more and more of my devotional life centres on the hope of Heaven. Paul Minear once said, 'Delete the thought of Heaven from man's lexicon and he is soon reduced to a one-dimensional environment, living without any invisible means of support.'

One of the greatest reasons for building our spiritual lives 'down here' is that it's the best possible preparation for the day when we will live permanently in the presence of God 'up there'. When we share hospitality it can be an anticipation of the heavenly banquet. Then there are a host of other ways to meditate on Heaven. I personally like to read hymns and poems about Heaven. I'm fond of practising 'heavenly contemplation' as the Puritan Richard Baxter called it, deliberately taking time out to meditate on it.

Then, I'm beginning to discover what has been labelled 'cosmic prayer'. That, of course, is all summed up by that simple petition in the Lord's Prayer, 'Your Kingdom come.' Heaven sums up how all the purposes of God are brought to completion. By meditating on Heaven, but with a newspaper beside me, I move into the realm of cosmic prayer, engaging with God about the way his purposes are being worked out 'on earth as in Heaven'. Exhilarating stuff when you get it right!

Chapter Nine

For All the Saints

John: There are two types of Christians, says St Paul. 'One man esteems one day as better than another, while another man esteems all days alike' (Rom. 14: 5). It's a comment that I think applies to saints and saints' days as well. I know people who make a beeline for the church once or even twice a week for a Eucharist to celebrate St Bloggs, St Ethelred or whoever happens to be on the church calendar. For those not so minded there are lots of Bible verses that will back up their position. In his writings St Paul, for example, uses 'saints' as a collective noun for the Christian people in the churches he founded. Christians, he says, are 'called to be saints' (Rom. 1:7).

For most of my life I would have cheerfully aligned myself with those who 'esteem every day alike'. I suppose as much as anything it was about opportunity: it just wasn't practical for our family to cultivate the habit of going to church on saints 'days. Underneath, however, was a mindset formed in reaction to Catholic practice. Chaucer's *Pardoner's Tale,* from more than two centuries before the Reformation, is just one indication of how veneration of the saints has always been open to humbug and corruption. The Catholic Church was well aware of the need for visual aids and stories, especially in a pre-literary culture. Accordingly it developed icons, windows and relics of the saints among a panoply of ways to illustrate the faith. Sometimes it got things just about right. Sometimes popular fervour got out of hand.

Evangelicals, too, know full well the value of people stories and visual aids in communicating the faith. So I've come to the conclusion that it's a mistake to fob off the issue of great Christians with the contention that 'we're all saints anyway' or 'why single out or elevate particular people?' How killjoy can you be? Yes, it's easy enough to go overboard, and human beings inevitably do. But to rule out celebrating great Christians is to deny an important fundamental ingredient in Christian devotion. As I'm fond of saying, we are pygmies who stand on the shoulders of giants. Biography – and even hagiography – can be an enormous source of help in the Christian life, whether it's a story about actual saints, people who are somewhat less than saints, or plain baddies.

As I've mellowed somewhat, I've begun to make more of saints in my own devotional life and in conversation. I have my favourites. I'm glad my father named me John and I'm the proud possessor of a mug that every day reminds me that it's a very special name and that God is gracious. Then, I find that asking a person what their name means is an innocent and highly effective icebreaker in personal evangelism.

I enjoy books that invite you on a journey of prayer with a particular person or saint. It's here that, along with a lot of other Christians of a more Protestant upbringing, I've found a way around the vexed question of prayer to the saints. Praying with them, if that means using their insights, I can do. Praying to them I can't buy. I know that through Jesus I can come boldly to God's throne of grace in praise, intercession, thanksgiving or confession. What more do I need?

Dwight: Are you sure there is such a person as St Bloggs? All these years I've been missing his feast day! Seriously, I appreciate your open-minded attitude about saints. There is much we can agree on here. Agreeing with Scripture, the Catholic Church also considers all the faithful to be' saints'. From the very beginning, however, the church has recognised that some of the 'saints' have been more saintly than others. Soon after the great persecution of the early church, the Christians saw the heroism of their martyrs, and realised they had emulated their Lord even to the point of death.

We know from the historical record that the martyrs were remembered faithfully. Their fellow Christians would gather at their grave on the anniversary of the death. Because they saw the saint's martyrdom as the day of his victory and entrance into life, they actually called the anniversary the saint's 'birthday' and celebrated a joyful Eucharist and agape meal. So the custom of celebrating a saint's feast day began. There is very early archaeological evidence for this custom at the graves of the early Roman martyrs. The first written evidence is from the second half of the second century, and refers to the glorious martyrdom of old bishop Polycarp. The early Christians not only remembered the martyrs, but they considered their mortal remains to have been made sacred by the holiness of their life and death. As a result, their relics were considered holy, and were venerated by the faithful. Even in the early days these customs led to superstition and abuse. Tertullian commented on the problems of these devotions in his writings in the early third century.

In the Middle Ages a fair amount of abuse and superstition surrounded the proper devotion to the saints. As a result, feast days, the veneration of relics and so on were some of the excess baggage the Reformers chucked overboard. Underlying the Catholic devotion to the saints, and the Protestant mistrust of saints, is a very different emphasis and understanding of the church. My evangelical upbringing stressed the personal nature of faith. Ours was a very individualistic approach to Christianity. We were expected to belong to a church, but the church could be one of our own choosing – the one we thought best, or liked best. As an Evangelical I felt the church was there for fellowship and not much more. The main thing was my relationship with Jesus.

I don't want to denigrate the personal aspect of faith, but Catholicism sees the church as much more crucial. From the moment of our baptism we become one with the body of Christ – the Church. We Catholics take very much to heart St

Paul's teaching about the body of Christ having many members. For a Catholic, it is virtually impossible to be a Christian without being a member of the church. As a Catholic Christian my individual faith is confirmed, validated and made complete by my fellow Christians. This includes not only all Catholics everywhere in the world, but all Catholics everywhere in time. As I worship at the Eucharist I am joined in a living and dynamic union with all of my brothers and sisters both living and departed. This 'communion of the saints' is a wonderful thing. It enriches my own life of faith immensely.

It is in this belief that our veneration of the saints has its context. While I appreciate your ability to pray with the saints by studying their lives and reading their writings, what Catholics do is more than that. Of course we look to the saints as our role models. We are instructed by their writings and inspired by their lives. But we also feel that we are in relationship with them. I can only describe it as the kind of intimacy we share with others through praying together. When you pray with another person you really get to know them and love them. So it is when we pray with the saints. We feel they have become our friends. We feel that they pray with us. That being the case, it is natural for us to ask them to pray with us and for us just as we would any other Christian friend here on earth. When a Catholic says that he 'prays to St Anthony' this is what he means. He is not praying to St Anthony instead of praying to God. Neither is he praying to St Anthony as some sort of lesser deity. He is simply asking his friend in Heaven to pray for him and with him.

Learning to share this experience has impressed upon me the reality of the resurrection almost more than anything else in my Christian experience. If the saints join in my earthly prayers, then I also join in their prayer and praise in Heaven. A greater appreciation of the communion of the saints helps my own worship to transcend this time and place and take me to the threshold of Heaven.

The book of Hebrews expresses the Catholic view on saints in language which is poetic and precise. In chapter 12 it says

> Since we are surrounded by so great a cloud of witnesses, let
> us lay aside every weight, and sin which clings so closely, and
> let us run with perseverance the race that is set before us,
> looking to Jesus the pioneer and perfecter of our faith; who for
> the joy that was set before him endured the cross, despising
> the shame, and is seated at the right hand of the throne of
> God.

The great cloud of witnesses are all those people who have
lived the faith in the ages before us. Encouraged by them, and
living in solidarity with them, we look together to Jesus, the
pioneer and perfecter of our faith. This is why saints are so
important to Catholics – because in the saints we see what
Jesus can do in an ordinary person's life. In the saints we meet
fellow pilgrims who help us on our journey. In the saints we
also get a glimpse of the great cloud of witnesses – the multitude that no man can number envisioned by St John in the
book of Revelation.

I believe that a greater appreciation of the communion of
saints is one of the riches Catholics can offer Evangelicals. Last
year I was in Rome to take part in an ecumenical celebration of
the martyrs. In front of the Coliseum the Pope led representa-
tives from every major Christian tradition. Together we heard
the stories of the heroic martyrdoms of this century from every
corner of the globe, and from every Christian tradition. I know
you like Tertullian's soundbite that 'the blood of the martyrs is
the seed of the church'. At that great ceremony I got a vision of
how the blood of the martyrs might also be the seed of church
unity in the future. As we heard the stories of the martyrs from
different traditions, the whole crowd was moved by their witness. Time and again they said how, in the fires of persecution,
denominational differences vanished. The Baptist was suddenly the brother of the Catholic. The Orthodox was locked in
embrace with the Presbyterian. The Anglican and the
Methodist were one. This is the fire in the heart of our love of
saints. Do you agree that a greater appreciation of the saints
from every age and every tradition must help to bring us all
together?

John: I agree with you about the special contribution of the Book of Hebrews, with its affirmation of the 'the great cloud of witnesses' which surrounds the church. As with the subject of angels, here is a theme that's much neglected by Protestants and Evangelicals.

A starting point in the search for common ground might be to focus on the stories of the saints (and martyrs) of the pre-Reformation, undivided church. That takes us back to Stephen, of course, and to the apostles. I can't recommend too highly the account of the life and death of Polycarp, the godly Bishop of Smyrna, nor can I read his last words without getting dewy eyed. `He who gives me the power will grant me to remain in the flames without the security you will give by the nails.'

Of course, the Catholic approach to mission has always left open possibilities of syncretism and excess. Whereas, on the whole, the Protestant missions to different parts of the world spent a lot of energy rooting out various practices that were considered incompatible with the Christian faith, many Catholic missions seem to have started the other way round, looking to try to 'baptise' the local spirituality. At the heart of these differences are distinct theologies of culture. I get the impression that Protestant missions, informed by a more transcendent focus for their understanding of Christ, tended to think that they were 'taking Christ' to unevangelised peoples. Catholics, on the other hand, informed by a more incarnational outlook, sought to discern Christ already present in the created order and in the various religious impulses and popular forms of expression. Some of this comes through into Anglicanism: churches on sites formerly dedicated to pagan worship, the takeover of traditional feasts like Whitsun and much more.

As you'll be well aware, all this can get very 'hairy' in some parts of the Catholic world: veneration of highly improbable relics of the saints, street processions with people following around statues draped in a costume with money pinned to it, and the even more controversial mixture of saint-devotion and voodoo that seems commonplace in Latin American countries, such as Haiti or Brazil. While the Catholic Church seems to have a generosity of spirit towards many of these devotional practices, they are not without their critics. Cardinal John Henry Newman could be very sharp tongued when it came to some of the excesses of popular Catholic piety.

Dwight: You've been pretty restrained in your criticism. Many non-Catholics would be more strident about what they see as not just excessive devotions – but downright paganism and idolatry. I agree with your analysis though. I think you're right that Catholic missionaries have been more inclined to accept what is good about the indigenous cultures. I'm reminded of the story about the Presbyterian ministers who went to the South Pacific and were shocked to find the women bare-breasted. The good Presbyterian ladies gave the native women tee shirts to wear. The women were delighted and came back to church the next week proudly wearing their shirts with two large holes cut in the front.

You are right that some Catholic veneration of saints is risky and easily misunderstood. Much of the misunderstanding is simply cultural. What we Anglo-Saxons find bizarre and pagan other Christians simply find a natural and wholesome expression of their love for God and his saints. On the whole, I'm glad our approach is more incarnational, and I'm willing to take the risk of a few problems to keep that physical under-standing of the faith.

John: Having picked on Catholic humbug, medieval and con-temporary, I need to come clean about aspects of evangelical hagiography and out-of-proportion hero worship. As it is part of my background, I suppose I should begin with some obser-vations about Brethren worship. Here, of course, it was said that worship should be spontaneous and led by the Spirit. The Lord's Prayer was never said because that was 'vain repeti-tion, in the manner of the Pharisees'. There was no written liturgy or creeds for the same reasons. But the service had a characteristic 'sameness' and even if it was the Spirit leading, he tended to lead the same people to play out more or less the same parts. So there was a spiritual elite and there were people past and present who were accorded a status tantamount to infallibility. I suspect that if you had said that St Athanasius was a man of straw, no one would have batted an eyelid, not least, I suspect, because few knew his significance in Christian history. But woe betide anyone voicing doubts about the plenary and verbal inspiration of the works of C I Schofield!

One of the great advantages with the way modern Catholics teach about saints and Christian heroes is that they're comfortable with their humanity. Catholics seem to be able to live with the shortcomings of their saints and heroes. As with the Bible's stories of the prophets and patriarchs, the human side comes out. So you people never see the need to put them out of reach on a pedestal. St Patrick rises to great spiritual heights, but there's a bit of the larrikin in him and that makes him accessible to people who know all too well that they're flawed.

Dwight: Maybe that's the case now, but I understand that Catholic devotion in the past *did* tend to suppress the human foibles and paint the saints with colours that were a bit too bright.

John: I think Evangelicals sometimes fall into this trap. They seem less comfortable with the human foibles of their great ones. Take for example the story of C.T. Studd, a former England cricketer and missionary hero of the nineteenth century. He developed a liking for cocaine – a fact that's not widely known. When this came to my notice, I talked to the chief of the publishing house that produced his biography in the 1930s. 'No, the biography didn't tell untruths or mislead', he told me. 'Yes, if you knew about the cocaine episode you would see it there subliminally.'

Coming more up to date, I have often asked myself why it is that Evangelicals tend to put their leaders on a pedestal. A serious problem arises if they then manifest lack of soundness, or blot their copybook. They will tend to be dropped altogether. It's all or nothing with Evangelicals, or so it seems. Catholic piety, on the other hand, through confession, penance and so on, has paths to rehabilitation that are largely unknown to Evangelicals. Of course, not all Evangelicals would approve of this.

Dwight: Whose side are you on here?

John: Ah. You would ask! Just observing the manifold strengths and weaknesses on both sides. Going on, a point that baffles me even more is why so many Evangelicals, who are by no means well off, give to ministries led by people with all the accoutrements of wealth: private jets, limousines, Rolex watches and the rest. In Nigeria it's standard practice for Anglican bishops to drive a Mercedes Benz and the people will tell you they would feel ashamed if their particular bishop didn't do likewise. There seems to be a vicarious pleasure on the part of those making sacrifices to see Christian leaders they support decked out that way. It seems to me that if Catholics have a tendency to consciously baptise the local culture, Evangelicals often imbibe it quite unconsciously.

Dwight: We're getting off track, but I agree with you. I've always been amused by the American Evangelicals who accuse the Pope of being a rich man in a palace while their own churches have million dollar budgets and their preachers zoom off to their television station in a Lear jet.

Let me get back to the saints. You touched on the issue of images when you mentioned processions with statues and so forth. I wonder where you stand on the question of images themselves. Some preachers in my evangelical background used to tell us that Catholics worshipped idols in their churches. Presumably you had the same teaching in your boyhood. Now that you're an Anglican, are you happy about images and statues, or does the Evangelical in you still balk at such things?

John: I seem to remember being taught that Catholics worship idols. As a boy, visiting St Mary's Catholic cathedral in Sydney,

I found a lot of circumstantial evidence that this was so, what with people kneeling before a statute of Mary and so on. My Anglican education had its beginnings in a somewhat austere 'reformed' and 'word-led' approach. The Diocese of Sydney has a reputation to keep! There's a famous story about a marble reredos being added to Sydney's Anglican cathedral. It's an exquisite work of art, wonderful material and gorgeous carving. Anyway, a group of a people, offended by the very Romish angels on it, somehow managed to get into the cathedral in the dead of night and to saw off the offending parts. Once I would have rejoiced in that. Now I would say it was mindless vandalism.

I have to say I love psalms that chide the pagan neighbours of the Jews for their idol worship. 'So you carve wood with your hands and kneel before it and call it your god. Then you gather up the leftovers, throw them on the fire and warm yourself.' Literal worship of idols is a mindless undertaking and the psalmist is right to sneer. Idols are dumb. To worship an idol is a betrayal of rationality. Statues are in another category. So too are icons, though they are not widely understood by Evangelicals. I've gradually begun to develop a sense of what might be labelled the beauty of holiness. It begins by understanding the value of a space that is something that's more than just a functional worship centre and which may even convey a sense of the presence of the Lord. It includes learning to appreciate the principles of iconography and enjoying the beauty of statues as works of art. The good Protestant in me would insist they contain no power or presence in their own right. They are capable, however, of pointing the mind and emotions to a higher plane and offering a rare glimpse or hint of what that higher plane may be like. I wouldn't want to go further than that.

Dwight: Ah! A civilized, tasteful Anglican point of view! You're right to appreciate Christian achievements in art and architecture. It's true that the greatest Western art, music, literature and architecture have been inspired by the Christian faith. More specifically, the vast majority of it has flowered from the heart of Catholicism – with its deeply incarnational understanding of the faith.

Now that I'm a Catholic I cannot understand why some Protestants want to prohibit all images in worship. They claim that this prohibition is biblical – indeed that it is based in the second commandment itself. But when God gave Moses the Ten Commandments he could not have intended a prohibition of all images because later in the wilderness he commands Moses to fashion a bronze serpent for the people to look to for salvation (Num. 21:8-9). Furthermore, the Lord's instructions for the tabernacle included various forms of religious imagery. The ark of the covenant was crowned with the graven image of two cherubim (Ex. 25:18-20) and the screens of the tabernacle were embroidered with images of angels (Ex:26:1). Solomon's temple, described in I Kings has carvings throughout, and the huge laver was set on the back of carved bulls (I Kings 7:25). Indeed, the descriptions of the tabernacle and temple with their rich and beautiful craftwork, carvings and embroidered vestments sound very like a highly decorated Catholic shrine – a far cry from the bare preaching halls of the Evangelicals.

Nevertheless, I can understand how the abuse of images has sent those with a more pure and abstract mindset howling. In the eighth century the church faced this problem head on. The Eastern church was struggling with the twin heresies of Monophysitism, which lessened the importance of Jesus' physical nature, and Manichaeism, which taught that the physical world was inherently sinful. The Emperor Leo III had been brought up under these influences and he thought the use of icons (the Greek word for images) was wrong. He also thought the use of icons was a barrier to evangelising the Muslims and Jews. So he decided to ban icons and destroy the existing ones. The church was immediately and bitterly divided by this interference. St John of Damascus was a Greek monk who argued the case for icons against the iconoclasts (destroyers of icons). His argument for the use of images in Christian worship is still relevant today. John argued that since Jesus Christ – the image of the unseen God (Col. 1:15) – took physical form, it was good and proper for Christians to use physical things in worship. He argued for the validity of images by saying

> The apostles saw Christ bodily, his sufferings and his miracles and they heard his words. We are double beings with a body and soul…it is impossible for us to have access to the spiritual without the corporeal, while listening to audible words we hear with our corporeal ears and thus grasp spiritual things. In the same way it is through corporeal seeing that we arrive at spiritual insight.

I don't want to labour the point, but it is important to distinguish between pagan idols and Christian images of saints. A pagan idol is a carved representation of a demon. The pagan doesn't worship the wood or stone as such. Instead he believes the physical image is a channel through which the demon will come once summoned. A Christian icon or statue is very different. It is not a fantastic image of a demon, but a physical image of a real, historical Christian who has lived and loved and died serving Christ. Images of the saints are like family photographs. They remind us of our loved ones and help put us in touch with them despite being separated from them physically. It's interesting that we now have photographs of the more recent saints. Somehow I get the feeling that a photograph of a saint is okay – but an icon is still suspect.

There is always the suspicion that Catholics are praying to the saints' images instead of to God. Indeed, it looks very like that sometimes. When you go into a Catholic Church, you may see an old lady light a candle in front of a statue of the Blessed Virgin Mary, then stand there praying while gazing up at the statue. It looks like she is praying to the statue. But if you were to ask her who she was praying to, even the most humble of Catholics would say they are praying to God. Even if they say they are praying to Mary they are clear that they are not praying to the statue. The best way to describe what that Catholic is doing is to say that she is using the image as a kind of window. The image is there to look through to get a little glimpse of Heaven and the saints.

While I'm grateful for your tolerance and even appreciation of Christian images, I should point out that the Catholic understanding does go further than simply appreciating the fine art involved. Why else do Catholics tolerate so much bad Christian art? We accept that a building, a stained glass window, a painting or a statue might be good art, but we regard it as more than that. It is not only a piece of art. It is a physical object which helps connect us to God and his saints. As such, some buildings and images can become objects of our veneration. Just as we come to treasure some special memento or photograph of our loved ones, so certain images down through time have become specially venerated by the faithful. These buildings and statues and paintings have been invested with the invisible love and prayers of thousands of our brothers and sisters down through time. They have become holy objects, and we venerate them as such. Of course they might sometimes become venerated instead of God, but this is an abuse, and abuses should never undo right uses.

I know some Evangelicals have a problem with the idea that a particular place or physical object can become holy. But if we believe in the incarnation, then we believe that God became man in a particular form, at a particular place and at a particular time. This physical-ness of the Catholic faith is something which has attracted me. I find it ever more profound and abundantly life-giving. This very physical emphasis is there in our churches, our flowers, windows, vestments, candles and images. It is there in our physical postures of worship. We kneel, we stand, we cross ourselves. The physical dimension to the faith finds its ultimate expression in our celebration of Mass. There in a particular time and place we believe Christ gives us his body under the most physical forms of bread and wine. We then do the most physical of actions: we eat and drink.

Chapter Ten

Holy Mary, Mother of God

Dwight: In the summer of 1987, I had just finished four years as an Anglican curate and had three months free before taking up my next post. I decided to make a hitch-hiking pilgrimage to Jerusalem from England. It was a fantastic journey with many memorable experiences along the way. One of the things I remember most about my time in the Holy Land was my visit to Nazareth.

If you've been to the big modern church in Nazareth, you know that beneath the floor level you come to some excavations which are presumed to be the remains of Mary's house. Whether they are or not doesn't matter too much. What is important is that in that town 2000 years ago the Virgin Mary received the message from the angel Gabriel telling her she was specially favoured of God, and asking her to accept God's will and bear his Son for the world. The church is a monument to that moment we call the Annunciation – or the announcement to Mary. It is also the point at which we believe Jesus Christ was conceived. I can remember kneeling at that shrine and suddenly being filled with a great sense of wonder. The poignancy and simplicity of the story struck me, but I was also hit by the enormous physical-ness of the event for the first time.

Here was a girl who seemed to be just another ordinary pious Jewish girl. Yet at that particular place and time she was asked to become the mother of God's son. One of the beliefs we all share as Christians is the Virgin Birth. We also believe that Jesus was true God and true man. In other words, his humanity was real – not pretend. But if we take this belief seriously then we are confronted with some rather amazing implications. If Mary really was his mother, then Jesus shares in Mary's physical make up. If Mary is his mother, then he is half-Mary. The first nine months of his life were spent in the nurture of her womb. During his childhood, he was dependent on her for food, warmth, love and shelter. From our mothers we learn how to love, and if Jesus was a man of love, then he learned that from Mary. Jesus not only shared Mary's genetic code, but God used her to help form the very foundations of Jesus' human personality. If we believe the incarnation, then there is an intimate and profound link between Mary and Jesus. That link is amazing and unique, and is something that has caused countless Christians to be filled with wonder and gratitude. This sudden understanding there in the Church of the Annunciation shook me up. I was still an Anglican, but from then on my understanding of the role of the Virgin Mary was one of respectful curiosity rather than my instinctive evangelical dismissal of her as 'too Catholic'.

Our images of the Blessed Virgin Mary most often portray her holding the Christ-child. Such images, like the realisation I had in the Church of the Annunciation, reveal the intimate bond between Mary and Jesus. This intimate bond between the Son of God and his mother is what led the early Christians to refer to Mary as *theotokos*, which means 'God Bearer'. The earliest record we have of Mary being referred to in this way is in the writings of Origen at the beginning of the third century. At the Council of Ephesus in 431 the title was upheld formally, and it has been maintained ever since. The reason it was used at Ephesus was not firstly to honour Mary, but to uphold and defend the doctrine of the incarnation. If God in Jesus Christ was truly born of a woman, then he had to be true God and true Man. It is from this intimate bond between Jesus and Mary, and the desire to defend the doctrine of the incarnation that all subsequent Catholic devotion to Mary springs.

In saying this, I have to admit that the Marian devotions and Marian doctrines of the Catholic Church were among the last pieces of the puzzle to fall into place for me. My Protestant background was pretty strongly 'anti-Mary'. I don't know about you, but we even seemed a bit embarrassed that she had to make an appearance at Christmas-time. Certainly I can't remember Mary being referred to in a sermon or Bible study, except in a derogatory anti-Catholic context. Looking back, I can't blame anybody because they were only passing on the gospel they had received. From my present perspective, however, there was something missing. Mary was missing, but I think her absence affected our view of Jesus. The humanity of Jesus was somehow lacking. I don't know about you, but I felt like the Jesus of my Sunday School days was rather like Superman – an All-American miracle worker whose feet never really touched the ground. Did you have that impression too? I wonder if it had anything to do with the fact that Mary was missing? Women are very down to earth and practical. Maybe if Mary and the feminine had been part of our religion, the Jesus we worshipped might have been more real too.

My own religious experience has supported this hunch. Since admitting Mary to my prayer life and acknowledging her role in redemption the whole thing has become more real to me than I can describe. It is as if I have been adopted into the family home when before I was still just a guest. From the point when I first started to allow Mary into my Christian life, the mysteries of the faith have become more real and concrete. I have also found less time to indulge my tendency to fantasise about life, love and religion. Everything's got more gritty. But if it's got more gritty it has also got more glorious.

I guess you'll want to challenge me on Mary, and I'm happy to be the target for your shooting practice. In the meantime, has anything I've said rung any bells for you?

John: It never ceases to amaze how, when the subject turns to the Blessed Virgin Mary, the brains of many an otherwise hard-minded Catholic seems to turn to putty! If you were to ask me to give my three best reasons why I'm not a Catholic, I'd simply say 'Mary, Mary and Mary'.

Now, having come out fighting, I'll deal an even dirtier punch. When, as an adult, you embrace another denomination or church, you generally do so with your eyes open. There are bits that are the very reasons why you wish to embrace it. There are bits that don't signal any change from where you were before. Then there are perhaps one or two items that you would honestly prefer weren't part of the package. But having concluded that either they're basically harmless, or at least don't constitute a sufficient reason for giving up, you grin and agree to bear them as part of the package. I won't press you to declare your hand. It might kill off the entire chapter before we get going!

Dwight: Let me butt in here. I know what you're talking about. You've put your finger on a very important matter in becoming a Catholic. Almost all the converts to Catholicism from evangelicalism express this problem with Mary. But they do not shrug their shoulders and go along with it just because they want to be Catholics. On the contrary most of them – like myself – are faced with considerable difficulties at the prospect of becoming Catholic. A major part of them doesn't want to become Catholic at all, and if the Mary thing can hold them back that's good because they're looking for any excuse *not* to become Catholic.

As a result, when they do actually 'get it' over Mary, the barriers are swept away and their conversion is complete. This almost always happens not as a result of the convert being reasoned through the Marian aspects of Catholicism by logic. Usually they have understood the logic of the Marian devotion but they still don't get it. What happens at that point is that instead of reasoning further they begin to use the rosary in prayer or they have some religious experience which brings them into a loving relationship with Mary. It's a difficult thing to explain. All I can say is that it is like falling in love. When it happens it might not make sense to you. It might turn your world upside down. You might look foolish in the eyes of others, but that doesn't matter because you know you've been given something precious.

John: Let me spell out my three problems with Mary and the Catholic Church. First, the Catholic Church has surrounded Mary with traditions that are not simply unbiblical, but run contrary to some important doctrinal principles. The gravest example concerns teaching about the role of Mary in salvation and attempts to have her officially recognised a co-redeemer. Second, the Catholic Church surrounds Mary with a whole lot of unnecessary clutter. To assert, for example, the perpetual virginity of Mary is a nonsense, not only because it's clear from the biblical record that Jesus had brothers and sisters, but also because in Jewish tradition denial of conjugal rights to Joseph would have been a violation of the marriage covenant. Third – and I'm sorry to be so tough – I think it sends out a wrong message about sexuality. As you know, for centuries before Jesus was born and well beyond, the cult of the girl flourished around the Mediterranean Basin. It was a cult that led to all sorts of aberrations including fertility rites, forms of worship that the Judaeo-Christian tradition from the prophets of Israel to St Paul utterly rejected. In our day, it takes a secular and materialist form and manifests itself in phenomena like Playboy magazine, page three girls and manifestations that are far worse. I fear that there's a displaced form of this phenomenon in the attitudes of some Catholics, especially males, to Mary.

Now, having launched an all-out assault, let me start again from what I see as first principles. It should be possible to salvage more than a few points in common. Here goes. In Heaven, when this old hack tries to blend in among the angels surrounding the throne hoping to get wind of a really good scoop, I'll fully expect to find that Mary occupies the highest place that Heaven can accord a human being. Speculations about words like *theotokos* will be well and truly lost in the mists of human time. They will have proved to be culture-bound, yet another of the many attempts of the Western mind to define and comprehend the incomprehensible. Mary herself will have seen to it that pious hymns like 'Hail Holy Queen' are banned from the heavenly hymnbook.

More seriously, I agree with you that the human Jesus is a blind spot for many Evangelicals and – apart from reaction to Catholic over-enthusiasm for Mary – this is a major reason why Mary is relegated almost out of sight. It doesn't help that we've made the Christmas/Nativity season so sugary. Happily, present-day Jesus' studies are redressing some of the losses and benefits are gradually percolating indirectly even to Evangelicals who consciously try to steer clear of such enterprises.

I would want to start to assess Mary's significance with reference to Mary's Song (the Magnificat) as recorded in Luke. The critics have wondered whether it's traceable to Mary herself. For my part I see no reason to sweep it aside as inauthentic. Here is a song of joy to a God who sets his people free, quite an irony considering that having a baby and taking on its care and nurture require big sacrifices of personal freedom.

Here is the ultimate act of hospitality. A young women gives her body to protect and nourish the God in human form whom she has conceived. She exults that the life within her will accomplish something that she doesn't fully comprehend, something of even greater significance in the history of her people than the Exodus. She expects nothing less than that the victory of God will be accomplished through the life within her. It's mighty stuff, and that is yet another reason why I think that all the sentimental guff about Mary that's crept into devotion to her is a serious distraction.

Here too is the ultimate act of humility and faith. It's very hard for post-modern people, especially males, to comprehend what Mary's choices implied. Right up until my mother's generation, which pre-dated modern contraceptive methods, women knew that marriage almost certainly meant child-bearing and thus the putting aside of any thoughts of independence or a career. Mary knows all that and much more. Notwithstanding she takes on social stigma, ridicule, vulnerability and the risk of loneliness. I can't begin to fathom the shadow side of her great elation in the Magnificat. I simply –

and truthfully – want to say 'Hail, Mary.' I want to say 'Blessed is the fruit of your womb, Jesus.' But I find myself swallowing hard at the phrase 'Mother of God'. Somehow it leaves everything upside down.

Dwight: Are you really banning 'Hail Holy Queen' from the celestial hymnbook? Think of all those disappointed Catholics! Seriously, the view of Mary you've just stated is understandable and attractive. I'm sure it is an acceptable position for most Anglicans and many Evangelicals. I want to congratulate you on actually taking Mary seriously rather than dismissing her out of hand. But let me challenge what you've said about Mary earlier on. I'll address the points in your order. First, I can understand a non-Catholic's fury and frustration at the prospect of the Catholic Church defining another dogma making Mary co-redemptrix and co-mediator with Christ. Personally, I hope the church doesn't define such a dogma because of the obstacle it would create in ecumenical relations. However, I do want to explain what we mean by such terms. We do not mean that Mary is a co-redeemer or co-mediator with Christ in such a way that she is equal to him. 'There is one mediator between God and man, the man Christ Jesus' (I Tim. 2:5). Mary is not another mediator. Instead we believe that she works with Christ for the redemption of the world. She mediates with Christ for the salvation of souls. As such she is a model of what we should all be doing. All of us are called to be 'God's co-workers' (I Cor. 3:9) and St Paul speaks of the possibility of 'completing what is lacking in Christ's afflictions' through the suffering in our own lives (Col. 1:24). In such a way we believe Mary co-operates with Christ for the salvation of the world. In doing so she shows the whole church how to share in his saving work.

I can understand your second point too. It looks like the Catholic Church has added lots of beliefs about Mary that are not substantiated by Scripture. I expect you'll pick up on one or two other items before we're finished, but let me first say that our Marian beliefs spring from the very earliest traditions of the church. Justin Martyr and Irenaeus – both writing in the second century – spoke of Mary as the 'new Eve'. As such she was considered totally pure.

Finally, you are unhappy with Mary because there was a 'cult of the girl' in ancient Rome. Your implication is that Mary is sort of like a good Catholic boy's pin-up. I'd be careful on this one. When you play the armchair psychiatrist and start finding deep sexual motivations for religious devotion it's a bit like opening Pandora's box. Before long you can theorise that homosexuals are attracted to muscular Christianity because they get to love the perfect man, and maybe Protestants, who can't stand Mary, have a mother-hatred complex. This kind of speculation is both sordid and specious. Furthermore, your theory doesn't account for the army of Catholic women who have a deep and abiding devotion to Mary. Anyway, for Catholics Mary has never been seen as the ideal wife or lover. Instead she is the ideal mother. When Jesus looked down from the cross at his beloved disciple and Mary he said, 'Woman, behold your son. Son, behold your mother.' We put ourselves in John's place and accept that maternal relationship with Mary which Jesus himself gave to his disciples.

I've been on the defensive here, and that's okay. But let me fire one back. In Luke 1:48 Mary says, 'From now on all generations will call me blessed.' Why do so many Evangelicals have this big Mary-block? You said we get emotional and our heads turn to putty when Mary comes up. I want to know why Evangelicals' heads and hearts both turn to stone when Mary comes up. Mary said 'all generations shall call me blessed.' Catholics rejoice to call her blessed. It's something we're enthusiastic about. So why do Evangelicals go all frosty and seize up?

John: Okay then. Perhaps all the stuff about the cult of the girl was a bit rough. I suppose it was an invitation to you to retaliate by trying to play therapist with one or two Protestant foibles. I'm glad you've resisted the temptation, for now at least.

Thank you for explaining the Catholic view of the role of Mary as co-redeemer and co-mediator. As with many bits of dogma, it's important to clear away misunderstandings so that the idea can be evaluated on its own terms. I suppose I have to say, grudgingly, that you have made the best possible case for a dogma which still leaves me uncomfortable. I'm glad that you for one see what an ecumenical liability it would be for the Catholic Church to go down the path of declaring Mary to be co-redeemer and co-mediator. Put on as plausible a 'spin' as you like, but for me it crowds the canvas in a domain that belongs to Christ alone.

Why do non-Catholics get so frosty and seize up when it comes to Mary? Perhaps it may be something to do with culture and taste, being spiritually underwhelmed amid a huge fuss. It's like visiting an exotic country, being invited to try one of the most famous local delicacies, only to find that you can't quite discern what it is that everyone's raving about. But I think there's more to it than that. We'll come to it when we get onto various other bits of Marian dogma.

Taken alone, all the different bits seem harmless enough. Take the dogma of the assumption of the Blessed Virgin. Yes, if Enoch or Elijah were transported directly into heaven, it doesn't seem the least bit unreasonable that this may have happened to Mary too. Her claims may indeed be greater than those of Enoch, whom we know very little about save that he joined God on occasional walks. For his part, Elijah was something of a man of blood and had some of the credentials of a manic depressive. But it's the way the Catholic Church gets to the dogma of assumption that troubles me. It all begins with an argument from silence. None of the early historians, beginning with Epiphanius, seems to know when and where Mary died. There is no tradition of a tomb for Mary. So once the church begins to speculate about Mary's role in salvation, a fragile but huge tower of cards begins to build up. She is the new virgin Eve, so we posit her perpetual virginity. As the new Eve she had to be sinless, so we have her immaculate conception. Then someone suggests that death comes through sin, so since Mary never sinned she must have escaped death. It's all very plausible, but there's not a shred of actual historical evidence to underpin all these ideas.

Dwight: You've stated the logic of it very clearly and succinctly. Thanks. About evidence – if Mary's body was taken up into heaven, as the tradition says, then there wouldn't be any evidence, would there? That's the point. The early church glorified the tombs of the apostles and venerated their bones. Given the traditions of the time, the fact that there is no tomb of Mary and no relics is pretty strong circumstantial evidence of the assumption of Mary into heaven.

John: Okay, but you can't build up a whole edifice on an argument from silence. Our belief in the resurrection, for example, includes the witness of contemporaries (see I Cor. 15). Data of this order about the assumption of Mary is simply non-existent. Let me go on to the issue of Mary's 'perpetual virginity'. From the New Testament there are three possible arguments against such a view. First, the word 'until' in Matthew 1:25 – Joseph and Mary did not make love 'until' the birth of Jesus – seems to imply that Mary and Joseph had marital relations after the birth of Jesus. Secondly, we are told that Jesus had brothers and sisters (Mt. 12:46-47; Mt. 13:55; Mk. 3:31-32; 6:3; Lk. 8:19-20; Jn. 2:12; 7:3, 5, 10; Acts 1:14). Lastly, Jesus is called Mary's 'firstborn' (Lk. 2:7), a point the redactors had plenty of time to adjust or change if needed.

Dwight: I don't really like getting into spats in which we sling Bible interpretations at one another, but there are some answers to your criticisms. Regarding Matthew 1:25 – it depends which translation you use. You're right that most translations say, Joseph did not have relations with Mary 'until' the birth of Jesus; but the main point of the verse is not to tell us whether Mary and Joseph ever made love, but that they hadn't before Jesus was born. In other words – this is a verse about the virgin birth – not the perpetual virginity of Mary. The Jerusalem Bible conveys this primary meaning. It says, 'he had not had intercourse with her when she gave birth.' Calling Jesus Mary's 'firstborn' doesn't necessarily mean there were other children. That was simply a technical term like 'the firstborn lamb'. It doesn't imply anything, one way or the other.

Finally, were the 'brothers of Jesus' referred to in the gospel the children of Mary and Joseph? Several things argue against this interpretation. First of all, in the Aramaic language the word 'brother' is used generally for kinsmen, cousins, uncles etc. They don't have a separate word in Aramaic for all these different relatives. Another example of this is where Abraham calls his nephew Lot his 'brother' (Gen. 13:8). Catholics have always argued that the 'brothers of Jesus' are simply his relatives – perhaps Joseph's sons by a previous marriage or the brothers of Mary or her nephews. A second point is that in the one incident of Jesus' childhood – when he was twelve years old – there is no mention of other children. The picture is of Jesus, Mary and Joseph. You claim earlier that the perpetual virginity of Mary conveys the wrong view of sexuality. This doctrine is not taught because Catholics think sex is nasty or dirty. It is maintained because it was the earliest tradition of the church and because it helps to explain the virgin birth. Think about it. If Mary and Joseph had had other children, would anyone have given any credence at all to the preposterous notion of the virgin birth? I doubt it. Jesus would simply have been Mary and Joseph's oldest boy.

John: Thanks for trying to clarify the issues. My comment would be that my case is bolstered precisely because of the kind of argument we're engaged in here. In the absence of an overwhelmingly clear tradition that is attested by contemporary eyewitnesses, the argument lives in a world of 'what if?' or 'yes but'. Going on, there is according to my reading hardly a shadow of an idea about the perpetual virginity of Mary among the early Fathers. There is not a hint in Clement of Alexandria or Tertullian. Origen floats the idea that Joseph may have been married and had children prior to his marriage to Mary and that Mary remained a virgin, not on the grounds of any evidence, but in his words that it 'is in harmony with reason'. Only when we get to Jerome, circa 335, do we see any attempt to flesh out the idea. It is done in the context of debate and speculation about the doctrine of salvation and a defence of Christian orthodoxy against various of the Gnostic sects. It's simply based on logical deductions from the speculations about how salvation accomplished. Of course, you can then go back and find there is Jewish precedent for being celibate while married – Moses may have been such a case – but that can do little more than create a plausibility factor.

Dwight: Sorry, but there is more about this in the early Fathers than you're letting on. The earliest evidence is the *Protoevangelium of James*. Written no later than 120AD it explains how and why Mary was a consecrated virgin. You've already mentioned Origen. If he defended it in the mid-third century it must have been known of earlier, mustn't it? Just after Origen the doctrine is very clearly stated. Hilary of Poitiers (315-367) asserts the perpetual virginity of Mary and Didymus (313-398) referred to her as 'ever virgin'. The doctrine was not only upheld by Jerome (342-420), but also by Ambrose (390) and defended by all the Eastern Fathers from the beginning of the fifth century.

John: I stand by my point. When Paul wrote of the resurrection there were people still alive who had witnessed the events and seen the risen Lord. This can't be said of Hilary or Didymus or Jerome or Ambrose, when this idea is beginning to be defined.

Let me try to explain how this happened. You can get an idea of why the Catholic Church has formed its Marian dogmas when you look more carefully at the way the early Fathers construed the doctrine of salvation. Take Justin Martyr's famous comment:

> [Christ] became man by the virgin, in order that the disobedience which began with the serpent might receive its destruction in the same manner as it derived its origin. For Eve, who was a virgin and undefiled, having conceived the word of the serpent, brought forth disobedience and death. But the virgin Mary received faith and joy when the Angel Gabriel announced the good tidings to her that the Spirit of the Lord would come upon her.

You can see from here how easy it was to create from this approach the edifice that both the Catholic and Eastern churches have built up. It's happy hunting ground for speculation, and contains not a small measure of romance. The great irony is that these ideas were offered to explain and defend the church's doctrine of salvation against its critics. Sadly, I think the ultimate result was to bring the doctrine of salvation into further disrepute by locking it into an obscure neo-Platonism. To put it another way, if I today were to try to construe a doctrine of salvation, I wouldn't start back there with Origen, Justin, Jerome and company! I suspect you wouldn't either, Dwight, but having embraced Catholicism then you are somewhat duty bound to include all this as part of the inherited furniture.

Dwight: You are taking us into different but very important territory here. You seem to be denigrating the development of Marian doctrines simply because they occurred in the fourth and fifth century. They weren't actually that late. Witness the *Protoevangelium of James*. Very early on the church was meditating on the role of Mary.

But there's an inner inconsistency with your thought. On the one hand I think you're suggesting that the Marian doctrines were elaborate and unnecessary. On the other hand, you've shown how the early theologians saw the Marian doctrines as crucial to a full understanding of the incarnation and salvation. You can't have it both ways can you? Either the Marian doctrines are elaborate, romantic speculation or they are a vital thread in the full tapestry of Christian theology.

I find the unity and inter-relatedness of Christian doctrine to be exciting. That the church reflected on Mary's person and role so very early is evidence that the Marian doctrines should be taken seriously. The fact of the matter is that the basic Marian beliefs developed very early within the theological development of the church. Protestants want to untangle all this and pull the Mary thread out of the whole tapestry. They want to say it was all a 'later development' by Catholics. The problem with this view however, is that other doctrines which conservative Protestants are keen to maintain were also developed at the same time, or even later. It's true that the church was reflecting on and formulating the basic Marian doctrines by the mid-fourth century. The problem is, the basic doctrines of the incarnation were also being formed at the same time. Just a bit later the doctrines of the Trinity were being hammered out. Furthermore, it was during the same century that the church authorities finally defined the canon of Scripture as we now have it. Protestants accept that church decision without question – indeed their whole edifice is constructed on it. If Protestants are happy to accept the theological development of the early church when it comes to the incarnation, the Trinity and the canon of Scripture, why do they reject the Marian doctrines which were developed and defined at the same time by the same theologians? Athanasius is a hero of the faith because he stood up for the incarnation. Well, Athanasius also called Mary 'ever-virgin'. Furthermore, it is only latter-day Evangelicals who reject the Marian dogmas. Luther, Calvin and Zwingli all believed in the perpetual virginity of Mary. Why do present day Evangelicals have such a problem?

You said the Marian beliefs were bound up in an obscure neo-Platonism which we carry as unfortunate baggage. Maybe you're right to a certain extent. I do think, however, that non-Catholics sometimes underestimate the freshness and vitality of Catholic theology. Since we allow for the development of doctrine we can always move on from a philosophy or worldview which has become outdated or obscure. Of course some early Christian writers were bound by their worldview or their philosophical assumptions. While we value their insights and wisdom, we are not bound by them. We are always trying to gather up the past and understand it in the present and in the light of the future.

The Marian doctrines in the Catholic Church illustrate perfectly how Catholics understand the Christian faith to be constantly unfolding. Non-Catholics sometimes criticise the fact that doctrine of the Immaculate Conception of the Blessed Virgin Mary was only defined in 1854 and that the doctrine of her assumption into heaven was defined in 1950. These doctrines are implied in Scripture and were there in kernel form in the early church. Through the centuries of prayer and reflection the church finally came to define them formally. As one reads church history it becomes clear that this development of doctrine didn't end at Pentecost. It didn't end at the Council of Nicaea. It didn't end in the fifth century or the fifteenth. Jesus promised his Spirit would be with the church until the end of time, and that he would continue to teach his disciples all things. We believe that God is still unfolding his truth to the world, and that the church has the authority to interpret that Truth and proclaim it for the salvation and redemption of the world.

When the church proclaims a dogma it is not simply a theological statement. Christian truth is always practical and relevant to the lives of ordinary people. The Marian truths show this most clearly. When we say Mary was conceived immaculately we mean she was conceived naturally by her parents, but by a special act of grace she was preserved from that tendency to fall into sin which every other person is born with. This 'immaculate conception' was necessary so that Mary could make a totally free choice to respond to God's invitation. If she'd had the usual tendency to choose selfishness and sin, then her choice would not have been totally free. This is why the early church fathers called Mary the second Eve – because like the first Eve, she had a free choice to obey or disobey God. This applies to us as well because, by virtue of our baptism we also are able to make a free choice to love and serve God. When we receive absolution we are able again to choose freely to obey God or not to obey. We constantly fall back into sin, but Mary shows us the possibilities of grace.

Her assumption into heaven also serves as an example to all of us. She shows us that the final result of our redemption is to be taken up into heaven to be glorified forever. Because she had a specially intimate relationship with Jesus she shows us what is possible for all those who wish to be one with him. She shared in his resurrection in a stupendous way and so gives us hope that we too shall rise on the last day.

In saying all this, I am not trying to preach too much, and I'm not trying to hammer people with Mary Mary Mary. I understand how the Evangelical still shakes his head and honestly says, 'I don't get it.' I am simply trying to share the enthusiasm Catholics have for Mary, and why she means so much to us. Mary is the example of the totally redeemed person. In her we see all that Jesus has done for the world, and all that he wants to do for each one of us.

John: We've hit one of those areas where we are going to have to agree to differ. I just can't buy a dogma that needs to be grounded in history but where for the first two or three centuries we only have silence to go on, after which there is a tentative trickle of speculation, leading finally to the statement of a doctrine. If we were to rely on this in the case for the resurrection we'd be laughed out of court. Nor do I find myself much moved by testimony that discovery of this seam of Marian doctrine has been a source of blessing. I can see that there may be spiritual blessing on offer but that is because the themes of obedience, grace, humility and so on are in themselves generic in the life of faith and will do their work on us if we allow it. I can recall having been much moved listening to Brethren preachers discerning all sorts of allegories about the person and work of Christ in the Tabernacle. The reason why I was so moved was that what they said about Christ was true, and the blessing was on offer in spite of the poor exegetical methods they deployed. In the case of Mary, in my view we have a story line that's flawed and which won't stand up to the rigours of critical historical scrutiny. So I should not feel compelled to believe it, though if I am of a certain temperament, perhaps it might have a place in my devotional imagination.

Chapter Eleven

The Reformation

Night and day I pondered until I saw the connection between the justice of God and the statement that 'the just shall live by his faith'. Then I grasped that the justice of God is that righteousness by which through grace and sheer mercy God justifies us through faith. Thereupon I felt myself to be reborn and to have gone through open doors into paradise. The whole Scripture took on a new meaning, and whereas before the 'justice of God' filled me with hate, now it became to be inexpressibly sweet…[1] Martin Luther

John: If my early years in faith were what might be best described as 'fundamentalist', my next years involved an exciting encounter with the high octane form of Christianity that is the Anglican Diocese of Sydney. For Sydney, the Reformation of the sixteenth century is the bedrock of everything that is important in Christianity. To this day, if a lay person does extension studies from Moore Theological college, Christian history studies begin not with the early Fathers (as in the Catholic and Anglo-Catholic traditions) but the Reformation. Taken alongside foundation courses in Old and New Testament and Systematic Theology, it is a powerful influence in the formation of the grass roots Christian activist from Sydney. So while I have been at great pains in the course of this book to demonstrate familiarity with the pre-

Reformation centuries of Christian history, I would still consider myself better schooled in the Reformation than anything else. Moreover, to this day I would say that its theological formulations provide me with the criteria against which I would judge other ideas in theology and church order.

Yet when I think about the Reformation, nearly a quarter of a century on from taking my leave of Sydney and coming to London, I find myself in sympathy with two contradictory lines of thought. The first is that the Reformation was one of those momentous misunderstandings, rather like a family row that gets out of control. A sharp word is blown out of all proportion. The rhetoric of both sides becomes more and more strident. Then, rather than lose face, both sides spend enormous energy justifying their position, using arguments that are increasingly extreme. In the end they take positions that are close to untenable and give the other side all the ammunition they need to pick off their position. The second is that a corrupt and pompous medieval church failed to appreciate a new mood in Western Europe, brought on by new ways of thinking and a communications revolution driven by the invention of the printing press. Rather than try to understand these new ways of thinking on their own terms, the medieval church tried to suppress it. The upshot was to shake Europe to its foundations, irrevocably dividing northern Europe from the south, and precipitating terrible wars and bloodshed that stand alongside the Crusades as the foremost scandals of Christian history.

Nevertheless every so often in Christian history there is a fresh wave of the Spirit and it throws up a new idea about how the Christian faith is understood and explained. I believe that this happened in the sixteenth century. Martin Luther discovered – perhaps it would be better to say rediscovered – something that met the deepest human need. This became a catalyst for the recovery of the place of the individual in a Western European society that was ripe for change. The old wineskins of the Holy Roman Empire were no longer able to contain the aspirations of a newly emerging culture. The medieval church, which fitted hand in glove with the old political order, found itself bewildered by the new forces at work. Only after a great fracture between north and south in Europe did it begin to try to come to terms with the changes and the new consciousness that created them. On the other hand, while the Reformation began as a piece of grass roots action, a monk in an obscure German town nailing a debating agenda on the doors of the local parish church, it too became politicised. In the Scandinavian countries, for instance, 'Reformation' was imposed from the top down with monarchs embracing new regimes of faith and order and the people more or less coerced into following. The English Reformation happened much later than the rest of northern Europe. A.G. Dickens has argued that the spiritual state of church and nation, both at national and local level, left it ripe for change. Others have contended that England was by nature and temperament a 'Catholic' country and as with Scandinavia the Reformation was imposed 'top down'.

I do not want to go into a whole lot of historical detail, but let me offer a reflection about the place of the Reformation in the respective consciousness of English Catholics and Protestants. I hope I will be able to set a keynote that enables us to get beyond the rhetoric and divisions of the Reformation and try to discover if common ground is possible.

Just about every day I drive down Prescot Street, London E1, a busy traffic precinct hidden away behind Aldgate High Street. Half way down stands a Catholic Church affectionately known by Catholic East Enders simply as 'English Martyrs'. Inside are memorials to hundreds of Catholics killed for their faith in the Reformation era. About a mile and a half away in Clerkenwell Green is the parish church of St James. Inside is a roll of honour to people who were burned at nearby Smithfield 'for the word of God and testimony of Jesus Christ'. The list stretches back to the Lollards of the twelfth century, but by far the biggest grouping is those who were burned at Smithfield under the persecution of Protestants by Queen Mary. Now there are, of course, other places in England that focus the distinct communal memories of Protestants and Catholics, Tyburn or the Oxford memorial to Bishops Ridley and Latimer. The point I want to make is that the lists in 'English Martyrs' and St James share no names in common. I take it, therefore that for over 400 years Protestant and Catholic communities in England have preserved and passed down to later generations distinctly different versions of the Reformation and its effects. We don't know each others' stories.

On many a wet Sunday afternoon I often used to choose for my reading *Foxe's Book of Martyrs*. It was, after all, much more lively fare than most other books prescribed by my parents. There are inspiring martyr stories from the early centuries, the venerable Polycarp, for example. But it is essentially an anti-Catholic tract. It recounts the chilling activities of the Spanish Inquisition. Wycliffe and the Lollards are claimed as part of a 'proto-Reformation'. But it is the account of the Marian persecution with high profile burnings that eventually claimed Archbishop Cranmer himself that is the main substance of the book. This book has been a major instrument for feeding anti-Catholic prejudice in England. The reader comes away with the impression that it is the Catholic Church that is the main persecutor and that only Protestants have suffered martyrdom and deprivation. This has become ingrained in English communal memory and may even be an ingredient in the current anti-European campaigning. The somewhat austere façade of 'English Martyrs' suggests that there may be more to the story. Dwight, what's your perspective?

Dwight: We may have had a copy of *Foxe's Book of Martyrs* at home, but I think I first came across it whilst I was at that fundamentalist university. In coming to England I was impressed with the Martyrs' Memorial in Oxford, and can remember going into the middle of Broad Street to find the plaque set in the road which marks the exact spot of the martyrdoms of Cranmer, Ridley and Latimer. Being brought up as an Evangelical and going to an evangelical Anglican college, I simply accepted the prevailing story of the Reformation. The Protestant martyrs were heroes of the faith who died at the hands of the wicked Catholic Church. As you've suggested, my teachers were strangely silent about what happened to the Catholics. I'm not blaming anyone. It's natural to take sides and genuinely not see the viewpoint of your opponent. That's why I'm grateful for your story about the two churches so close together which commemorate two different sets of martyrs.

Part of my journey to the Catholic Church included reading the monumental work of Cambridge historian Eamon Duffy. His book is called *The Stripping of the Altars* and it painstakingly compiles a huge amount of evidence to show that the pre-Reformation church in England was not the corrupt, clergy-ridden church painted by Protestant propagandists. There were problems, but by and large it was a healthy, vigorous church that was struggling to adapt to the new technologies and social structures. It was enlivened by hearty involvement of the lay people, who were surprisingly well-educated in their faith. It's a big door-stop of a book, but I recommend it to anyone for a fresh view of that period.

That changed my mind, but what made me really see things in a different light was a visit to Poland. I listened to the Catholics there telling me what it was like under communist rule. In Eastern Europe the communist state imposed a new religion – atheism. They closed the Catholic schools, confiscated monasteries and convents, took their land, stripped the riches from the churches, closed seminaries and forbade any kind of Catholic religion. Any resistance to this state-wide persecution of the church was seen as treason and disloyalty to the state.

Suddenly I saw the experience of English Catholics in a fresh way. As far as Catholics are concerned, the persecution of their religion in England was far worse than what happened under seventy or so years of communist rule in Eastern Europe. In England, for four hundred years, Catholics were persecuted by the state in a systematic, complete and oppressive way. Starting with Henry VIII, then under Edward VI and Elizabeth, their monasteries were closed and destroyed. Their churches were taken – lock, stock and barrel. Their land was given to the king's cronies. The churches were stripped and the rich ornaments melted down, vestments made into curtains and precious artwork hacked to pieces and burned. Monks and nuns were kicked out of their homes and pressured to marry. A new religion was imposed – the religion of the monarch. Any resistance was seen as treason and was punishable by torture and death. This systematic and total oppression of Catholicism continued, albeit in a less oppressive way, until the mid nineteenth century. A scrap of it still exists in the legislation which does not permit an heir to the throne to be Catholic or marry a Catholic.

It's natural for Catholics therefore to commemorate their own heroic martyrs. After fleeing the country, men like Edmund Campion actually came back into England as Jesuit priests to serve the Catholic community in secret. They were caught, then hung, drawn and quartered for treason, despite their constant declaration of loyalty to the Queen. These men were trapped in a catch-22 situation. If they came back into England openly they would be caught and killed as soon as they set foot in England. So they came in disguise, and since they were disguised they were perceived as spies, sneaks and secret plotters. The same thing happened to Christians under communist rule. If they met openly they were persecuted. If they met underground it proved they were spies and traitors.

I know I've painted in broad strokes here. In fact the whole situation was very complex. Politics and religion really were woven together, and it was difficult not to see Catholics as traitors when the Spanish king and the Pope were working together to launch a military invasion of England. But I've painted in broad strokes to try to convey the Catholic perspective. We don't really want them back, but some Catholics see all the ancient parish churches in England, which are now Anglican, as a painful reminder of what has happened.

That's the Catholic perspective. Putting that on one side, I agree with you. It's important for both sides to commemorate their martyrs. It is also important for both Protestants and Catholics to really listen to the stories of the other side. When I hear the stories of the Reformation martyrs now I see tales of heroic faith – full stop. I'm inspired by the Protestant martyrs just as much as I'm inspired by the Catholics. I think those who killed to defend either their religion or their kingdom are equally demonic. Perhaps this is the way forward – to catch a new vision altogether and see that the real enemies were the evil people who were willing to kill their brothers and sisters simply to preserve their own power. It that is so, then the enemies were not Protestants or Catholics, but killers and tyrants. Don't you think in Heaven all the martyrs who really gave their lives for their Lord Jesus Christ on both sides will be brothers and sisters? I do.

You mentioned Martin Luther. I like to compare Martin Luther to St Francis. Both men were driven by a fiery passion. Both men made a plea for simplicity of faith and practice in a church which was wealthy, powerful and corrupt. Both were accused of heresy. The political situations were completely different, but somehow in the twelfth century Francis was able to stay within the church, but in the sixteenth Luther was not. Francis sparked a renewal movement in the church which continues today. Luther broke away. I'm sure part of the problem was on both sides, but how much better it would have been if the strengths and good insights of Luther and the other Reformers had been kept within the unity of the Catholic Church. The division has been terrible. As a former Evangelical I miss the good things of evangelicalism on a regular basis. I feel Protestants miss out on an enormous amount by being separate from the ancient Catholic Church, but Catholics are poorer too for having lost so many of our brothers and sisters in the faith.

I want to talk about two recent events which have helped to heal the divide. One of these is the concordat between Lutherans and Catholics on justification which was signed in 1999. I hope we'll come to that, but first I want to challenge you a little. In March of the year 2000, the Pope led seven cardinals of the church in an astounding service of contrition in St Peter's. In the service they read out a list of sins against others which Catholics had been guilty of down through the ages. The Pope publicly admitted the sins of the church during the Reformation age and asked forgiveness of God and from those who were still offended by the terrible events. To my mind this was a humbling, courageous and remarkable public apology. I wonder what you think about that event, but I also wonder when we are going to have a similar event led perhaps by the Archbishop of Canterbury or even the Queen – who is, after all, the titular head of the Anglican Church.

John: Wow. I've found responding in other parts of this book intellectually challenging. Often we've laughed together. Maybe now it's time for some tears. Eamon Duffy's magis- terial work is unanswerable in general and in detail. If readers don't feel inclined to take his word, then look at the relevant sections in Jeremy Paxman's remarkable book *The English*. Paxman has no special axe to grind. His account and commentary on English bloodthirstiness in the matter of the Catholic persecutions is an eye opener. It helps puncture myths that the English tend to want to believe about themselves, in particular that they are a compassionate people who value fair play above all else. Events in Continental Europe were of course a somewhat different story.

Let me add a haunting anecdote about what happened when Henry dissolved the monasteries. In London, St Thomas' and St Bartholomew's Hospitals were originally monastic foundations caring for the sick. The upshot of Henry's order was that the sick were literally thrown out on the street. That's a matter of public record. It took some time for the civic authorities to make arrangements for their care. But this act had wider ramifications. It was tantamount to closing down the National Health Service, training and research functions included. It left a huge vacuum and it took a long time before medicine could get back on its feet. Eventually medical research and training re-emerged, but in the first instance it did so over the borders in the relative safety of Edinburgh. What folly.

Taking another perspective, my wife and I have the good fortune of having a Spanish friend whose academic career has focused on the Spanish Armada of 1588. She put together an exhibition in London marking the 400th anniversary of that event. In secondary school history, we are encouraged to accept uncritically nonsenses like how the tiny English ships were somehow able to get underneath the guns of the Spanish galleons. It's a great challenge to be faced with a thoughtful and measured Spanish perspective.

In this chapter we already seem to have turned over some stones and found some horrible realities beneath them. So, then, should the Queen or the Archbishop of Canterbury take a lead from the Pope and utter a series of public *mea culpas* in this matter? For my part I'm reluctant to prescribe this specific route. It's very fashionable to issue apologies for events past, and I'm not entirely convinced as to the value of this. As a white Australian, there is the constant issue of the treatment of our indigenous peoples and calls for apologies and reparations. I'm not quite sure, for instance, how I can make valid apologies for events set in train even before the time of my great-great grandparents? I know Christians who are taking it on themselves to apologise for the Crusades. Others feel the need to apologise for the apartheid years in South Africa. Still more want to utter apologies for sins of the colonial past. Where does it all end?

Then we have a situation where grass-roots Christians in the United Kingdom and Western Europe are already deeply discouraged by the trends of decline in the fortunes of the church. Cynical race that the English are, we expect that any such gesture would be greeted with scorn. That would hardly be a morale booster.

But I sense there needs to be some form of closure, if nothing else so as to enable the Catholic Church in England to experience a sense of healing and be released to move on. If it were to be done, I suspect the person best placed to offer some kind of gesture would be our present Queen. If it was she who took a lead, I also suspect many of the voices that would otherwise howl criticisms might hold their tongues out of respect for the combination of the office and Her Majesty's personal credibility. What the exact gesture should be I do not know. I have no idea how receptive the Royal household would be to the idea, nor who might put the proposition. I certainly think it's a future topic for ecumenical talks.

Having said all this, I need to make one or two points both as a response to what you said about the pre-Reformation English church and concerning the violence surrounding the Reformation. I suspect there will be an almost eternal debate among the historians as to the exact health of the pre-Reformation church. We know from the 400 years following the Henrican revolution that the spiritual and moral state of the church ebbed and flowed. There can be no doubt that at the time the Wesleys emerged on the English scene, the Church of England had hit one of its all-time lows. Many of the clerical elite weren't doing their jobs. Great cities like Manchester had emerged with the onset of industrialism but the parish system had not been adjusted to take this on board. He may be classified as a hostile witness, but if you read the writings of William Tyndale, Bible translator and one of the highest-profile Protestant martyrs, you don't come away with an overwhelming admiration for the quality of leadership that the church of the time was receiving from the bishops and officials from Rome.

Then Henry's divorce petition brought forth papal duplicity and ineptitude. Citing other authorities in *The Church of England, Where it's Going*, Monica Furlong shows that there had been several royal divorces with papal authorisation in the two hundred years before Henry, some of them for no stronger basis than personal incompatibility. So why did the Pope say no this time round? No small part of the answer was that he couldn't find a way to be above the politics of Europe. All sorts of factors made if prudent to take the side of Spain. This was home to Henry's estranged wife, Catherine of Aragon, and the Pope felt vulnerable to the armies of Catherine's nephew, Charles V.

Once the break with Rome had come, and it was decreed that the Pope had no jurisdiction in England, the position of the Catholics was precarious indeed. The temporal claims of Rome meant that Catholics were construed as being loyal to a foreign power. In a regime that spoke of itself as one nation united under one faith and one king, the implications for Catholics were dire. And the early papal responses to Henry's new regime stoked up the inferno. The terms of the excommunications of Henry and later Elizabeth, with pronouncements that this action released English citizens from their allegiance, was a death warrant for loyal Catholics. They were powerless in the face of the state security systems. Nor were they in any position to fend off the effects of the state propaganda arm that quickly learned to put the strongest possible anti-Catholic 'spin' on events like the Spanish Armada or the Gunpowder Plot.

There was craziness on both sides. One example I often cite is how the English monarchs, having finally accepted Tyndale's case for the creation of a Bible in the English vernacular, utterly refused to allow the same to happen in Ireland. Now there is one of the great 'what ifs' in the Reformation story.

By the way, I found your comparison of Luther with Francis very interesting. I've always admired Luther, not least because he is the most transparently human personality among the Protestant reformers.

Dwight: I accept your points about 'craziness on both sides.' I don't think the Catholic leadership responded well to the challenge of the Reformers. They were too caught up in temporal power and politics. Likewise, some of the Reformers themselves had rather too much interest in temporal power and political alliances. Think of Luther throwing in his lot with the German princes and Calvin setting up his own government in Geneva. I hope as we enter a new millennium, we can all begin to leave the 'craziness' behind and work and pray for a new unity within Christ's church.

Serious ecumenical work has been going on now for about forty years. The grass roots work is just as important as the high-level agreements amongst theologians. I don't know about you, but I don't think this is a task that will be accomplished overnight. We've already been working at it for nearly half a century. We may not be finished for another half century. Nevertheless there have, and continue to be, some remarkable milestones along the way.

One of the milestones which I find most promising is the *Joint Declaration on Justification* which was signed by Lutherans and Catholics in 1999. The declaration was the result of many years' work by an international commission of Catholic and Lutheran theologians. The two sides were able to say, 'This declaration shows that a consensus in basic truths of the doctrine of justification exists between Lutherans and Catholics.'[2] During the Reformation and Counter Reformation both sides had issued formal condemnations of the opposite side. In 1999 they were able to say, 'The teaching of the Lutheran churches presented in the Declaration does not fall under the condemnations from the Council of Trent. The condemnations in the Lutheran Confessions do not apply to the teaching of the Roman Catholic Church presented in this declaration...the earlier mutual condemnations do not apply.'[3] The whole document is a profound, biblically based meditation on justification. It was worked on very carefully by the highest authorities in both churches and is the fruit of much study, prayer and listening.

I know this isn't the end of the story. The declaration itself is a theological document. It is limited in its scope. Both sides agreed that further work needs to be done, and continued joint study and prayer is required. Nevertheless, the declaration is an astounding step forward. If the Lutheran view of justification influenced the whole evangelical movement, then this new declaration ought also to influence every Evangelical. The basic message is: Catholics and Protestants no longer disagree on the basics of justification. Do you agree that Evangelicals, if they haven't done already, need to take a serious look at this document?

John: Sadly, speak of justification and these days an alarming number of people brought up in the evangelical stable are just as likely to think you're talking about word processing: whether to square off the right side of the page or leave the ends ragged! Of course, as I've mentioned in an earlier chapter, the Anglican-Roman Catholic International Commission (ARCIC) published *Salvation and the Church*[4] where the main aim was to address justification. Catholic-Lutheran official dialogue overall has been far more heavyweight than its Anglican-RC counterpart. ARCIC, I think, made the mistake of creating the impression that the sixteenth-century dispute over justification was all a misunderstanding. Evangelicals who care about doctrine will never buy that position. For my part I would not want to see Luther's position, particularly, relativised away. At stake, as I said above, was how the human race's deepest need, being put right with God, was to be met. The great thing about the Catholic-Lutheran document is that it digs more deeply and it's pushed the Catholic Church far harder than ARCIC managed. I think the Lutherans, who generally display more theological rigour than Anglicans, have managed to push the Catholic Church far harder. I think the outcome is impressive.

Dwight: Good observations. I agree.

John: Another comment on the 'craziness on both sides' theme. Take, for example, the treatment of the Anabaptists by the continental reformers. Having, mercifully, escaped punishment themselves, in no time it seems they were using inquisitional tactics against these people. Likewise, when their radical wing started to build on the implications of the reformer's doctrine of freedom and incited the peasants of the Black Forest to rise in revolt against their overlords, to his eternal shame Luther counselled sending in the army and terrible bloodshed followed. There was the spectre of the Saxon Visitation, and other inquisitional acts to ensure that people were 'on message'. Then Calvin's Geneva became an oppressive tyranny, among whose acts included execution of the dissenter Michael Servetus. It reinforces my strongly held view that faith and political power are a highly dangerous mixture. The point is borne out today in the context of Afghanistan where the Taleban are perpetrating a deadly trail of vandalism, terror and oppression in the name of doctrinal orthodoxy.

For me, a big question is whether the world and the church can learn the lessons of history and in the twenty-first century help build a world that truly honours the way of the Prince of Peace. My attitude to Catholics is one small litmus test of whether I truly honour Christ and am 'on board' with him in bringing 'shalom' in the place of anger, hatred, war and death.

For readers fiercely loyal to the Reformation, that means willingness to honestly consider what I've pinpointed as some of its failings, rather than hastening to accuse me of selling out. Dwight, a fly on the wall during our many hours of conversation that have accompanied the creating of this book and the radio series that goes with it, would attest that straight-talk has been one of its main hallmarks. I know I've occasionally thrown a dirty punch, and that I regret. I've also known what it means to have put my faith and my whole life on the line to honest scrutiny. There have been uncomfortable moments, but I believe that what we have set out to do honours Christ as the Lord of the church for which he suffered and died. The former Bishop of Chester, Michael Baughen, is fond of saying that facing our differences requires us to be 'G&T Christians' – people who keep grace and truth in proper proportion. I think I've learned a bit more about what that's all about.

Dwight: I'm totally with you. You've made me remember what grace and truth are in the evangelical way, and made me see again how much the Catholic Church 'has a piece missing' because of the sad divisions between us. I've enjoyed our 'scraps' because they've been frank and good-humoured. We haven't pulled any punches, but that's okay.

You've sometimes expressed a worry that you haven't 'stood up to the Catholics' enough to please hard line Evangelicals. If it makes you feel better, I expect I haven't been rigorous enough to please the hard line Catholics either. Just like there are some Evangelicals who think Catholics are a pagan cult, I'm afraid there are some Catholics who still regard all Protestants as heretics fit for burning. I guess you know why Catholics burnt Protestants in the old days? They believed by delivering their bodies to fire here they might just deliver their souls from eternal fire. This is the crazy thing – they convinced themselves that by burning people they were doing them a favour. Figure that one out! My point is that I fear there might be a few Catholics who still hold this view. They don't burn anybody at the stake, but they believe all the Prots are headed for hell.

A Catholic bishop (now quite a 'big name' on the Catholic scene) once said to me, 'I believe the age of Reform is over.' He didn't mean that in the new millennium all the Reformed churches would just die out and everybody would become Catholic again. The history of the Holy Spirit never moves backward. He meant something bigger – that Christ's church has been through a terrible time of pruning in the last five hundred years, that what we call the Reformation is only one part of that pruning, and that the whole process has been much bigger and has included the effects of the discovery of the new world, the missionary movements, the Counter-Reformation, the 'Enlightenment' and the terrible events of the twentieth century. He hinted that we are moving forward into an exciting new phase of the Christian story. He's said publicly that this is a time of 'hope and joy' for the church. I'm sure if the Spirit is bringing us into this new era, then church unity will be high on the agenda. How and when that will happen still remains to be seen. There is still a lot to play for. The stakes are high, and how it all turns out depends on how we co-operate with the Holy Spirit. That's what makes the whole enterprise endlessly fascinating and incredibly exciting.

---

1 Martin Luther at the Diet of Worms in H.C. Bettenson, *Documents of the Christian Church*, based on Luther's *Opera Latina*, (Frankfurt, 1865-73)

2 L'Osservatore Romano, (24 November 1999), p5, *Joint Declaration on the Doctrine of Justification*, para 1

3 As above

4 *Salvation and the Church:* Agreed statement of the Anglican-Roman Catholic International Commission, (London: Church House/ Catholic Truth Society, 1988)

Chapter Twelve

The Future Church

Dwight: When I came to England over twenty years ago I left a rather narrow band of Christianity for something I thought was bigger and older. I wanted to be part of the 'ancient church in England.' Some people thought I was betraying my evangelical upbringing. They thought I was turning my back on all I had been taught and rejecting the truth. I didn't see it that way. For me, becoming an Anglican was not a denial of what I had before, but an addition to it. I wanted to keep all the good traditions of my evangelical background, I simply wanted more than that. C.S. Lewis had spoken of 'mere Christianity'. I wanted 'more Christianity'.

From my family I had picked up a positive world view. With it was a form of Christianity which was devout, loving and open to the Spirit – despite the narrow sectarian world in which we lived. This openness to all God might have in store gave me the courage and interest to seek more of his goodness within the Anglican Church. It was the same force which eventually brought me into the Catholic Church. In the Catholic Church I have found a universality and antiquity which I see now I was looking for within Anglicanism. Again – it isn't so much a denial of all the good things in Anglicanism as an addition and amplification of them. In my experience, what was good in evangelicalism and Anglicanism is magnified and completed within Catholicism.

I'm saying this not to be triumphalistic. I'm certainly not perfect and I don't pretend that the Catholic Church is humanly perfect. We have lots of problems. I'm also not saying this in order to twist people's arms to convert. If the Spirit leads others to seek full communion with the ancient yet ever youthful church of Rome that's marvellous, but that's not my first aim. Instead I am sharing my own experience in the modest hope that it might be a paradigm not only for others, but for the whole church. As we move into the new millennium of the Christian age I wish all Christians could put the enmity of the past behind them and move into 'more Christianity'.

The world is getting smaller every day. More and more people are travelling and learning firsthand about other cultures, religions and peoples. World religions are mixing and moving and learning from one another. With new communications, a global economy and an integral system of finance the catchphrase 'global village' makes more and more sense. I can see that the Christian church is moving in this direction too. In the new millennium our five hundred year old Catholic-Protestant problems will simply not make sense. They will be seen as hopelessly tied to outmoded expressions of truth, outmoded political identities and outmoded ways of communication and worship. As these cultural shifts occur it seems impossible for the Christian church not to come into closer union.

I know this is a problem for many people. Conservative-minded Catholics fear the possibility of giving away the ancient patrimony of the faith. Conservative-minded Protestants fear being swallowed up by that old dragon, the Church of Rome. I don't think either scenario is necessary. I wish we could leave behind our suspicions, our fears and our prejudices and see that God is always bringing us into something better – not something worse. One of my guiding mottos is a little saying by the Anglican thinker, F.D. Maurice – 'A person is most often right in what he affirms and wrong in what he denies.' This means seeing the best in all things and trying to gather up all that is good and true wherever it is, while rejecting all that is negative and destructive wherever it is. For me this is the true spirit of Catholicism. It is also the true spirit of the Christian church, and is the same Spirit that came down to us at Pentecost.

Many people feel that the church is moving into a kind of new Pentecost. Cardinal Newman called it 'the second Spring'. If the Holy Spirit really is bringing us into a 'second Spring' or a new Pentecost, then surely we must move forward with a sense of faith and hope. A valuable story in this context is told in Acts 10. Peter has a dream in which he sees unclean animals. His religion forbids him to eat such creatures, but the voice in the vision says, 'Rise, Peter, kill and eat.' Being a good Jew, Peter rebels against such a command. But in the end he accepts this new law as from God. What interests me is that Peter is being commanded to go against all his religious instincts and reach out in trust and faith to welcome the Gentiles into the church. His action was controversial and his brothers in the faith took a fair bit of convincing. I don't think it's any mistake that it was Peter who had this experience. The present successor of Peter has been pretty revolutionary in his ideas and actions, and I wouldn't be surprised if the next Pope takes some pretty radical decisions too. I only hope the whole church – Catholics and Protestants alike – will be able to respond with creativity, vision and obedience to the call of the Spirit in the years to come.

I believe part of the call will be for Catholics to continue re-examining the rich heritage and traditions of non-Catholic Christians. Likewise, a new generation of Evangelicals will need to continue discovering the riches of the Catholic tradition. This will require courage, vision and obedience, like it did for Peter. But the rewards will be great and will help to bring us together again. When I speak in these terms my evangelical friends sometimes get defensive. They suspect I'm doing a charm offensive – a little amateur spin doctoring. They want to know what I really think. They press me to show my hand and admit that what I really want is for all non-Catholics to convert and come under the thumb of the Pope once more.

The fact is, I'm not sure that is the way forward. I think the Pope has to have some sort of role to play as a leader of the whole church, but how that happens, and what form that leadership takes, is open to discussion. What I'm convinced of, is that both sides need to step out in faith, looking for a fresh way forward together. I actually see many signs of this happening already. Do you agree? You've worked more closely with the Anglican power structure, and you know the evangelical world better than I do. Do you see signs of this happening already or am I being naïve and indulging in some serious fantasising here?

John: As I've worked on this project, I've often rehearsed scenarios for the stage we've reached now. It might have been time for something dramatic, like an announcement from me that I'd put in train becoming a Catholic, or convinced I'd won all the arguments, my issuing an invitation to you to join my side.

Something very different has taken place. We've become friends. When we've met for face-to-face dialogue, it's been lively and full of wit. There's been what my ecumenical friends call a 'convergence'. A generation ago the ecumenical movement shifted emphasis away from merger talks. This emphasis, begun in earnest after World War Two, had consumed vast amounts of time but yielded few tangible results. So instead of focusing on merger schemes, the ecumenical movement tried to reinvent itself by encouraging Christians at all levels to find ways to understand each other better. The underlying conviction was that by relating in this way, Christians would realise that what they held in common was far greater than what divided them. I think this has happened in the course of writing this book and making the series of accompanying broadcasts.

As a teenager, I remember seeing the film *Martin Luther* and I can keenly remember snatches from it. I recall yelping with delight when the radicals went on a rampage, smashing statues and other church artefacts and being amazed when Luther upbraided them. Obviously my spiritual formation had left me with more in common with the Anabaptists and radicals than with mainstream Lutheranism.

Dwight: Why read theology into it? Maybe you were just a rambunctious kid who was thrilled to have a bit of action in an otherwise dull religious flick.

John: Well, that too, plus the theology. I was a very serious-minded kid. Anyway, I then recall being utterly amazed at a reconstructed conversation between the young Luther and his confessor. The soon-to-be reformer questions why the church insisted on worship in Latin. I found the answer utterly unconvincing: Latin was a universal language and had served the church well, so why change? According to my spiritual formation, for worship to be in spirit and in truth it needs to be in my native tongue and should preferably be spontaneous, not printed in a book. Later, at university, I learned a lot more about Johannes von Staupitz, Luther's confessor. Here was a man of great compassion and insight and happily history now judges him in a far more favourable light than my recollections of the film. Most memorable of all, however, is the scene at the Diet of Worms in 1521. The powers that be demand that Luther should recant his writings. The camera zooms in as he answers:

> Unless I am convinced by Scripture and plain reason ... I do not accept the authority of popes and councils, for they have contradicted each other ... my conscience is captive to the Word of God. I cannot and will not recant anything, for to go against conscience is neither right nor safe. Here I stand. I cannot do otherwise. God help me. Amen.[1]

Over the last few months I have felt great empathy with Luther. I have had some hard things to say about the faith in which I was brought up and I fear that my motives may be misunderstood. Then as one used to being wheeled out by Evangelicals as a media spokesman, and having been entrusted with the job of editing *The Church of England Newspaper*, I sense that some members of this constituency may mutter than I've sold out.

In his statement at Worms, Luther appeals to reason, to conscience and to the word. I would take my stand there too over my role in this enterprise. However, I'm well aware, like St Paul, that I reason only in part and so what I've said is in at least one important aspect provisional. I would concede, too, that even though I'd claim to be a life-long student of the word, the emphasis is on student. I have no doubt that the word has much to teach me still, not least on those texts that touch on the great controversies between Catholics and Evangelicals. Therefore conscience has emerged as supremely important. When I have been tempted to score a debating point rather than offer an honest answer, conscience has come to the fore.

Dwight: I hope we have both been honest and resisted scoring points. I appreciate your irenic style and I don't think you've sold out at all. You've been very articulate in expressing just where many Evangelicals are at the dawn of the new millennium.

Allow me a little grumble about Luther's courageous statement. I saw the movie too. I remember the scene well. It makes excellent drama. We Catholics thrill to a similar scene in the film *A Man for All Seasons* in which Thomas More stands up on trial in England and makes an eloquent and courageous confession of his faith. The two are well compared because the two heroes state clearly the position of the two sides. Luther, in all sincerity, stuck up for the word of God, reason and individual conscience. Thomas More sticks up for the authority of the church. I want to echo the point I made in our discussion on authority. This is the bottom line. Where do we turn for the final answer? Luther – for all his courage and eloquence – is sticking up for what is essentially individual reason, individual interpretation of the word of God and individual conscience. These are important, but if they are the final source of authority then every man's a pope and the result is continual division in the body of Christ, heterodox doctrine and schism. Christ prayed for his church to be one. For me the full unity of the church can be found in full communion with the ancient Church of Rome.

John: Okay. I hear you. I think we've made a lot of progress, but I have to honestly tell my Catholic readers where my conscience leads me as far as they are concerned. There still remain three huge barriers. Each one of them is being worked on at the highest level of theological reflection and official ecumenical dialogue. The trouble is that the Catholic Church is a big ship and there can be a huge gap between the best Catholic thinkers and, say, the parish priest in my local area whose ecumenical thought world extends little further than the anathemas of the Council of Trent.

First, the issue of the pope and his authority remains. I don't want to go back over the ground we covered earlier. I simply have to reiterate that I cannot accept that any human can claim that their utterances should be deemed infallible. I know you have blown a lot of air into the issue of papal infallibility, but for me it remains a barrier. I think there are myriads of Protestants, Evangelicals, charismatics and pentecostals who would say 'Amen' to that.

Then we have Mary. I think this issue is even more vexed than the question of papal authority where there has been at least some ecumenical convergence. This is not least because there seems to be a rampant pro-Mary lobby group within the Catholic Church, who seem determined to put even more clear blue water between themselves and people who already find the Catholic position on Mary difficult, if not impossible.

Finally, I believe there remains an issue that takes us back to the justification debates of the sixteenth century. Some will say I've sold the pass by suggesting that some Evangelicals have made too much of the outward show of 'making a decision'. But I want to insist that there must be a way on this side of the grave for me to know that I belong to Christ. Evangelicals in various dialogues have tried to safeguard this by insisting on 'the necessity of personal conversion'. St Paul believed it was possible to know and experience salvation in the here and now, 'If you confess with your mouth the Lord Jesus, and believe in your heart that God has raised him from the dead, you will be saved' (Rom 10:9-10). The Catholic Church has, I believe, moved a long way in this debate, which I see as a great sign of hope. I think it will move even more.

There's another point and I'm sorry to raise it as what appears almost to be an afterthought. I remain concerned that in at least some predominately Catholic countries, minority Christian groups and other faith communities live with a degree of second-class citizenship. There are even reports of persecution, even from France. This grows out of another of the themes I have returned to quite often: when the church gets political power it can often, perhaps even unwittingly, abuse it.

You have suggested that you believe the church is moving towards some sort of new Pentecost. I have to say that while I genuinely welcome much of the reform that's discernible in the Catholic Church, I don't feel as hopeful. One reason why I assert the futility of Catholic claims such as that of papal infallibility is that the thought world that brought them into being is now passing away. We are already witnessing an alarming erosion of the size and influence of the church in the Western world. The post-modern person indulges a pick'n'mix spirituality. They will not be constrained by popes, patriarchs or any person to whom an earlier generation would accord the status of an authority figure. So the institutional base of the church is eroding fast and at an increasing rate. I do not buy the idea that the Catholic Church is exempt from this. When I first visited Rome in 1980 I learned that in the previous year the local diocese had produced just two candidates for the priesthood and one had died of old age while in training. I know things ebb and flow and the achievements of some of the Catholic Church's lay movements are considerable, though I find many of them quite reactionary, both in theology and politics. Then, people tell me that the hope of the institutional churches lies with Christians from the so-called Third World. Again, I'd like to believe that but I'm not convinced. Visit a city like Lagos or Nairobi and you find that the very same forces at work eroding the church in the West are working there too.

Dwight: Maybe, maybe not. History shows that the pendulum swings back and forth. Is the present climate anti-authoritarian, subjective, post-modernist and pick 'n' mix? All the more reason to propose that there is a greater and greater hunger for authority, truth and reason. If every other source of authority and reason and truth is eroded to nothing, it's arguable that the Christian faith is ready to step into the vacuum.

History also shows that the church of Christ has tremendous resilience and the ability to pick herself up, dust herself off, and march on. Time and again the church has been persecuted from without and troubled by corruption within. Then the Spirit has blown. The fires of repentance have burned and often through great pain and turmoil she has been renewed and reformed. Come on John, the Lord said the gates of hell will not prevail against his church. Where's your optimism?

John: I hear that text all the time from leaders of the Anglican Church who refuse to admit to the deep institutional crisis we're in. Change is possible. But it's tough, and I don't see many church leaders with the stomach for it. When he was President of the USSR, Mikhail Gorbachev likened the Soviet system to a massive ocean liner. Turning it around involved an enormous manoeuvre. Others, like the Anglican evangelist Robert Warren, have said that the church is long overdue for a visit to the garage for an MOT. I don't find either analogy helpful. More radical measures are needed. One of my problems with the current crop of Christian leaders is that they seem to be in denial about the deep crisis that the Western church is in. We need to realise that in the economy of God, it is often when things are at their lowest, and people realise it, that the voices of the prophets begin to be heard and new shoots begin to appear.

We have seen how church merger talks have sometimes succeeded in exhausting an entire generation with nil outcomes. I don't know whether we have the luxury of a generation to put things right with the institutional church. The first Pentecost was ignited by a tiny group of people who already knew from the events surrounding the death of their founder that trying to change the old system was absolutely futile.

But I don't want to dwell on a negative note. I want to propose a way forward for Catholics and Evangelicals, not on the basis of theological debate or even sharing stories, but on the basis of the way we treat each other and the way we present the beliefs and concerns of the other side. The place to look for a cue is neither official Catholic-Lutheran nor Anglican-Catholic dialogue. The real cutting edge stuff is to be found among the findings of the official Catholic-Pentecostal dialogue. As you will know, Pentecostalism has burgeoned, not least in South America which used to be the exclusive domain of the Catholic Church. These two traditions probably represent at least three-quarters of the total number of the world's Christians.

Their Final Report (1990-97)[2] pledges both sides to refrain from:

- all ways of promoting our own community of faith that are intellectually dishonest, such as contrasting an ideal presentation of our community with the weaknesses of another Christian community;
- all intellectual laziness and culpable ignorance that neglect readily accessible knowledge of the other's tradition;
- every wilful misrepresentation of the beliefs and practices of other Christian communities;
- every form of force, coercion, compulsion, mockery or intimidation of a personal, psychological, physical, moral, social, economic, religious or political nature;
- every form of cajolery or manipulation, including the exaggeration of biblical promises, because these distortions do not respect the dignity of persons and their freedom to make their own choices;
- every abuse of the mass media in a way that is disrespectful of another faith and manipulative of the audience;
- all competitive evangelisation focused against other Christian bodies (c.f. Rom. 15:20).

Now if we could get our readers, Catholic and non-Catholic, to pledge to treat one another in that way, I think this whole exercise will have been worthwhile.

Dwight: I'll sign up. I think we agree about the value of the different high level talks between Rome and the different religious groups. Rome has initiated discussions not only with the Pentecostals, but with the Anglicans, with a confederation of Evangelicals, with the Lutherans as well as the different Orthodox groups.

While these initiatives are necessary and good, there has to be more than this. In addition to the official discussions there have been several startling initiatives on an unofficial level. In 1994 the well known American evangelical Charles Colson launched a consultation with Catholic theologian Richard John Neuhaus called *Evangelicals and Catholics Together*: From that consultation came two documents: *The Christian Mission in the Third Millennium* and *The Gift of Salvation*.[3] The statement recognised the already existing partnership between Evangelicals and Catholics in the areas of mission, social responsibility, sexual ethics and the defence of Christian belief. Evangelicals and Catholics are realising that even in the area of doctrine, they agree on far more than they disagree. When they fight each other they're wasting time and bullets shooting their own troops. A conservative evangelical hero – the scholar J Gresham Machen – spent many years fighting the relativistic and destructive liberal Protestant scholars. He understood the wide gap between Evangelicals and Catholics, but he observed, 'Profound as it is, the gap seems almost trifling compared to the abyss which stands between us and many ministers of our own church.'

Leading Catholic theologians are also recognising the need to build a common future with Evangelicals. In a quote which might have given us the title for this book, Cardinal Avery Dulles has said the Catholic Church needs:

> …To welcome the more traditional and conservative churches into the dialogue. For the Catholic Church it may not prove easy to reach a consensus with the conservative evangelicals, but these churches and communities may have more to offer than some others because they have dared to be different. Catholics have the right and duty to challenge the adequacy of some of their positions, but they should be invited to challenge Catholics in their turn.[4]

I hope this book and our own radio discussions have made a small contribution to the wider discussion. I also hope our conversations may prompt our readers to initiate their own talks with their opposite numbers on the local level. Maybe our own discussions can continue as well. Who knows, I might convert you yet!

John: Don't hold your breath! I have no doubt, however, that the map of world Christianity will be redrawn radically during the next generation and in my lifetime I expect to be part of something quite different from what pertains now. In Anglican terms, except perhaps in rural areas, the ideal of the parish is dead. So too is our Anglican insistence on territorial jurisdictions. These things tie up rather than release resources and inhibit the extension of the gospel. We are set in a culture that is seeking spiritual answers. Sadly, the church is just about the last place they would go for answers. As well as inhabiting physical communities, the church of the future will need to learn to be incarnational in cultures that exist around us but don't fit in with what goes on inside our buildings, and should never be expected to.

In the area where I live in east London we have few choices but to create strategic alliances with the Catholics, who have fewer church buildings than we do but whose congregations are stronger. Likewise, it is the various forms of Pentecostalism that have sprung up around us which have great energy and evangelistic zeal. I believe our community would be best served not by church mergers but by each of these traditions being prepared to thoroughly endorse one another and contribute what they do best from the basis of their distinct traditions.

Evangelicals of a number of varieties have voiced suspicions about the Evangelical-Catholic accords that underlie *Evangelicals and Catholics Together: The Christian Mission in the Third Millennium*. Predictably, of course, the Protestant supremacists will have nothing to do with it. Then there are Evangelicals such as South American Rene Padilla, one of the main voices in the Lausanne Movement, who tells me he fears it's an instrument of the Religious Right.

For some years now I sensed the possibility of a re-alignment in world Christianity that will bring Catholics and Evangelicals much closer together. It's clear, for instance that both traditions share more in common than most of their adherents realise. There is certainly more in common between Evangelicals and Catholics than between Evangelicals and the modern-day successors to the people who hounded J Gresham Machen out of his professorship a couple of generations ago. Since Vatican ll, lay Catholics have opened up the Bible. I find myself increasingly using Catholic material both in academic study and lay groups. There are two reasons for this, first the reliability and rigour of the underlying scholarship, and secondly that without what I can best describe as 'evangelical baggage' the material has a freshness to it.

There are other straws in the wind. A few years ago I discovered a group in Dublin, members of the Catholic Church, who happily wore the label 'Evangelical Catholics'. In England, Catholic Alpha is well and truly on the map. I have friends who have moved to France who attend a Sunday house church. It includes indigenous Catholics who go to a formal mass on Saturday night and play a full part in a much less formal manifestation of church on Sundays. In the academies we have phenomena such as the Radical Orthodoxy movement. This is made up mainly of Catholics but also includes prominent Anglicans such as Archbishop Rowan Williams. This enterprise is revisiting the contributions of thinkers such as Aristotle, Aquinas and Augustine in philosophical theology.

This is a time that's as volatile for the church as the sixteenth century, and I sincerely believe a new form of church has to emerge and will emerge. For my part I hope it will have learned the lessons of two thousand years and freed itself from the trappings of power and political influence, to be what Charles Colson has called 'the little platoons of society'. The church must become communities who go against popular sentiment by welcoming the asylum seeker, feeding the hungry, visiting the prisoner and washing feet. After all, that's what following Jesus has always been about.

Dwight: Three cheers – I knew you were optimistic underneath it all. I also see signs of convergence from ordinary experience. In Europe I've been interested not only by the Taizé community which was started by a Protestant pastor, but also by some other Christian communities which could be labelled Evangelical, Charismatic and Catholic. In France, the Community of the Beatitudes was also started by a former reformed minister who turned Catholic. The community's inhabitants live together as celibates and married, priests and lay people. They practise perpetual adoration of the Blessed Sacrament, but they also carry out evangelical works like handing out tracts, street preaching, summer camps for kids, evangelical broadcasting and publishing. At the end of their worship they are likely to stay for free worship, speaking in tongues and healing. Similar new movements within the Catholic Church have sprung up in Italy and the Third World.

In the States, not only are Catholics and Evangelicals meeting together to talk theology, but they are active together in politics, in the pro-life cause, in action to break poverty and in ministry to those on the margins of society. In addition, the good side of the post-modern phenomenon is that Evangelicals are more and more likely to be experimenting with Catholic forms of spirituality and worship – and vice versa. I heard about one Southern Baptist minister who thought the Catholic custom of putting ashes on heads for Ash Wednesday was very biblical. He wasn't sure where to get the ashes though, and when he found out that the ashes are produced by burning the Palm crosses from the Easter before he grinned and said, 'Shucks, all this Catholic stuff is connected.'

There's much to be done, but all these signs make me optimistic. I'll let you finish, but I'd like to bow out with a quotation from Pope John Paul's encyclical on Christian unity called *Ut Unum Sint*. In it he makes a plea that in the midst of our talk and work together we also remember to pray.

Love is the great undercurrent which gives life and adds vigour to the movement towards unity. This love finds its most complete expression in common prayer. When brothers and sisters who are not in perfect communion with one another come together to pray, the Second Vatican Council defines their prayer as the soul of the whole ecumenical movement. This prayer is a 'very effective means of petitioning for the grace of unity ... a genuine expression of the ties which even now bind Catholics to their separated brethren.' Even when prayer is not specifically offered for Christian unity...it actually becomes an expression and a confirmation of unity. The common prayer of Christians is an invitation to Christ himself to visit the community of those who call upon him for 'where two or three are gathered in my name, there am I in the midst of them.'[5]

John: A final rain check on where we are. For a long time, both the Catholic Church and the newly emerging post Reformation churches acted as though they expected the other side to capitulate. That is the tone of the infamous anathemas of the Council of Trent. That, too, is the mindset behind the burnings and bloodletting that occurred in England. You and I have been engaged in a process that shows that things have moved on. We have been engaged in a conversation that has had a transforming effect, even though neither of us has changed our minds on many fronts. In the process we have exhibited:

● self insight;
● a capacity to empathise with and understand the other side;
● the honestly to identify and discuss important differences;
● generosity and breadth of mind enabling the discovery of common ground (including, even, some doubts and uncertainties);
● a growth in mutual respect;
● a deepened appreciation of the nuances of the other side's position;
● new ways of communicating (not least sharing our stories).

Processes like this need to happen at grass roots between ordinary people, leading to the diffusion of mutual suspicions and identification of new ways of working together. We have noted in passing that the theologians have been able to pave the way by reframing many of the theological 'chestnuts' that were at the fore in the sixteenth century and have since become slogans, opening even further the great divide between the churches. We need the theologians to carry on their task and help people in the pews to rewrite these old chestnuts in popular parlance.

In this dialogue you, Dwight, have been billed as a Catholic and I have been billed as an Evangelical. For my part I'm not the least bit ashamed of that tag. What greater aspiration can a Christian have than to be a gospel person – one who's formed by it and lives by it? In truth, however, neither of our traditions really have the right to appropriate those names solely for themselves. God's church is both evangelical and Catholic. To be evangelical, as Oxford theologian John Webster has said, is to be 'determined by and responsible to the good news of Jesus Christ'. Thoughtful Catholics would want to claim that about themselves too. In his article The Self-Organising Power of the Gospel of Christ,[6] Webster insists that we might 'equally say that all Christian theology is catholic, in that it seeks reflectively to trace the universal scope of the gospel'. I buy that too! I wonder how these seeds will grow as the twenty-first century opens up?

---

1 Martin Luther at the Diet of Worms in H C Bettenson, *Documents of the Christian Church*, based on Luther's *Opera Latina*, (Frankfurt, 1865-73)

2 Final Report, Pentecostal-Roman Catholic Ecumenical Dialogue: cited in the *International Review of Mission*, Jan-Feb 2001.

3 Charles Colson and Richard John Neuhaus, *Evangelicals and Catholics Together: Towards a Common Mission*, (Dallas: Word, 1995)

4 Thomas P Rausch, *Catholics and Evangelicals, Do They Share a Common Future?*, (Downers Grove: InterVarsity Press, 2000), p29

5 John Paul ll, *Ut Unim Sint*, 21

6 John Webster, The Self-Organising Power of the Gospel of Christ: Episcopacy and Community Formation, *International Journal of Systematic Theology* Vol 3, No 1, March 2001.

Recommended Reading

Chapter One – Only the Bible?

Scripture and Truth, D.A. Carson and John D. Woodbridge (eds) Inter Varsity Press. As good an introduction as there is, explaining and expounding a contemporary evangelical view of the inspiration and authority of Scripture. **JM**

Dei Verbum, Vatican II Document, Catholic Truth Society. A pamphlet which explains the teaching of the Catholic Church regarding Scripture. **DL**

Tradition and Traditions Yves Cardinal Congar, Basilica. An in-depth theological consideration of the history and role of tradition in the life of the church. **DL**

Not by Scripture Alone, Robert Sungenis, Queenship. A scholarly but readable explanation of the Catholic view that Scripture and church tradition are both necessary. **DL**

Chapter Two –Apostolic Authority

New Testament Background Documents, C.K. Barrett, SPCK, 1964 Still in print, this is an exhaustive collection of source material from the political, religious, and social landscape of the New Testament. **JM**

The Early Christian Fathers, Henry Bettenson, Oxford University Press. Choice excerpts from the early church fathers are arranged according to author and topic. **JM**

Early Christian Creeds, J.N.D. Kelly, Longmans, 3rd edn, 1982. Probably the classic study of the formation of key doctrines in the first three Christian centuries. **JM**

Early Christian Writings, Maxwell Staniforth (ed) Penguin. The complete texts of the earliest Christian writings outside Scripture. **DL**

One, Holy, Catholic and Apostolic, K.D. Whitehead, Ignatius. A book which shows how the early church has survived as the Catholic Church, and how Christians can find new zeal in the lives of the saints. **DL**

Chapter Three – Prince of the Apostles

Jesus, Peter and the Keys, Butler, Dahlgren and Hess, Queenship. Detailed evidence from Scripture and the early church fathers for the papacy. **DL**

The Tomb of Peter: The New Discoveries in the Sacred Grottoes of the Vatican, Margherita Guarducci, Hawthorn Books. The archaeologist who uncovered Peter's tomb tells the story of her discoveries. **DL**

Chapter Four – The Papacy

The Gift of Authority, ARCIC, Catholic Truth Society. The third report on the question of authority in the Church from the Anglican Roman Catholic International Commission. **JM/DL**

The Office of Peter, Hans Urs von Balthasar, Ignatius. A history and defence of the papacy by one of the foremost modern Catholic theologians. **DL**

Saints and Sinners, Eamon Duffy, Yale University Press. An excellent, objective illustrated history of the papacy. **DL**

Pope Fiction, Patrick Madrid, Basilica. The author answers thirty common misconceptions about the papacy. **DL**

Chapter Five – Channels of Grace

The Church, Mystery, Sacrament, Community, John Paul II, Pauline. The Pope explores the life of the Catholic Church as the foundation sacrament. **DL**

Pardon and Peace, Francis Randolph, Ignatius. A positive and practical explanation of the value and reason for the sacrament of confession. **DL**

Understanding the Sacraments, Peter Stravinskas, Ignatius. A straightforward explanation of the Catholic view of sacraments, and an exploration of the seven sacraments and their meaning. **DL**

Chapter Six – The Real Presence

The Final Report, ARCIC, 1981, SPCK/Forward Movement Publications. The report on the first segment of the Anglican Roman Catholic International Commission which deals with Eucharist, Ministry and Authority. **JM**

The Hidden Manna, James T O'Connor, Ignatius. A readable historical study of the Eucharist from apostolic times to the present day. **DL**

Holy Mass, Adrienne von Speyr, Ignatius. A meditation which prayerfully explains the meaning of each detail of the Mass. **DL**

Not by Bread Alone, Robert Sungenis, Queenship. A scholarly but approachable defence of the Catholic position on the Eucharist. **DL**

Chapter Seven – Brother Are You Saved?

Salvation and the Church, ARCIC, Catholic Truth Society. The text of the 1986 agreed statement on salvation from the Anglican Roman Catholic International Commission. **JM**

Joint Declaration on Justification, Catholic Truth Society, 2000. The text of the agreement on justification between Lutherans and Catholics. **DL**

The Logic of Evangelism, William J Abraham, Eerdmanns, 1989. One of the best expositions of the meaning of evangelism from an evangelical-reformed perspective. **JM**

Evangelicals and Catholics Together: Towards a Common Mission, Charles Colson and Richard John Neuhaus, Word. The second document which came from this Evangelical-Catholic dialogue is called 'The Gift of Salvation' and deals with justification. **JM**

Making Sense of the Cross, Alister McGrath, Inter Varsity Press, 1992. A helpful little book that explores some of the many biblical images that inform an evangelical understanding of the Cross and its significance. **JM**

Not by Faith Alone, Robert Sungenis, Queenship. An exploration of the Faith vs. Works issue from a Catholic perspective. **DL**

Chapter Eight – Heaven, Hell and Purgatory

Heaven, the Heart's Deepest Longing, Peter Kreeft, Ignatius. An exploration of our desire for heaven based on psychological, philosophical and theological dimensions. **DL**

The Great Divorce, C.S.Lewis, Fount. A fantasy journey to the realm beyond death which offers profound insights on heaven, hell and purgatory. **JM**

Purgatory, Michael Taylor SJ, Our Sunday Visitor. An explanation of purgatory and prayers for the dead based on Scripture and tradition. **DL**

Chapter Nine – For All the Saints

Dictionary of Saints, Donald Attwater with Catherine Rachel John, Penguin. A classic resource for Catholic saints. **DL**

Christifideles Laici, John Paul II, Pauline. Pope John Paul outlines the mission of all Christians and the call to universal holiness. **DL**

Chapter Ten – Holy Mary Mother of God

Mary of Nazareth, Kenneth Howell, Queenship. A convert from Presbyterianism gives a Scriptural meditation and defence of Catholic beliefs about Mary. **DL**

Mary and the Fathers of the Church, L Gambero, Ignatius. A comprehensive survey of the development of Marian doctrines over the first eight centuries of the Church. **DL**

Mary for All Christians, John MacQuarrie, HarperCollins. An Anglican theologian shows how the Marian doctrines can be more widely understood and accepted. **JM**

Mary: God's Yes to Man, John Paul II, Cardinal Ratzinger, von Balthasar, Ignatius. The text of Pope John Paul's encyclical about Mary along with commentary by Cardinal Ratzinger and theologian Hans Urs von Balthasar. **DL**

Mary's Story, Mary's Song, Elaine Storkey, SPCK, 1994. Archbishop's Lent Book for 1994. An example of how evangelicals are beginning to find a fuller appreciation of Mary and her role. **JM**

Chapter Eleven – The Reformation

The Age of the Reformation, Roland H Bainton, D. Van Nostrand, 1956. An excellent collection of Reformation documents from the author of one of the finest biographies of Martin Luther. **JM**

Characters of the Reformation, Hilaire Belloc, Tan Books. Belloc's classic analysis of the strengths and weaknesses of 23 major Reformation figures. **DL**

The Stripping of the Altars, Eamon Duffy, Yale University Press. An exhaustive scholarly re-examination of the English Church before and just after the Reformation. **DL**

English Reformations, Christopher Haigh, Oxford University Press. An objective and scholarly reassessment of the Tudor and Elizabethan period. **DL**

Chapter Twelve – The Future Church

Catholics and Evangelicals – Do They Share a Common Future? Thomas P. Rausch (ed) Inter Varsity Press, 2000. Seven theologians from both sides of the fence discuss their own experiences in evangelical-Catholic dialogue and consider the future. **DL**

Evangelicals and Catholics Together: Towards a Common Mission, Charles Colson and Richard John Neuhaus, Word, 1995. A pioneering document with contributions from Catholic and Evangelical theologians on how to work together in evangelism and cultural issues. **JM**

Reclaiming the Great Tradition, Evangelicals, Catholics and Orthodox in Dialogue, James S Cutsinger (ed.) InterVarsity

Press, 1997. Essays by theologians from all three traditions which seek to find common ground in the shared history of the ancient church. **JM**

General Reading

The Catechism of the Catholic Church, Geoffrey Chapman. Clear exposition of Catholic belief with exhaustive notes and cross references to Scripture and the teaching of the church down through the ages. **DL**

The Catholic Faith, W.H. Griffith Thomas, London Church Book Room Press, first published 1904. Still one of the classic evangelical presentations of the case for Anglicanism. **JM**

Evangelical is Not Enough, Thomas Howard, Ignatius. A famous convert explains the usefulness of liturgy, tradition and the church year. **DL**

What Catholics Really Believe, Karl Keating, Ignatius. A question and answer exposition of Catholic beliefs. **DL**

Catholic and Christian, Alan Schreck, Servant Books. A Catholic charismatic Christian explains the Catholic faith from a viewpoint of Scripture and the renewal movement. **DL**

Essentials, John W.A. Stott, and David L. Edwards, Hodder and Stoughton, 1988. A frank and honest dialogue between one of the great evangelicals of the twentieth-century and one of the foremost spokesmen for liberalism. **JM**

Jesus and the Victory of God, N.T. Wright, SPCK, 1996. Understanding Jesus and his mission is the heart of the evangelical enterprise and this is the most important of Wright's works. **JM**

Websites and Magazines

Pontifical Council for Christian Unity
http://www.vatican.va/roman_curia/pontifical_councils/chrstuni/index.htm The Vatican's official ecumenical website is the best starting point for accessing official documents from the Catholic Church's dialogues with other churches including Anglican, Lutheran, Methodist, Pentecostal and Reformed.

The Evangelical Catholic
http://www.evangelicalcatholic.com/ In Europe and North America there are growing numbers of Christians who would claim to be both Catholic and Evangelical. This website is an excellent starting point for locating the huge and growing body of statements and publications dedicated to this theme.

ARCIC Documents
http://www.prounione.urbe.it/dia-int/arcic/e-arcic-info.html This website catalogues all the documents from the Anglican Roman Catholic International Commission. The full text of all the documents are available to download.

Catholic Answers
http://www.catholic.com/ A Catholic Apologetics website with lots of links to many other Catholic sites. Many pages full of pithy answers and loads of quotes and references.

Touchstone Magazine
http://www.touchstonemag.com/ Describes itself as a Journal of Mere Christianity. The editors are from Evangelical, Catholic and Orthodox background and are concerned to see the three great traditions work together and grow together.

First Things
http://www.firstthings.com/ First Things is the magazine of the American Centre for Policy and Religion. It includes viewpoints from Catholics, Evangelicals and Orthodox on current affairs in the USA and worldwide.

Notes

DL – Most of the books which I have listed are in print and available through the internet booksellers, Amazon.com. They are also available through Catholic bookshops, and to order from most large booksellers.

In the UK they are also available through Family Publications who provide an excellent mail order service: Family Publications, 77 Banbury Road, Oxford, OX2 6LF, tel: 01865 514408. Email: fameduc@aol.com
Website: www.family publications.co.uk
JM – Most of the books I have chosen are in print and are available from SPCK bookshops, through Amazon.com or to order from any good Christian bookshop. Where they are out of print I have included the publication date. These will have to be found through libraries or second-hand booksellers.